geog.sc

geography for scotland

< rosemarie gallagher >< richard parish >< susan mayhew >

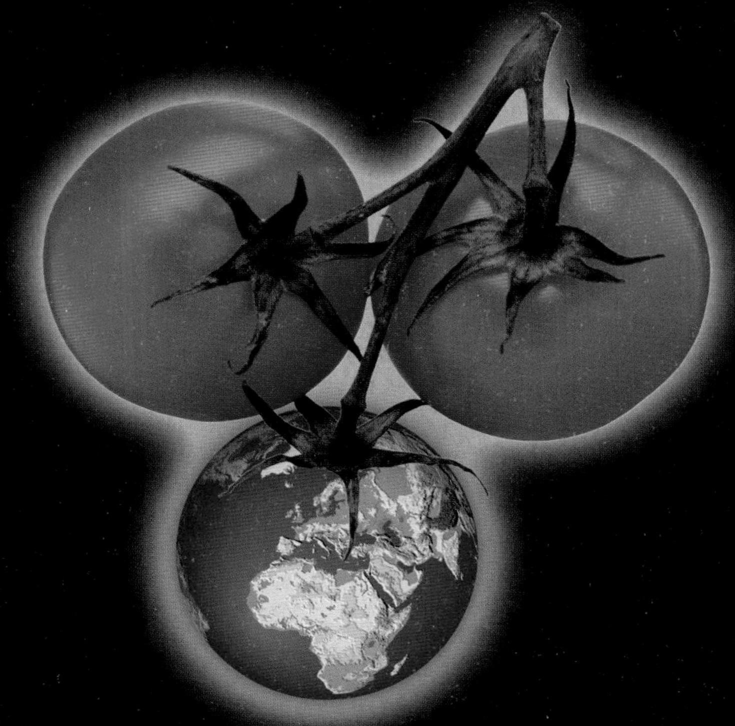

editorial advisors
< ollie bray >< malcolm mcdonald >< pauline mcclellan >< simon mein >

Great Clarendon Street, Oxford OX2 6DP

Oxford University Press is a department of the University of Oxford. It furthers the University's objective of excellence in research, scholarship, and education by publishing worldwide in

Oxford New York

Auckland Cape Town Dar es Salaam Hong Kong Karachi Kuala Lumpur Madrid Melbourne Mexico City Nairobi New Delhi Shanghai Taipei Toronto

With offices in

Argentina Austria Brazil Chile Czech Republic France Greece Guatemala Hungary Italy Japan Poland Portugal Singapore South Korea Switzerland Thailand Turkey Ukraine Vietnam

Oxford is a registered trade mark of Oxford University Press in the UK and in certain other countries

First published 2007

British Library Cataloguing in Publication Data

Data available

ISBN: 978-0-19-913476-2

10 9 8 7 6 5 4 3 2 1

Printed in Singapore by KHL Printing Company PTE Ltd.

Assembled in Cambridge by Hart McLeod.

Acknowledgements

The publisher and authors would like to thank the following for permission to use photographs and other copyright material:

p4 Wolfgang Kaehler/Corbis UK Ltd. ; p9l Jean Dominique DALLET/Alamy ; p9c Worldwide Picture Library/Alamy ; p9r Trevor Smithers ARPS/Alamy; p10tl Corel/Oxford University Press; p10cl Corel/Oxford University Press; p10bl Corel/Oxford University Press; p10tc Corel/Oxford University Press; p10bc ©LWA-Sharie Kennedy/Corbis UK Ltd.; p10tr Corel/Oxford University Press; p10cr Corel/Oxford University Press; p10br Corel/Oxford University Press; p10c Corel/Oxford University Press; p11 Corbis UK Ltd.; p13cl B. Apicella/Photofusion Picture Library; p13l E. Guigenan-Christian Aid/Still Pictures; p13cr Ed Eckstein/Corbis UK Ltd.; p13r Harmut Schwarzbach/Still Pictures; p15 Anna Tully/Panos Pictures; p20 PA WIRE/Empics; p24tl Jorgen Schytte/Still Pictures; p24cl John Isaac/Still Pictures; p24bl Michael MacIntyre/Hutchison Picture Library; p24tc Pat Bennett/Alamy; p24bc Penny Tweedie/Corbis UK Ltd.; p24tr Ron Giling/Still Pictures; p24cr Michael MacIntyre/Hutchison Picture Library; p24br Ron Gilling/Still Pictures; p25l Jorgen Schytte/Still Pictures; p25c Ron Giling/Still Pictures; p25r Popperfoto/Alamy; p26tl Gary Cook/Alamy; p26tr Hutchison/Eye Ubiquitous/Hutchison; p26b Pat Bennett/Alamy; p28 Jorgen Schytte/Still Pictures; p29 Jorgen Schytte/Still Pictures; p30 JORGEN SCHYTTE/Still Pictures; p31t Greenshoots Communications/Alamy; p31b JORGEN SCHYTTE/Still Pictures; p32l Nick Haslam/Hutchison Picture Library; p32r Corbis UK Ltd.; p33 Liba Taylor/Panos Pictures; p34l TopFoto; p34c Michael J. Balick/Still Pictures; p34r Janine Wiedel Photolibrary/Alamy; p36tl Caroline Penn/Corbis UK Ltd.; p36tr PA Photos/EPA/Empics; p36b Jorgen Schytte/Still Pictures; p37 Jorgen Schytte/Still Pictures; p38l ISSOUF SANOGO/AFP/Getty Images; p38r Greenshoots Communications/Alamy; p39 Greenshoots Communications/Alamy; p40tl Sygma/Corbis UK Ltd.; p40cl Koichi Kamoshida/Getty Images; p40bl Bernd Mellmann/Alamy; p40bc JTB Photo Communications, Inc./Alamy; p40tr Iain Masterton/Alamy; p40cr Gavin Hellier/Robert Harding World Imagery/Getty Images; p40br Franck Robichon/Epa/Corbis UK Ltd.; p42 Mike Agliolo/Science Photo Library; p44tl Robert Harding Picture Library Ltd/Alamy; p44bl Chad Ehlers/Alamy; p44tr FocusJapan/Alamy; p44br JTB Photo Communications, Inc./Alamy; p46l Oote Boe Photography/Alamy; p46r David Vintiner/Zefa/Corbis UK Ltd.; p47 superbshots.com/Alamy; p48t Charles O'rear/Corbis UK Ltd.; p48b Christopher Farina/Corbis UK Ltd.; p51 ImageState/Alamy; p52t AP Photo/Katsumi Kasahara/Empics; p52b Roger Ressmeyer/Corbis UK Ltd.; p53t AP Photo/Kyodo News/Empics; p53b Eriko Sugita/Reuters/Corbis UK Ltd.; p54 JTB Photo Communications, Inc./Alamy; p55t Hemis /Alamy; p55b Ko Sasaki/The New York Times/Redux Pictures; p57 Empics; p58 Andrew Milligan/PA/Empics; p60 Illustrated London News; p62t Jochen Tack/Das Fotoarchiv/Still Pictures; p62b *Beltra/Greenpeace Pictures*; p63tl Peter Johnson/Corbis UK Ltd.; p63bl Lynsey Addario/Corbis UK Ltd.; p63tc geogphotos/Alamy; p63bc Bob Krist/Corbis UK Ltd.; p63br Vic Pigula/Alamy; p64t Intergovernmental Panel on Climate Change; p64b Jason Hawkes/Corbis UK Ltd.; p65 United Nations Photo Library; p66l Cath Mullen/Frank Lane Picture Agency/Corbis UK Ltd.; p66r © Anthony Upton 2003/npower renewables; p67 Marine Current Turbines TM Limited; p68 Photographers Direct/Peter Watson Photography Ltd; p69 Lews Castle College; p70cl National Renewable Energy Laboratory; p70bl Ecoscene; p70bc National Renewable Energy Laboratory; p70cr Lineair/Still Pictures; p70br Simon Grosse/Alamy; p70t David R. Frazier Photolibrary, Inc./Alamy; p70c Still Pictures; p71 N. Francis/Robert Harding Picture Library Ltd/Alamy; p72l National Renewable Energy Laboratory; p72r National Renewable Energy Laboratory; p73tl National Renewable Energy Laboratory; p73tr National Renewable Energy Laboratory; p73b National Renewable Energy Laboratory; p78tl Don Ryan/AP Photo; p78cl George Hall/Corbis UK Ltd.; p78bl Daniel O'Leary/Panos Pictures; p78tc Getty Images; p78bc Duomo/Corbis UK Ltd.; p78tr Getty Images; p78br foybles/Alamy; p78c Anat Givon/AP Photo; p80 Corel/Oxford University Press; p81 Toby Adamson/Still Pictures; p82t Chris Stowers/Panos Pictures; p82b Paul A. Souders/Corbis UK Ltd.; p83 Martin Sookias/Oxford University Press; p84t Ron Giling/Still Pictures; p84c Dunfermline Press Ltd; p84b David Gibson/Photofusion Picture Library; p86tl Paul A. Souders/Corbis UK Ltd.; p86cl Bettmann/Corbis UK Ltd.; p86bl Lito C. Uyan/Corbis UK Ltd.; p86tr Charles O'Rear/Corbis UK Ltd.; p86cr Paul A. Souders/Corbis UK Ltd.; p87t Donald Stampfli/AP Photo; p87b Corbis UK Ltd.; p88tl Anders Gunnartz/Panos Pictures; p88cl Harmut Schwarzbach/Still Pictures; p88bl David Reed/Panos Pictures; p88tr Ron Giling/Still Pictures; p88cr Mike Williams/Peak Pictures; p88br Catherine Karnow/Corbis UK Ltd.; p89t Ray Tang/Rex Features; p89b David Turnley/Corbis UK Ltd. ; p92l Corel/Oxford University Press ; p92r KTB - Archive of the GeoForschungZentrum Potsdam ; p97 (Source: World Ocean Floor map by Bruce C. Heezen and Marie Tharp, 1977. Copyright © 1977 Marie Tharp. Reproduced by permission of Marie Tharp, 1 Washington Ave., South Nyack, NY10960)/Marie Tharp ; p99 AP Photo; p100bl Shehzad Noorani/Still Pictures; p100br Caren Firouz/Reuters/Corbis UK Ltd.; p100t Wolfgang Rattav/Reuters/Corbis UK Ltd.; p102 JOHN RUSSELL/AFP/Getty Images; p103tl DigitalGlobe/Getty Images; p103tr Digital Globe/Zuma/Corbis UK Ltd.; p103b ullstein - Mehrl/Still Pictures; p104l J. Allan Cash Photo Library; p104r Lyn Topinka/United States Department of the Interior/U.S. Geological Survey; p105t Rex Features; p105b Katz Pictures; p108tl Yannis Kontos/Sygma/Corbis UK Ltd.; p108cl Patrick Robert/Sygma/Corbis UK Ltd.; p108bl Alan Andrews Photography/Alamy; p108tc Peter Turnley/Corbis UK Ltd.; p108bc Thomas J. Casadevall/United States Department of the Interior/U.S. Geological Survey; p108c Jacques Langevin/Sygma/Corbis UK Ltd.; p108tr Peter Frischmuth/Still Pictures; p108cr Bryan F. Peterson/Corbis UK Ltd.; p108br Popperfoto; p109 Sipa Press/Rex Features; p112t Jackie Chapman/Format Photographers/Photofusion Picture Library; p112b Joanne O'Brian/Format Photographers/Photofusion Picture Library; p113 CR World; p114 London Aerial Photo Library; p117tl Michael Yamashita/Corbis UK Ltd.; p117cl Inge Yspeert/Corbis UK Ltd.; p117bl Purcell Team/Corbis UK Ltd.; p117tc London Aerial Photo Library; p117bc Mark Edwards/Still Pictures; p117tr Barnaby's Picture Library; p117cr London Aerial Photo Library; p117br Art on File/Corbis UK Ltd.; p117c Martin Sookias/Oxford University Press; p119t Martin Sookias/Oxford University Press; p119b CR World; p120tl Gallo Images/Paul Velasco/Corbis UK Ltd.; p120tr Martin Sookias/Oxford University Press; p120b Oxford University Press; p121t Martin Sookias/Oxford University Press; p121c Barnaby's Picture Library; p121b Bill Varie/Corbis UK Ltd.; p122tl Francis de Mulder/Corbis UK Ltd.; p122bl Michael Yamashita/Corbis UK Ltd.; p122tc EPA/PA Photos; p122bc Rik Ergenbright/Corbis UK Ltd.; p122tr Eye Ubiquitous/Patrick Field/Corbis UK Ltd.; p122br Ute Klaphake/Photofusion Picture Library; p123t Popperfoto; p123b Martin Sookias/Oxford University Press; Department of Trade and Industry; p66br and p67tl and tr.

The publisher and authors would like to thank the many people and organizations who have helped them with their research. In particular, and in topic order: Kate Kilpatrick, Oxfam; Tamsin Maunder and other staff of WaterAid; Joe Ewins, Angela Wratten and Sally Marine, all of the Department of Trade and Industry; Kevin Cloutter of Future Energy Solutions; Jack Stone of the National Renewable Energy Laboratory, USA; Akanksha Chaurey of the Tata Energy Research Institute, New Delhi; Dr Nick Fyfe of the Department of Geography, University of Dundee; Chris Morris, GIS Analyst at Brent Council; Phil Spivey and Martin Garrad of the Community Safety Department, Sussex Police; Jane Oakland of Wembley Police; Ross Hayman of National Grid Transco.

We would like to thank our editorial advisors: Ollie Bray, Malcolm McDonald, Pauline McClellan, and Simon Mein for their unfailingly helpful and thoughtful advice and comments. Our thanks also to George 'Arthur' Readshaw. Thanks to Omar Farooque for his help and support.

Every effort has been made to contact copyright holders of material reproduced in this book. Any omissions will be rectified in subsequent printings if notice is given to the publisher.

Contents

1 Rich world, poor world

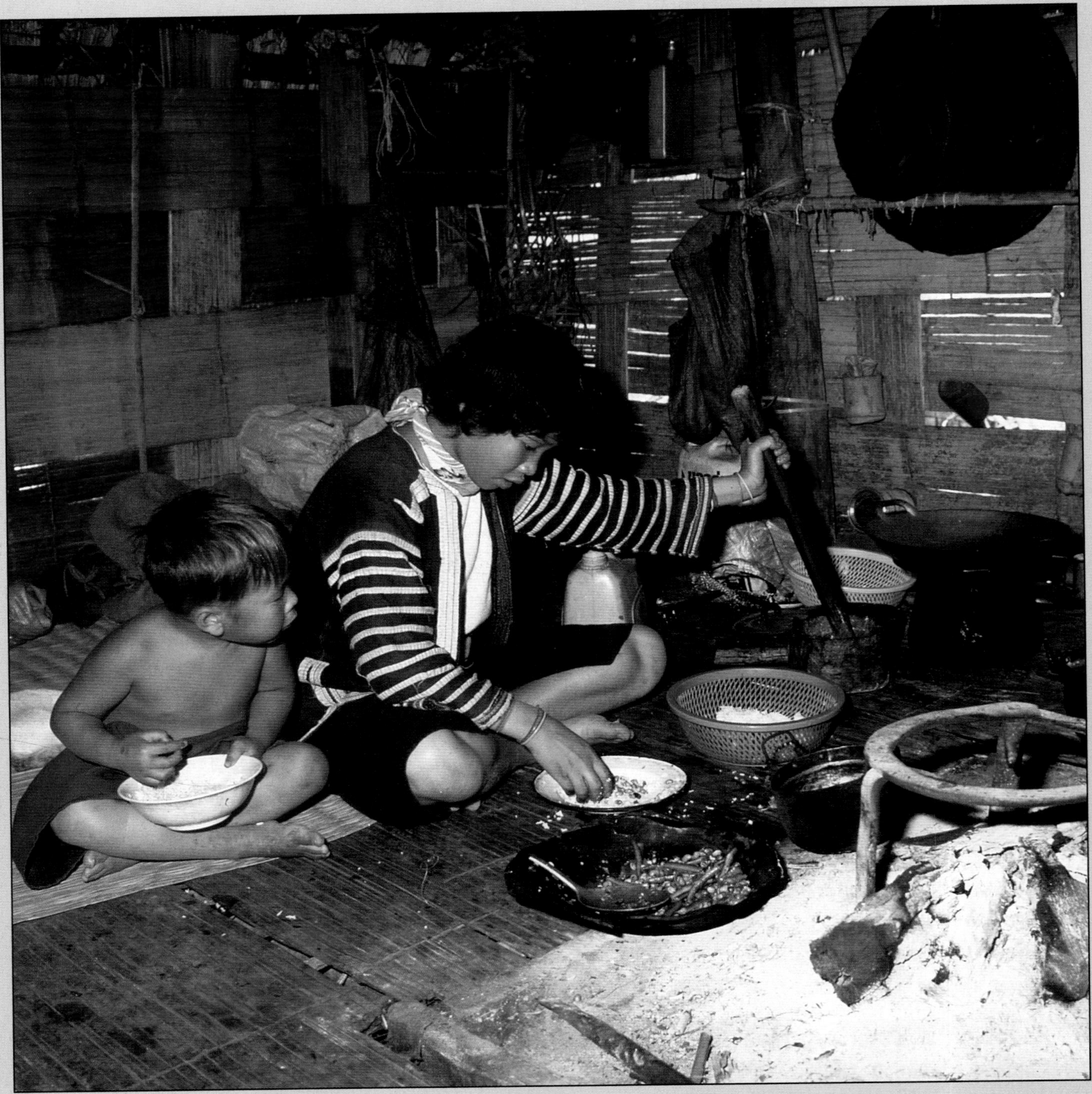

The big picture

This chapter is about **development** – the process of change for the better. These are the big ideas behind the chapter:

- Development is about improving people's lives.
- It goes on in every country, at every level. (It is going on around you!)
- Every country is at a different stage of development.
- There is a big gap in development between the richest and poorest countries – so the world is a very unequal place.
- Helping the poorer countries to develop is one of the big challenges facing our world.

Your goals for this chapter

By the end of this chapter you should be able to answer these questions:

- About how big is the world's population, and how is it changing?
- Which are the most crowded, and the most empty, parts of the world?
- Why is the population distributed like this? (At least two reasons.)
- Development has many different aspects. Having enough money to live on is one. Which others can I list? (At least four.)
- What are *development indicators*, and what six examples can I give?
- Which areas of the world are wealthiest? Which poorest?
- What do these terms mean, and which countries can I give as examples? (At least two different countries for each!)

  LEDC *MEDC* *NIC* *Third World* *rich north* *poor south*

- Poorer countries share many characteristics. So do richer countries. What examples can I give? (At least five for each group.)
- What reasons can I give, to explain the differences in development around the world? (At least five, with an example for each.)
- What are *the Millennium Development Goals*? And where could the money come from, to meet them?

And then …

When you finish this chapter you can come back to this page and see if you have met your goals!

Did you know?

- About 30 000 children die each day, because of poverty.
- Most die quietly, out of sight, in the world's poorest villages.

Did you know?

- The world's population is expected to reach 8 billion by the year 2025.
- It was 6 billion in 2000.

Did you know?

- Almost half the people on this planet live on less than $2 a day (for all their needs).

Did you know?

- Almost 1 billion people, aged 15 and over, can't read or write.

Your chapter starter

This photo shows Jintana and her younger brother. She's cooking dinner.

What five things do you notice about her kitchen?

In what ways is it like your kitchen? In what ways is it different?

Do you think most kitchens around the world are like yours, or like Jintana's?

1.1 People everywhere

Here you'll see how the world's population is distributed – and explore some reasons.

Here we go !

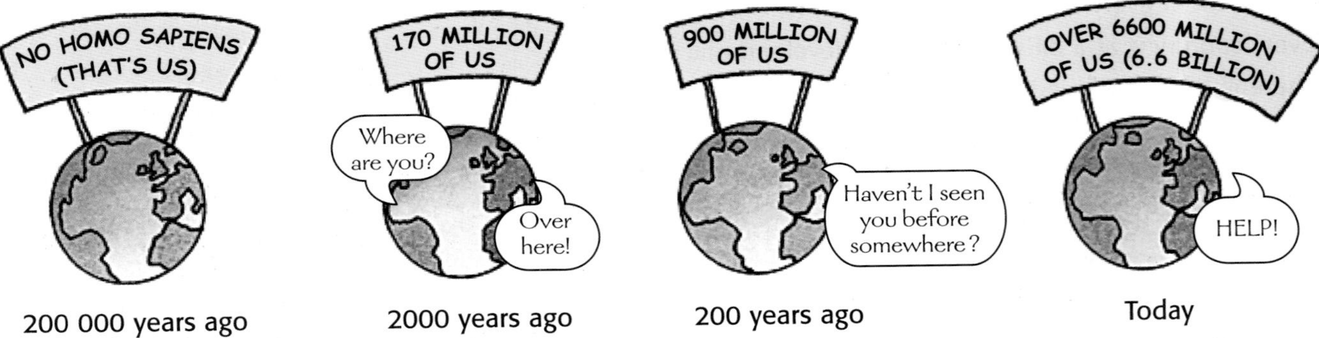

We humans are a very successful species. Our numbers are rising fast. The world population is growing by about 8780 people an hour. Try to imagine that number of new babies, every hour!

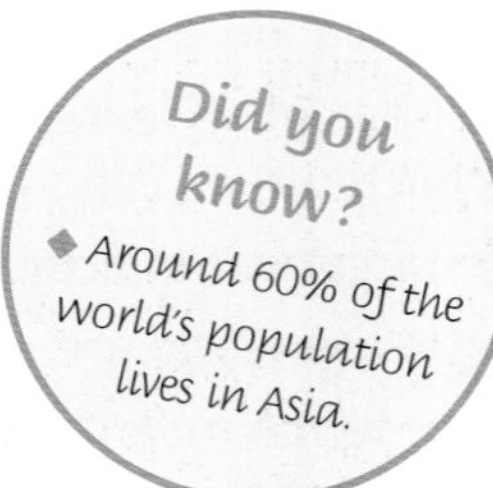

Did you know?
◆ Around 60% of the world's population lives in Asia.

So where on Earth are we?

We are not spread evenly around the Earth. Some places are still quite empty, for example the deserts and the tundra. Other places are very crowded.

The map below shows how we are spread or **distributed** around the Earth. There are many reasons why we are spread like this. You will explore some of them in **Your turn**.

World population distribution

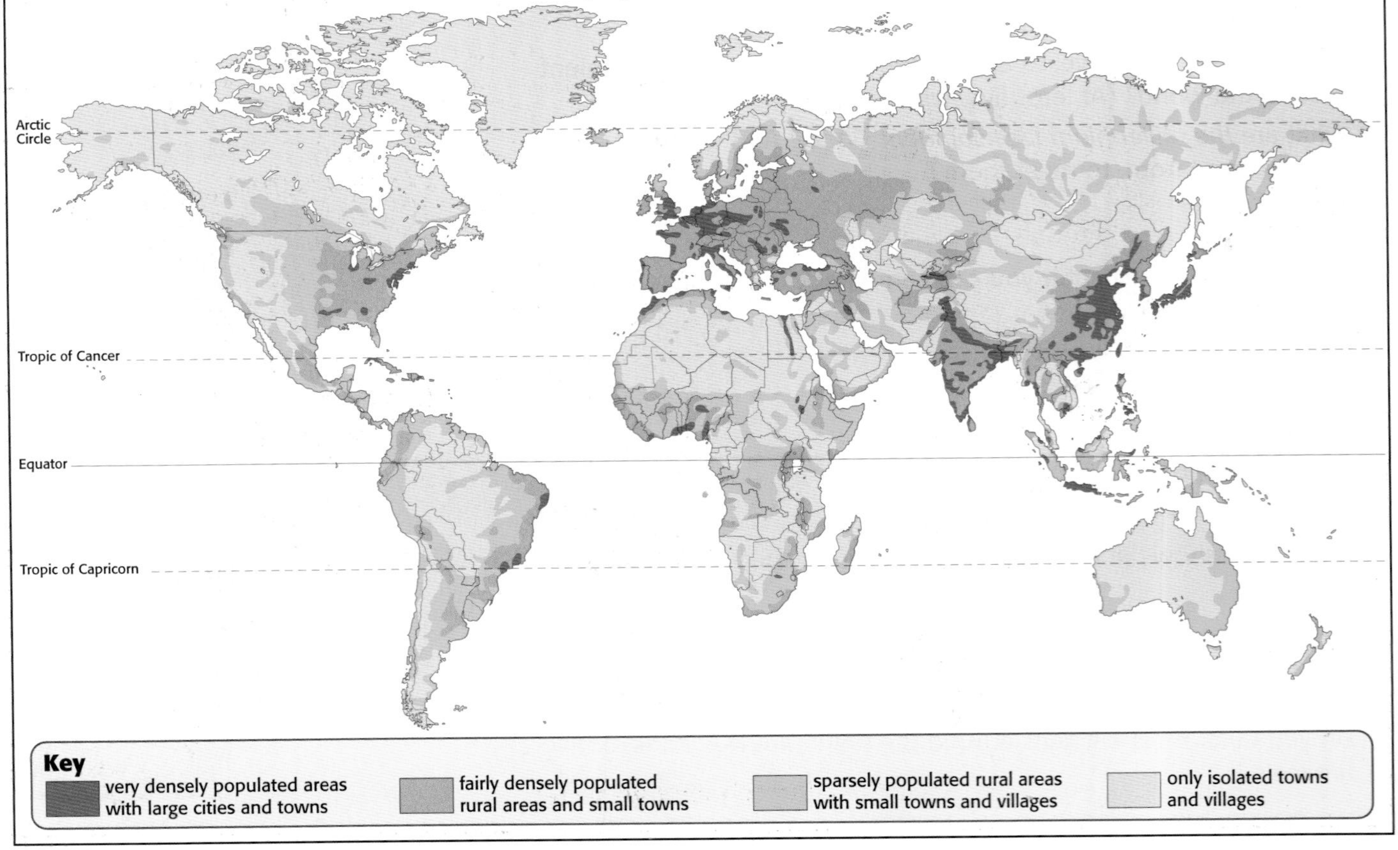

Arctic Circle

Tropic of Cancer

Equator

Tropic of Capricorn

Key

- very densely populated areas with large cities and towns
- fairly densely populated rural areas and small towns
- sparsely populated rural areas with small towns and villages
- only isolated towns and villages

Your turn

The world map on pages 128–129 will help with these.

1 Look at the key for the map on page 6.
What does this term mean?
a sparsely populated b isolated
(Try to answer without looking in the glossary.)

2 Name two countries that are:
a very crowded, overall b very lightly populated

3 In general, where do more people tend to live?
a in the middle of continents
b on or near the coast
See if you can come up with a reason for this.

4 Climate affects all living things. It is one reason why some regions are less crowded than others.
a What's the climate like, at **A** on the map below?
b This shows what crops need:

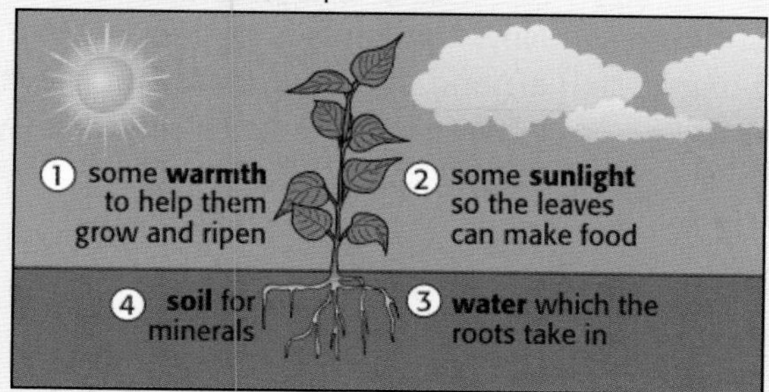

Will crops grow well at **A**? Give reasons.
c Is the population density at **A** high, or low? Give as many reasons as you can to explain why.

5

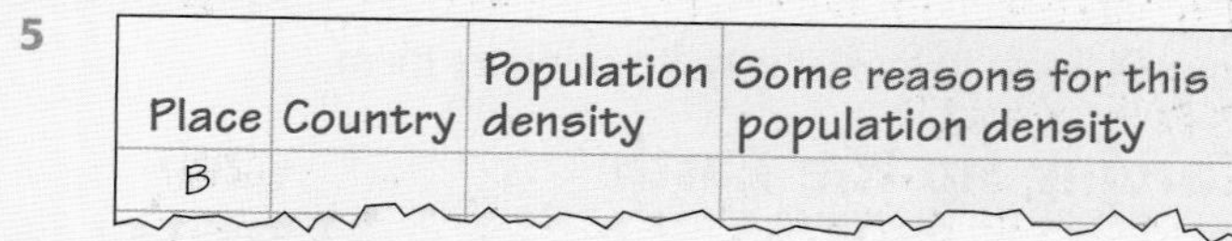

Place	Country	Population density	Some reasons for this population density
B			

Make a table like the one started above, but much larger. Leave room to write quite a lot in the last column.
a Write the letters **B** – **F**, from the map below, in the first column.
b Name the countries they're in, in the second.
c In the third column, describe the population density at each place, using one of these phrases:
very high *fairly high* *fairly low* *very low*
d In the last column, see how many reasons you can give, to explain why the population density is like this. (Can you think of other reasons besides climate?)

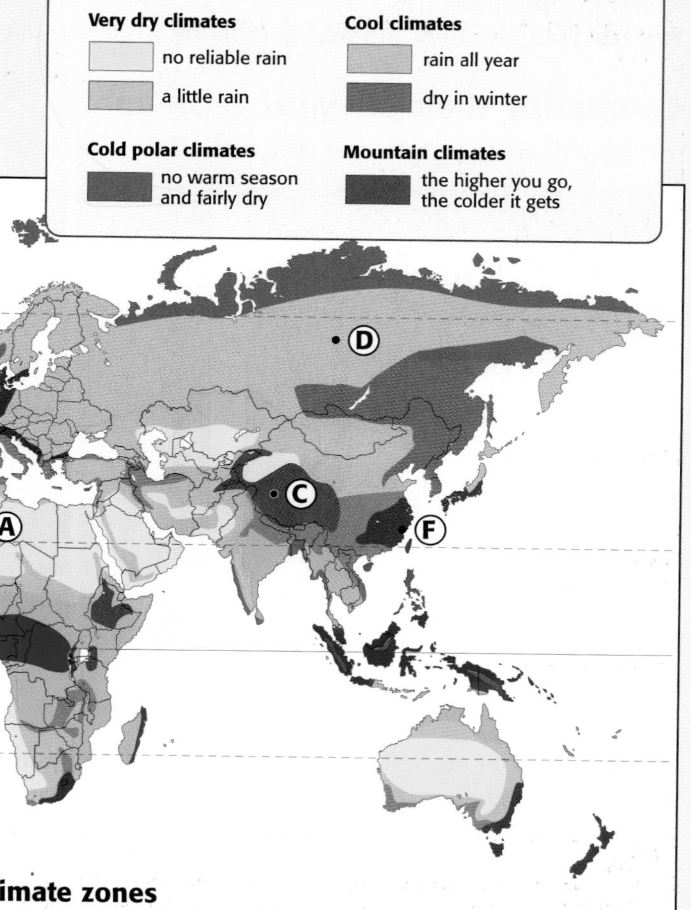

The world's climate zones

Comparing countries

There are around 200 countries in the world – and they are all different. In this unit, you will begin to look at ways to compare them.

Carving up the Earth

10 000 years ago, we think there were only around 5 million humans on the Earth. And no separate countries, with borders to keep people out!

We were on the move in those days, hunting animals for food, and gathering fruit and seeds.

The idea of borders and countries developed later, after we'd begun to farm, and build settlements.

Now the Earth is carved up into around 200 countries. And moving between them is not always easy.

How do you compare countries?

Every country is different. Some are very large, some tiny. Some are wealthy, some poor. It is very useful to be able to compare them. You can compare their physical geography, and how their people live.

Comparing their physical geography

It is easy to compare physical geography, for countries.

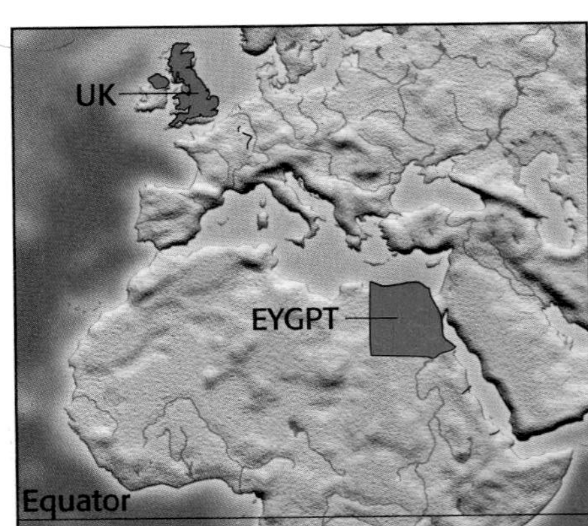

For example **Egypt** is over 4 times as large as the UK. It is nearer the Equator, so is much warmer. In fact it is mostly hot desert (the Sahara).

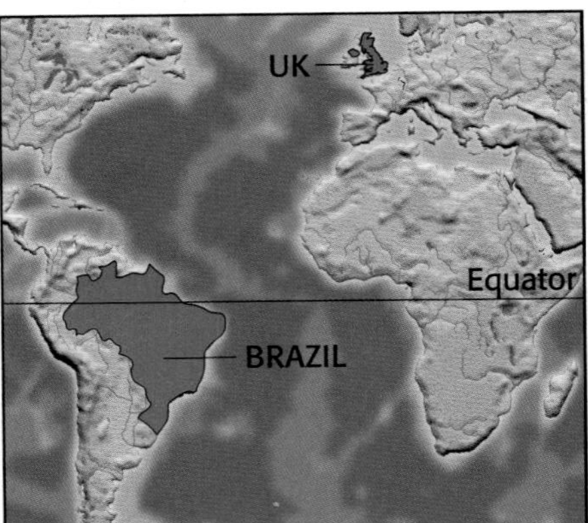

Brazil is 35 times as large as the UK. It is warmer, but has a big range of climates, since it is so large. And 40% of it is rainforest.

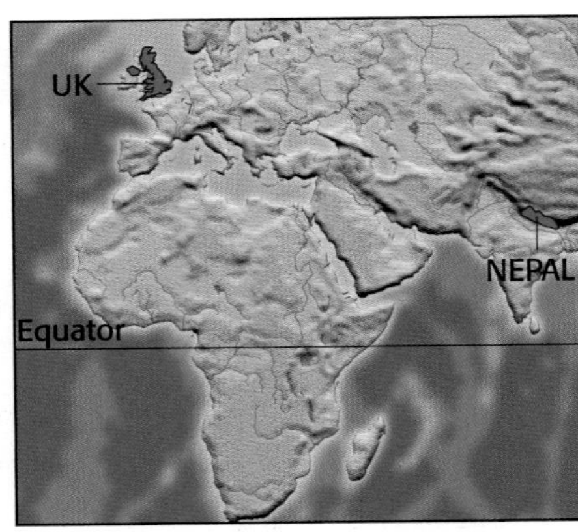

Nepal is only about 60% of the size of the UK. It is much more mountainous, since it lies in the Himalayas. And it has no coast.

You can find out an amazing amount about the physical geography of countries, using an atlas. You can find out about their climates, and ecosystems, and resources. It's fun.

But to *really* get to know about countries, and compare them, you also need to find out how their people live.

Comparing how people live

We are all humans, with the same needs. But there are big differences in the way we live, in different countries. In language, and culture, and customs – and in the standard of living.

For example, here in the UK we are well off compared to most people. Everyone has electricity. Almost all adults can read and write. And, on average, there is one doctor for every 430 people.

So how does the standard of living in those other three countries compare?

In Egypt, nearly all homes have electricity. But over a quarter of adults can't read or write. There is one doctor for every 1850 people. 44% of the people have less than $2 a day (or £1) to live on.

In Brazil about 6% of homes do not have electricity. Over one-tenth of adults can't read or write. There is one doctor for every 870 people. And 21% of the people have less than $2 a day to live on.

Three-quarters of the homes in Nepal do not have electricity. Half the adults can't read or write. There is one doctor for every 4760 people. And 69% of the people have less than $2 a day to live on.

It's all about development

The data above tells you about the level of **development** in those three countries. In a **developed** country, most people have a good standard of living.

Every country is at a different stage of development. And some countries have fallen very far behind. This is one of the big challenges facing the world today.

So we focus on development in the rest of this chapter. We'll start in the next unit by looking more closely at what development means.

Your turn

1 Here are some statements about countries. Which ones are about physical geography? Give their letters.

- A Only 60% of its children of primary school age actually go to school.
- B It is a low flat country, with many rivers that flood.
- C It has a quarter of the world's known oil reserves.
- D It is the home of sumo wrestling.
- E It is the world's biggest island.
- F It has the most wealth per person in the world.
- G It has the least wealth per person in the world.

2 Which of the statements in 1 tell about development?

3 Each statement in 1 matches a different country in the list below. See if you can match the statements to the correct countries. Give your answer like this: A =

Saudi Arabia Greenland Luxembourg
Bangladesh Sierra Leone Japan Nigeria

4 Look at the data under the photos above. Use it to help you put the three countries in order of development, with the most developed first.

So what is development?

In this unit you'll learn more about what development means.

It has many different aspects

Development is about **improving people's lives**. It is not just about getting richer, or buying more stuff. It has many different aspects.

Everybody's doing it

Every country in the world is striving to develop. But some are further along than others. Some are developing very slowly – or even going backwards.

So there is now a huge gap in development between the most and least developed countries. That is one of the biggest problems facing our world.

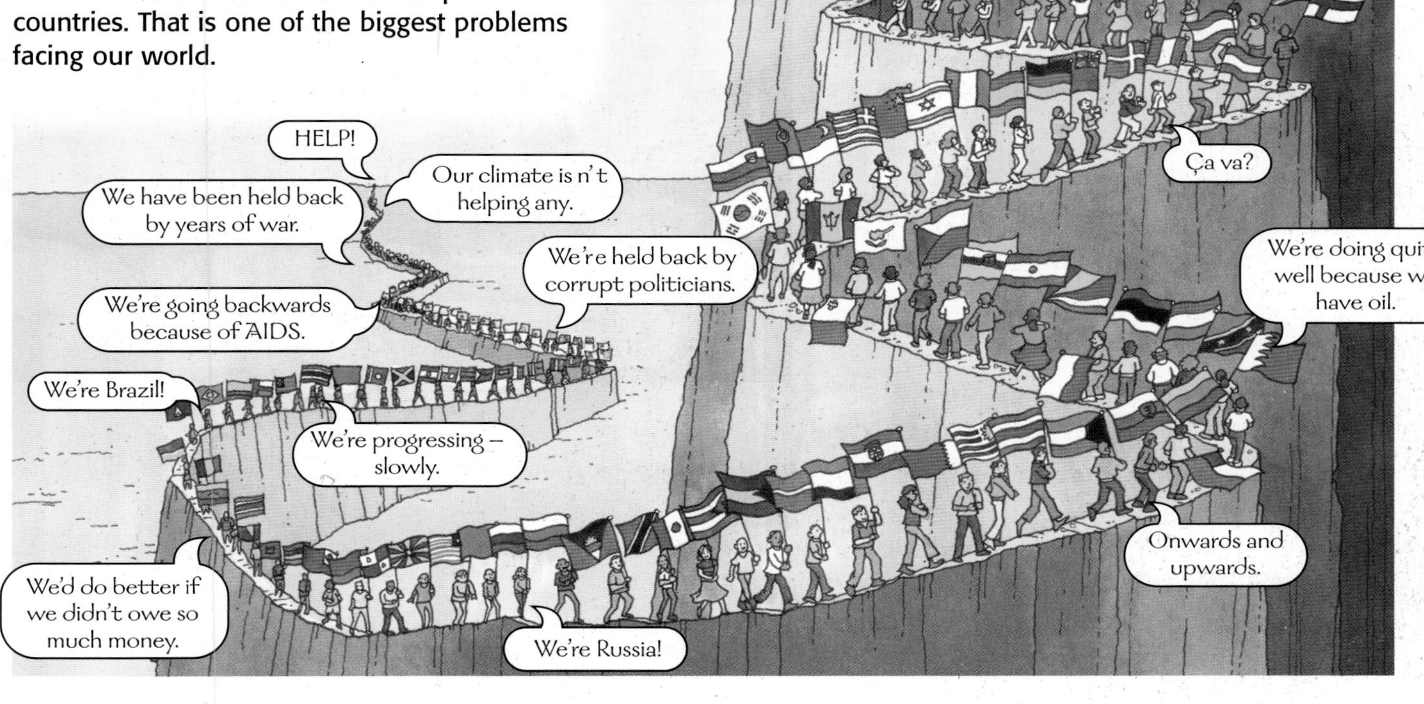

Your turn

1 Look back at page 10. The key aspects of development are outlined in red.
   a Write down this heading:
   Development – change for the better
   b Under your heading, list the other key aspects of development. Put them in what *you* think is their order of importance, the most important one first. (For example would you put *the chance of a good education* first?)
   c Do you think everyone in the world would choose the same order as you? Explain your answer. (Compare lists with a partner, to check!)

2 Look at the drawing above.
   a What do you think it's trying to show?
   b What does it tell you about the UK?

3 Development costs money. For example it costs a lot to provide a clean water supply for everyone.
   From page 10, write down:
   a four other changes you think would cost a lot
   b two that may need people to change their attitudes
   c two that may need a government to pass new laws.

4 The photo below was taken in Iraq in 2003, after it was invaded by the USA and UK. War can halt the development of a country, or even reverse it. Explain why. You can give your answer as a spider map.

5 Which aspects of development do you think the UK needs to do more work on? Write a letter to the Prime Minister giving your list, and your reasons.

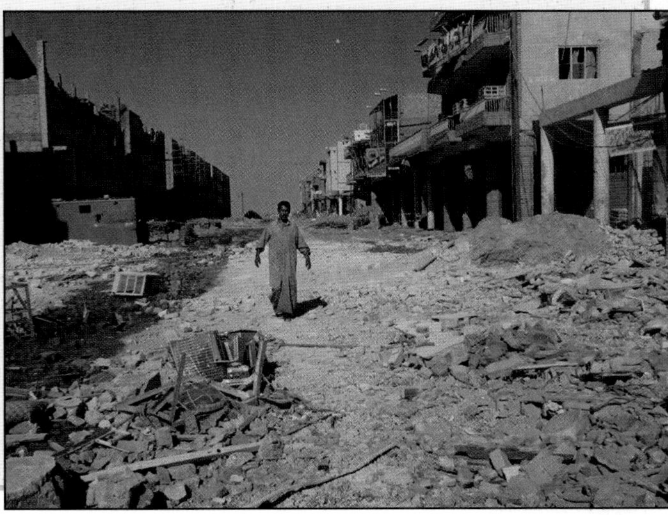

1.4 Measuring development

Here you'll see how development indicators can be used to compare countries.

Measuring development

On page 10 you saw that development has many different aspects.

So to get a clear picture of *how developed* a country is, you need to ask questions like those on the right.

And then collect data to answer them !

Luckily, the data is already collected every year, for most countries in the world.

It is published by the United Nations, in tables of **development indicators**.

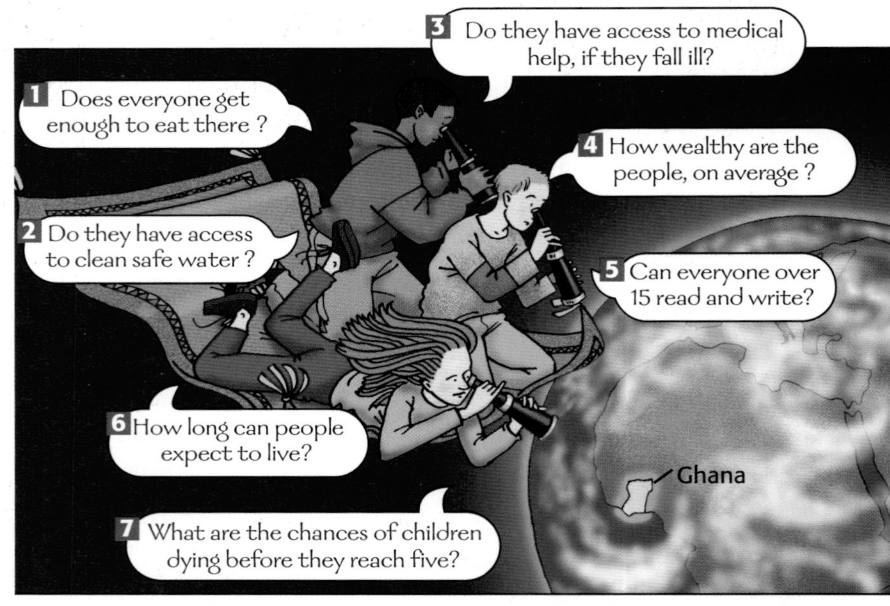

1 Does everyone get enough to eat there ?
2 Do they have access to clean safe water ?
3 Do they have access to medical help, if they fall ill?
4 How wealthy are the people, on average ?
5 Can everyone over 15 read and write?
6 How long can people expect to live?
7 What are the chances of children dying before they reach five?
Ghana

What is a development indicator ?

A **development indicator** is just data that helps to show how developed a country is.

Look at question 6 above. **Life expectancy** is how long people can expect to live, on average. It is one example of a development indicator.

For people born in Ghana in 2004, for example, the life expectancy was 57 years. For people born in the UK, it was 79. In other words, people in the UK are likely to live 22 years longer. (You'll try to explain why, later.)

◆ live longer than men
◆ earn less than men.

Using wealth as a development indicator

One indicator that's used a lot is **gross domestic product** or **GDP**.
It's the total value of the goods and services a country produces in a year. You can think of it as the wealth the country produces.

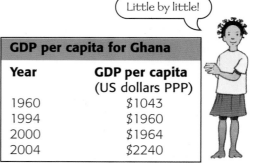

GDP is given in **US dollars (PPP)**. (**PPP** or *purchasing power parity* means the GDP is adjusted to allow for the fact that a dollar buys more in some countries than others.)

But some countries have far more people than others. Dividing GDP by the population gives **GDP per capita**. This gives you a better way to compare countries.

Little by little!

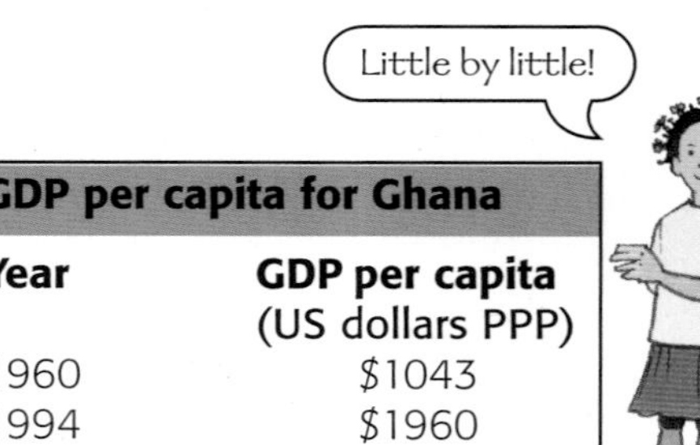

GDP per capita for Ghana

Year	GDP per capita (US dollars PPP)
1960	$1043
1994	$1960
2000	$1964
2004	$2240

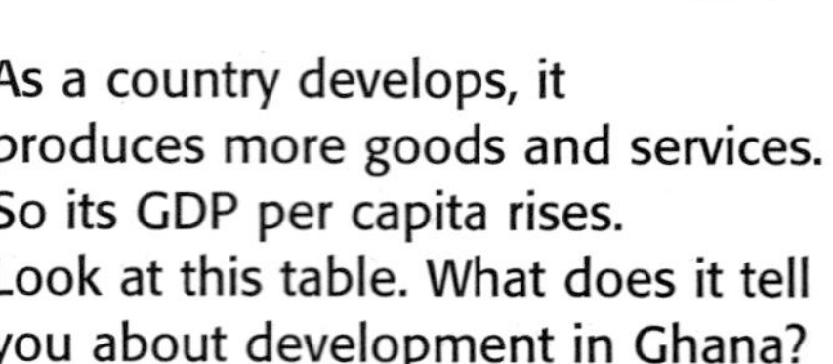

As a country develops, it produces more goods and services. So its GDP per capita rises.
Look at this table. What does it tell you about development in Ghana?

But GDP per capita does not tell us whether people have safe water, for example, or enough doctors. That's why we need other indicators too.

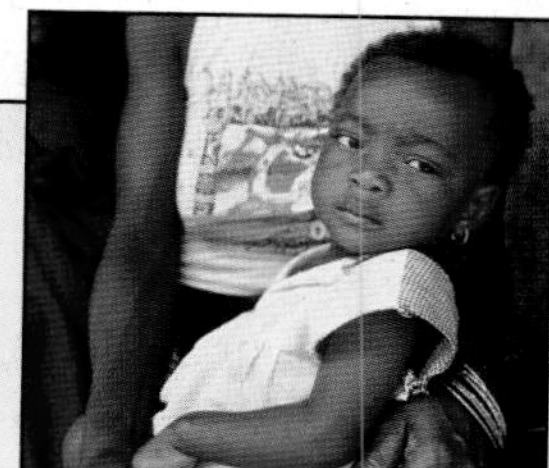

Akosua, Ghana
Life expectancy: 57
Chances of –
dying before age 5: 1.1%
going to primary school: 58%
a safe water supply: 75%
GDP per capita: $2240 (PPP)

Molly, UK
Life expectancy: 79
Chances of –
dying before age 5: 0.6%
going to primary school: 100%
a safe water supply: 100%
GDP per capita: $30 820 (PPP)

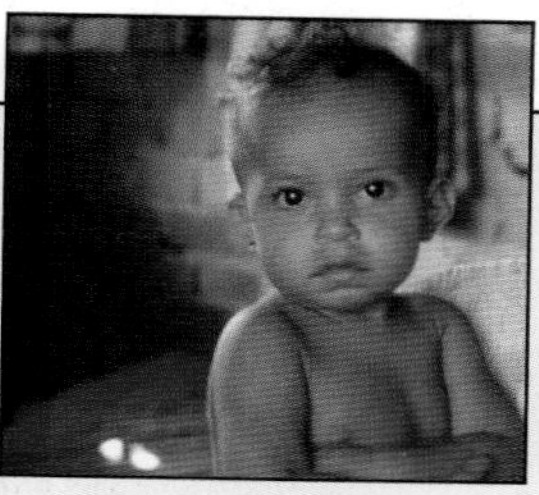

Maria Teresa, Brazil
Life expectancy: 71
Chances of –
dying before age 5: 3.4 %
going to primary school: 93%
a safe water supply: 90%
GDP per capita: $8200 (PPP)

Prema, India
Life expectancy: 64
Chances of –
dying before age 5: 8.5%
going to primary school: 76%
a safe water supply: 90%
GDP per capita: $3139 (PPP)

▲ *Comparing four countries, using development indicators.*

Your turn

1 This table shows some development indicators.

The question	The matching development indicator	Its value for Ghana in 2004
	GDP per capita	$2240 (PPP)
	life expectancy	57 years
	adult literacy rate	58%
	under-5 mortality rate	11 in 1000 (or 1.1%)
	% with access to clean safe water	75%
	number of doctors per 100 000 people	15
	% undernourished	12%

a Make a larger copy of the table. (Leave room to write quite a lot in the first column.)

b Now write questions 1–7 from page 12 in the correct rows in the first column. (Glossary?)

2 Life expectancy is lower in Ghana than in the UK.

a See if you can think up some reasons for this.

b Do you think it will change as Ghana's GDP per capita rises? How? Why?

3 Next you'll compare Ghana with three other countries.

a First make a table like this one.

	Score for ...			
	Ghana	UK	Brazil	India
Life expectancy	1	4		
Under-five mortality rate				2
Enrolment in primary school				
Access to safe water				
GDP per capita				
Total score				

b Now look at the data for the four baby girls above. Using this data, give each country a score 1 – 4 for each indicator. (This has been started for you.) The country with the *best* result each time gets 4.

c Find the total score for each country.

d Using the totals to help you, list the four countries in order of development, the most developed first.

4 The **human development index** or **HDI** gives a quick way to compare countries. It combines data for GDP per capita, life expectancy, adult literacy, and enrolment in education, to give each country a score between 0 and 1. The higher the better!

Human development index (HDI), 2004

Australia	0.957	Kenya	0.491
Brazil	0.792	Mali	0.338
China	0.768	Nepal	0.527
Egypt	0.702	Nigeria	0.448
France	0.942	Pakistan	0.539
Germany	0.932	Saudi Arabia	0.777
Ghana	0.532	Spain	0.938
India	0.611	UK	0.940
Japan	0.949	USA	0.948

HDI, 2002
1
← Mali
0.5
0

a Make a much larger copy of this vertical scale. Use a whole page. (Graph paper?)

b Mark in each country from the table above, on your scale.

c Now draw two horizontal lines, cutting the scale at 0.8 and 0.5, as started here.

d Above 0.8 = high human development. From 0.5 to 0.8 = medium human development. Below 0.5 = low human development.

i Shade each group of countries (high, medium and low HDI) on your scale. Use a different colour for each, and add a key for your shading.

ii To which group does Ghana belong?

iii To which group does the UK belong?

5 So – how developed is Ghana? And is it growing more developed, or less, or even going backwards? Give evidence to support your answers. (This little table may help.)

HDI for Ghana

Year	HDI
1980	0.467
1990	0.511
2000	0.555
2004	0.532

Mapping development around the world

Here you'll see how an indicator can be mapped, to compare development around the world. And then you'll take a look at some patterns in less developed countries.

An unequal world

The world is a very unequal place. You can show just how unequal it is by mapping a development indicator. Look at the map below. It shows the **GDP per capita** (PPP) for different countries.

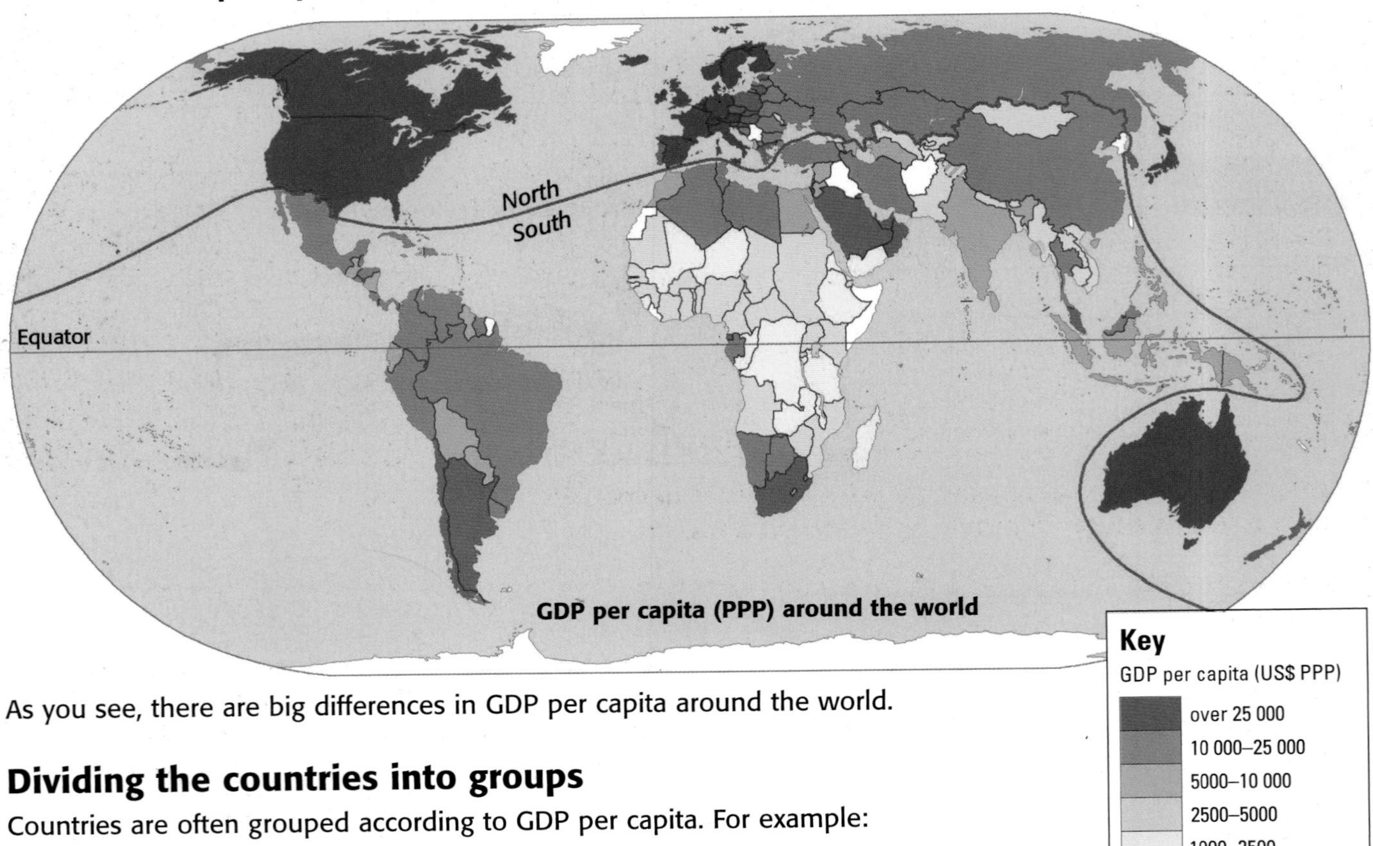

GDP per capita (PPP) around the world

Key

GDP per capita (US$ PPP)

- over 25 000
- 10 000–25 000
- 5000–10 000
- 2500–5000
- 1000–2500
- under 1000
- no data

As you see, there are big differences in GDP per capita around the world.

Dividing the countries into groups

Countries are often grouped according to GDP per capita. For example:

- The poorer countries are often called **less economically developed countries** or **LEDCs**.
- The richer countries are called **MEDCs**. (What does that stand for?)
- The poorest countries are also called the **Third World**. But many geographers don't like this term because they think it is patronising.
- The richer countries are sometimes called the **rich north**, because most are up in the northern part of the world. (Look at the red line.) So the poorer countries are called the **poor south**.

But it is always changing ...

Several LEDCs are now developing very fast, and will soon catch up with MEDCs. India, China, Brazil, and South Korea are examples. The table on the right shows how fast the GDP per capita for China is growing.

These countries are developing fast by setting up industries. So they are often called **newly industrialised countries** or **NICs**. (The UK and some other European countries began to industrialize about 250 years ago.)

GDP per capita for China

Year	GDP per capita (US dollars PPP)
2000	$3976
2001	$4020
2002	$4580
2003	$5000
2004	$5896
2005*	$6800
2006*	$10 518
2007*	$11 694

* estimated by the World Bank

More about the less economically developed countries

The poorer countries, like all countries, are quite different from each other. But they do tend to share some patterns.

But as you saw, countries are always changing. And even the poorest countries have some wealthy people, and better-off areas.

Your turn

1 Look at the map on page 14. In which range of GDP per capita (in US dollars PPP) is:
 a the UK? b Ghana? c Brazil? d Japan?
 The map on pages 128–129 will help.

2 Name:
 a five other countries in the same group as Ghana
 b five other countries in the same group as Brazil
 c five of the world's very richest countries
 for GDP per capita.

3 Assume for now that the MEDCs have a GDP per capita (PPP) of over $10 000.
 a What does *MEDC* stand for?
 b Name two MEDCs you haven't named already.

4 Write out each sentence. After it, write *True* or *False*.
 A Overall, Africa is the poorest continent.
 B Iceland is in the highest income group.
 C Mali is one of the world's poorest countries.
 D Everyone in Mali is really poor.
 E Overall, Libyans are better off than Egyptians.
 F The GDP per capita for Japan is $20 000 (PPP).
 G The poorest countries are also the most crowded. (The map on page 6 will help here.)

5 If you map *life expectancy* on a world map, you will get a pattern very like the one on page 14.
 See if you can draw a diagram like the one started below, to explain why. Add more boxes and arrows!

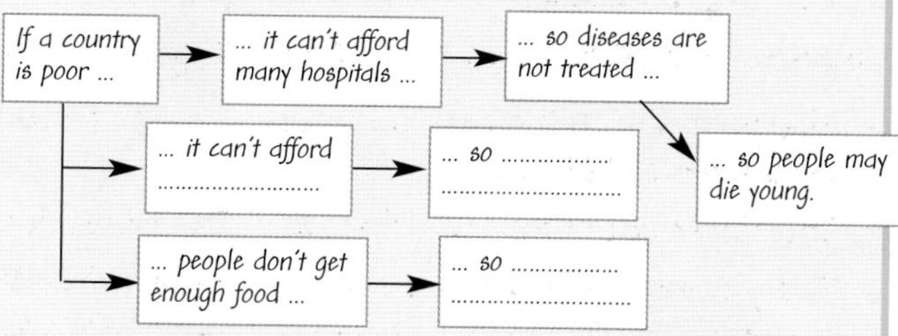

6 Find Cambodia on the map on page 14. Then, using the spider map above to help you, write 6 bullet points about development in Cambodia. Start like this: *I think Cambodia is likely to have ...*

7 *Why* are so many countries poor?
 Could it be to do with their climates? Location? Leaders? Other countries?
 a Give all the possible reasons you can think of. (But no silly ones!)
 b Underline reasons to do with physical geography in one colour, and to do with the people in another.

1.6 How did the development gap grow? (part I)

In this unit, and the next, you will learn about the main reasons for the big differences in development around the world.

Some reasons for the development gap

1 Historical reasons

The pattern of development around the world changes over time. 2000 years ago, India and China were the richest countries in the world – and Italy and Greece the richest ones in Europe.

But by 1500 AD, Western Europe was developing fast, thanks to good farmland, a good climate for crops, and the growth of industries such as shipbuilding and textiles.

Then came the Industrial Revolution. It began around 1750 in Britain and spread to its neighbours in Europe. It led to a big jump in wealth and development for several countries.

By then, Europeans had settled in North America. They began to develop industries, using the new ideas and inventions – and North America soon grew wealthy too.

Meanwhile, European explorers had been exploring Africa, South America, and Asia. They found lands rich in natural resources. Trading, and conflict, soon followed.

It usually started with friendly trading for things like gold, tobacco, timber, and spices. But as time went by, the Europeans grew greedier …

… and took over their trading partners by force, as **colonies**. They took their raw materials, and sold them finished goods – and that made many Europeans very rich!

In time, the Europeans were forced out. They left behind countries in a low state of development – with little industry, or education, or skills, and often a great deal of unrest.

Between them, Britain, France, Spain, Portugal and some other European countries carved up Africa, South America and much of Asia, as colonies. Those ex-colonies are LEDCs today – and many are still unstable.

2 Reasons to do with physical geography

The physical geography of a country – its location, and climate, and natural resources – can play a huge part in helping it develop.

Over the years its coal, oil, gas, and good farmland, have all helped the UK develop. And the sea has been great for fishing, and for trading.

But in a hot dry country far from the sea, isolated by mountains, with poor soil and few other resources, development may be very difficult.

Some countries have the opposite problem – good soil, but too much rain, and severe floods. Years of hard work just get washed away.

3 Social and political reasons

A country has a better chance of developing if it is stable and secure, with a strong government.

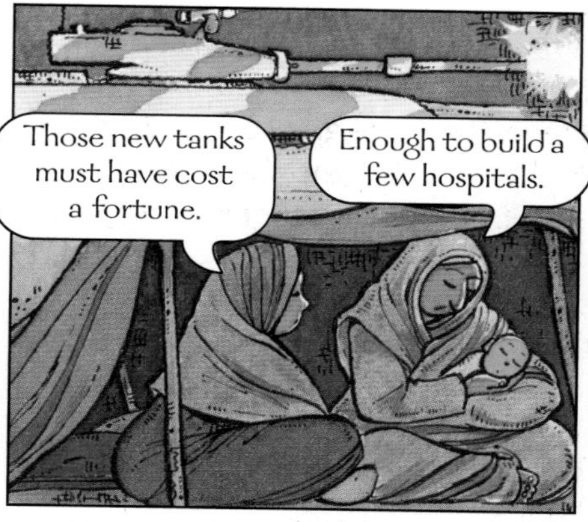

But many of the world's poor countries have wars going on, with a big waste of lives, and money.

And in many countries, corrupt leaders have made themselves rich, while their people live in poverty.

You can read about more reasons in the next unit.

Your turn

1 A – I are facts about different countries. For each, explain why this could have held back development.

A It is mountainous and hard to reach.
B A tribal war has been going on there for ten years.
C Millions of its people are suffering from AIDS.
D It suffers severe flooding almost every year.
E It was a British colony for over 50 years.
F A small group of people owns most of its wealth.
G Others refuse to trade with it, because of its politics.
H It has poor soil, and the rains are not dependable.
I The country that colonised it made sure that its people did not get much education.

2 Look at the facts in 1. Which of them are:
a historical (about things that happened in the past)?
b to do with physical geography?
c to do with society and politics?

3 Now see if you can write 10 similar statements that would explain why a country is *more* developed.

How did the development gap grow? (part II)

Here we carry on from the last unit, and look at two more reasons to explain the big development gap between countries.

4 The heavy debts of the poorer countries

Poor countries want to develop fast – but that needs money, and they don't have much. So they have borrowed lots. Some from ...

... ordinary **banks** like we all use. Some from the **World Bank** and the **International Monetary Fund**, set up jointly by over 180 countries.

And some straight from other **governments**. To get the money, the poor countries often had to make some promises in return.

When you borrow money, you pay interest on the loan. Many bank loans were made in the early 1970s when interest rates were low.

Then interest rates shot up. So the poorer countries had to use more and more of the money they earned, just for interest payments.

And that meant they had less for schools, or hospitals, or a water supply, or the other things their people badly needed.

High levels of debt, and high interest payments, have been a very big factor in some countries, in holding back development.

You can find out what's happening about these debts, in the next unit.

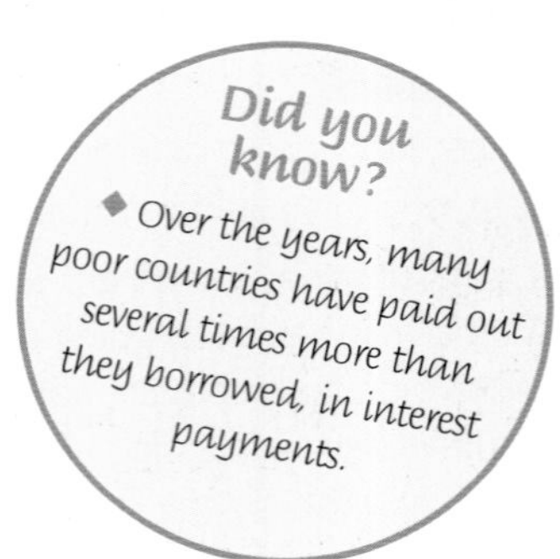

Did you know?
◆ Over the years, many poor countries have paid out several times more than they borrowed, in interest payments.

5 Unfair trade

Today, unfair trade is a key reason for the development gap. These two terms will help you to understand why:

- **Subsidies**. These are a sort of grant. Farmers in Europe and the USA get many subsidies from their governments, for growing crops.
- **Tariffs.** These are taxes a government may place on imported goods. The government gets the money. But tariffs can put people off importing goods, since they make them more expensive. So the tariffs help to protect the country's farmers, and industries, from competition.

Many poor countries depend on exporting crops such as sugar, cocoa, and coffee. So let's see how subsidies and tariffs – and big international companies or **TNCs** – have helped to keep these countries poor.

When the poorer countries sell their crops to the richer countries, the richer countries may slap big tariffs on them.

At the same time, the world price for many crops has been falling. Partly because many poor countries are competing to grow them …

… and partly because the big food TNCs, who buy up most of the crops, are so powerful that they can force the price down.

The tariffs mean the poor countries can't sell so much. The falling world prices mean they earn less from what they do sell. But their problems don't end there …

… because meanwhile, farmers in rich countries grow many of the same or similar crops – and get subsidies for doing so.

These crops are then exported to the poorer countries. At prices so low that the local farmers can't compete, and go out of business.

The poorer countries can't stop these imports, because the World Bank has forced them to drop tariffs, in exchange for loans.

So poor countries that depend on exporting crops may stay poor, no matter how hard people work.

What can be done to help them catch up, and close the development gap? The next unit has some ideas.

Your turn

1 Explain what these terms mean. (Glossary?)
  a the World Bank **b** the International Monetary Fund
  c debt **d** the interest rate **e** TNC

2 You live in a poor country. Your government wants to borrow money from a rich country, to build schools – but wants your advice first. What will you say?

3 You must explain to a 10-year-old how tariffs help countries to protect their industries. What will you say?

4 Your country, which is poor, has just been forced to drop all its tariffs against food imports. Write a letter of protest to the local paper, explaining how this will:
  a harm your country **b** benefit other countries

1.8 Tackling the development gap

Here you'll learn about the development goals that world leaders have set, to help the poorer countries catch up.

Did you know?

- We have the money, and the know-how, to end world poverty.

A Happy New Millennium?

This is how our world looked at the start of the new millennium:

1 January, 2000 — World population: 6 billion

- 20% of the world's people barely survive (on less than $1 a day)
- 14% do not get enough food to eat
- 18% do not have access to a clean safe water supply
- 40% do not have access to adequate toilets
- 8% of children die before age 5, most from preventable causes
- 20% of people aged over 15 can't read or write
- 17% of children of primary school age don't go to school

The Millennium Development Goals

In September 2000, world leaders held a **summit meeting**, to discuss the state of the world. They agreed a set of goals, to be met by the year 2015. Here are some of them:

We can do this...
... if we put our minds to it.
It's not rocket science!

The Millennium Development Goals

By 2015 we aim to:

- halve the % of people living on less than 1 dollar a day
- halve the % of undernourished people
- halve the % of people without access to a safe water supply
- cut under-5 deaths by two-thirds
- ensure that all children everywhere complete primary school

This is only fair.
And it will make the world more stable.

A first step: cancelling some debt

- In 2004, the British government cancelled some of the debts owed to it by the poorest countries, to help them climb out of poverty.
- In 2005, at a summit meeting in Scotland, the leaders of the G8 countries agreed to cancel $40 billion of debt owed by the poorest countries. (The G8 are the world's 7 richest industrial nations – the USA, the UK, Japan, Germany, France, Italy and Canada – plus Russia.)
- In return these poor countries promised to use the money to help their poorest people.

It is working. For example, in the past, poor people in Zambia could not afford to go to the doctor. But in 2006, Zambia was able to make health care free for everyone – because it had $6.5 billion of its debts cancelled. (That left Zambia with debts of $500 million.)

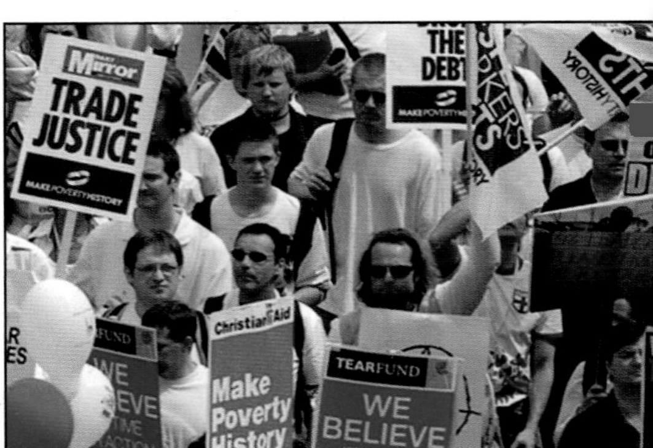

▲ *Speaking up for the world's poor, before the summit of G8 leaders, at Gleneagles in Scotland in 2005.*

The money to meet those goals

The rich countries will need to come up with a huge amount of money, to help the LEDCs meet the Millennium Development Goals. How can they provide this money? There are three ways:

Just think what we could do with this.

20 billion dollars

% of GNI given as aid in 2004

Country	%
Australia	0.25
Canada	0.27
Denmark	0.85
France	0.41
Germany	0.28
Japan	0.19
Netherlands	0.73
Norway	0.87
United Kingdom	0.36
United States	0.17

They promised 0.7%.
Give us a fair price for our crops.
Stop subsidising your farmers, and ...
Drop all tariffs against us.
... give us a chance to compete with them.

1 Cancel *all* old Third World debt
This would free the LEDCs from a huge burden, and help them to make a fresh start.

2 Give more aid
Rich countries keep promising to give aid. But most give far less than they promised.

3 Make world trade fairer
This would help LEDCs to earn more, which they could then use for their own development.

Of these, fair trade is the one that would make most difference for the future. Farmers in poor countries say they want fair trade, not charity!

So can the goals be met?

Everyone hopes so. But progress is very slow. It will take lots of careful planning and hard work, as well as money. And 2015 is getting close.

Talks about debt and fair trade *are* going on, but really slowly. And meanwhile the LEDCs take out more loans, to try to help themselves.

Your turn

1 Imagine it's the year 2000, and the world is a village of 100 people. Using the statistics at the top of page 20, say how many of the 100 people:
- a are undernourished
- b have under a dollar a day – around 50p – to live on (for their food, fuel, clothing, medicine, everything)
- c have no access to safe water
- d have no access to adequate toilets

2 Look at the Millennium Development Goals.
- a Why don't they aim for safe water for *everyone* by 2015?
- b Arrange the goals in what you think is their order of importance (most important first), and explain why you chose this order.
- c The cost of meeting these goals will be enormous. Give some reasons why.

3 Look at the table above. It shows the % of gross national income (GNI) that ten MEDCs gave as aid, in 2004.
- a What is *gross national income*? (Glossary?)
- b Draw a vertical scale like this one, and mark in the countries at the correct places.
- c They had promised to give 0.7% of GNI as aid. Mark in a dotted line at 0.7. How many had kept their promise?
- d Write an open letter to the leaders of the other countries, asking them to keep their promise on aid. Be as persuasive as you can.

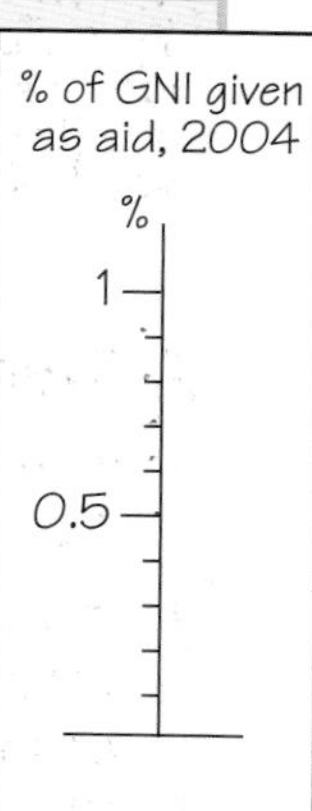

4 This is one person's opinion. What will you say in reply? Write it down as a set of bullet points.

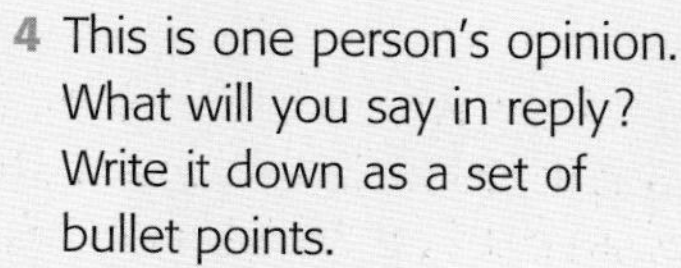

We should stop helping other countries, and give the money to poor people in our own country!

About Ghana

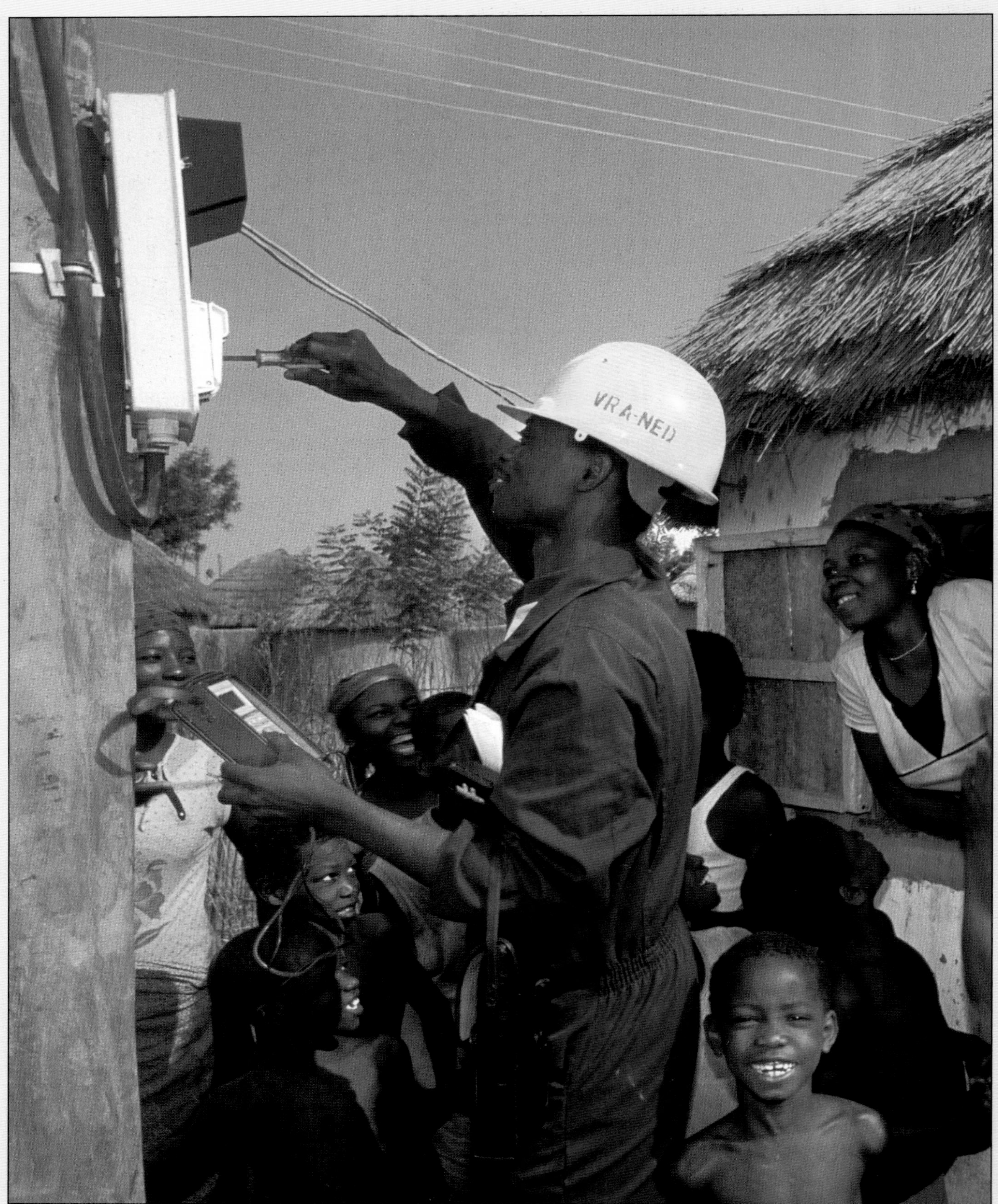

The big picture

This chapter is about **Ghana**, a country in West Africa that's linked closely to the UK by history. These are the big ideas behind the chapter:

- Ghana is rich in natural resources.
- Even so, it is a less economically developed country, or LEDC. A great many of its people live in poverty.
- There are many reasons for this, including historical reasons.
- Ghana is working hard to lift its people out of poverty.

Your goals for this chapter

By the end of this chapter you should be able to answer these questions:

- Where is Ghana, and ...
  - what are its main physical features, climate zones and ecosystems?
  - what natural resources does it have, and what are its main exports?
- Why has Ghana got close links with the UK?
- What is life like, in poor rural villages in Ghana?
- Where in Ghana is Accra, and what can I say about it? (At least five statements!)
- Why has Ghana lagged behind in its development? (At least five reasons.)
- Earnings are low, and unsteady, for Ghana's cocoa farmers. Why is this?
- Who gets most of the money, when I buy a bar of chocolate?
- With Fairtrade chocolate, the cocoa farmers get a better deal. How does this work?
- Why can small projects, like water wells, help development?
- Ghana has a better chance of developing faster now than in the last 50 years. Why is this?

And then ...

When you finish the chapter, come back to this page and see if you have met your goals!

Did you know?

- On 6 March 2007, Ghana had its 50th birthday.
- On 6 March 1957, it gained its independence from Britain!

Did you know?

- The Ghanaian government gave motorbikes and bikes to thousands of teachers in rural villages.
- The aim was to persuade them to stay!

Did you know?

- Ghana's two main exports are gold, and cocoa beans (used in making chocolate).

Did you know?

- Ghana's army plays a big part in helping to keep peace in other African countries.

Your chapter starter

Look at the photo on page 22.

Something new has arrived in this village in Ghana. What is it?

Why is everyone looking so happy?

Why didn't they have this thing before (like you do)?

About how many people around the world do you think still don't have it?

2.1 Meet Ghana

This unit introduces you to Ghana – the African country we explore in this chapter.

Welcome to Ghana

Welcome to Ghana, linked to the UK by history and the Prime Meridian. Where you'll find …

▲ *… a warm welcome for visitors …*

▲ *… some great wealth …*

▲ *… a great sense of style …*

▲ *… tropical rainforest to explore …*

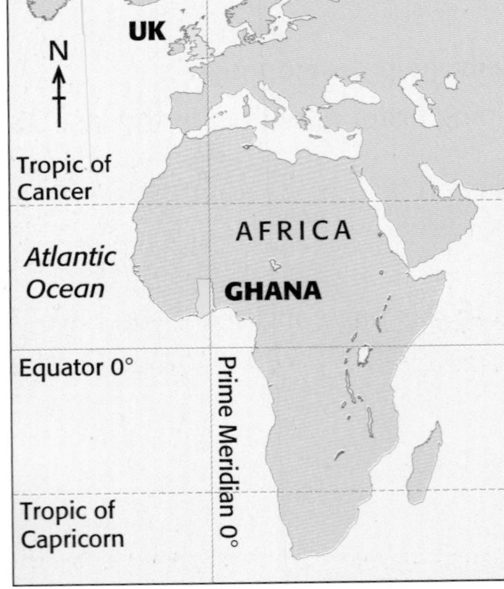

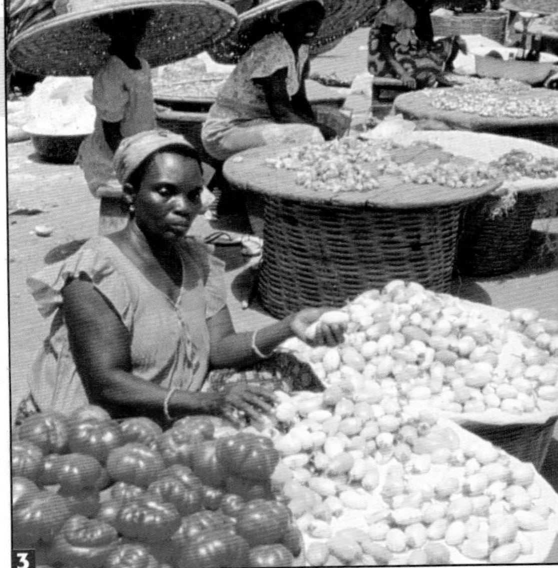

▲ *… outdoor markets everywhere …*

▲ *… traditional ceremonies and rituals …*

▲ *… music, dancing, laughter …*

◀ *… gold and diamond mines …*

▲ ... hundreds of small rural villages ...

▲ ... millions living in poverty ...

▲ ... and a passion for football.

Ghana's physical geography

Look at the map on the right. You can see that over half of Ghana is quite low and flat.

The main river is the Volta, fed by the Black Volta and White Volta. A dam was built on the Volta in 1965, to give hydroelectricity. A huge area behind the dam was drowned, forming Lake Volta, the world's largest artificial lake. It covers about 8500 sq km – or nearly 50 times the area of Glasgow.

Now look at the shape of Ghana. It's quite neat and tidy! That's because it was carved out of separate kingdoms by the British, by drawing lines on a map.

You'll find out more about its history later.

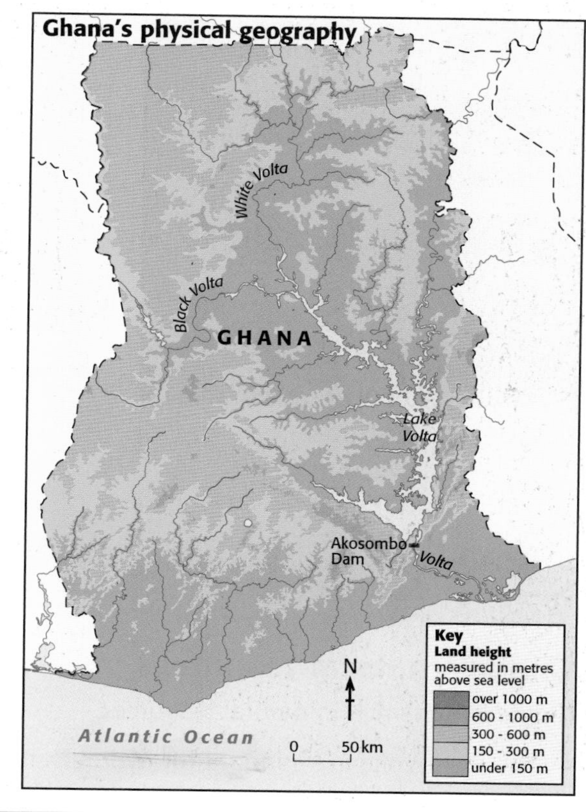

It's an LEDC

There are about 21 million people in Ghana. Around 8 million of them live in great poverty.

Compared with many countries, Ghana is poor. It is called a **less economically developed country** or **LEDC** for short. You will look at its development more closely later.

Your turn

1 Where is Ghana? Use these words and terms in your answer: ocean, meridian, West Africa, tropic, equator.

2 Name the countries that border Ghana. (Page 129.)

3 Using the map above, write a paragraph about Ghana's features. (For example where is the highest land? How high? What about lakes? Rivers? Coast?)

4 Using this table to help you, write a paragraph comparing Ghana and the UK. Give the *population density* for each country in your answer. (Glossary?)

5 a Ghana is an *LEDC*. What do the letters stand for?
b What evidence can you see in the photos, that Ghana is an LEDC? (Give the photo numbers.)

Some statistics	Ghana	UK
Area (thousands of sq km)	240	245
Population (millions)	20	60
% in rural areas	55	10
Life expectancy (years)	58	77

2.2 A closer look at Ghana

Here you'll learn a little more about the geography and people of Ghana, before we go on to look at its development.

Ghana's climate and ecosystems

Ghana is in the tropics. That means it's hot! But like most countries it has different climate zones – which means different ecosystems too.

1 hot and wet

- hot all year round
- about 2 m of rain a year

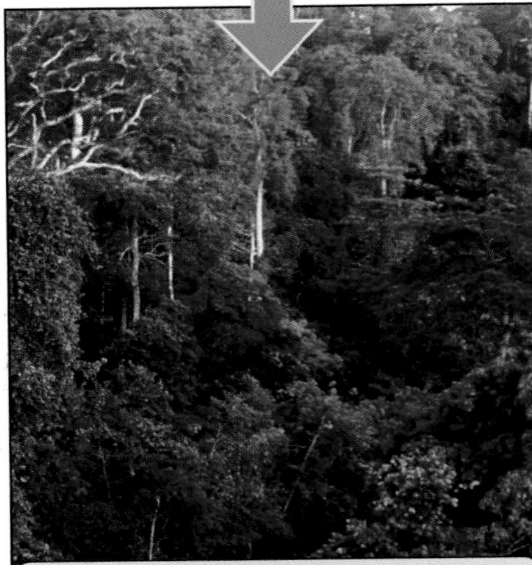

Tropical rainforest

- Ghana used to have a lot of rainforest. Only a quarter is left.
- It was cut down by loggers, by farmers clearing land to grow cocoa, and by people collecting firewood.

Ghana's climate zones

a hot dry NE wind called the *harmattan* blows December–March

Z • Y • X • 1 2 3

Lake Volta

prevailing wind

Atlantic Ocean

2 hot and very dry

- it gets hotter than the rainforest
- one rainy season a year – and droughts are quite common
- the further north you go, the drier it is.

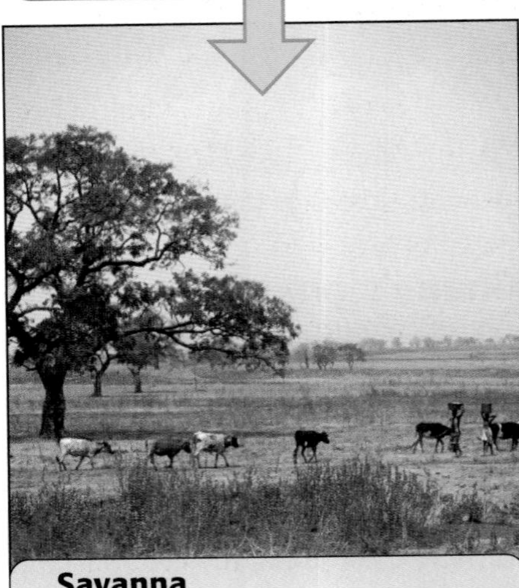

Savanna

- The grass grows tall in the rain, then shrivels in the dry season.
- You won't find many trees. Most are acacia trees, like this one.

Did you know?

- About 400 000 tourists visited Ghana in 2000.
- They expect over a million tourists a year by 2010.

3 quite hot and dry

- quite hot all year
- two rainy seasons a year

Coastal savanna

- You'll see tall grass, thick-leaved shrubs, and giant baobab trees.

Ghana's natural resources

Ghana is quite rich in natural resources.

- The River Volta is important for hydroelectricity and fishing. The power station at the dam provides about two-thirds of Ghana's electricity.
- The rainforests are a source of timber. (So they are getting cut down.)
- It has gold, diamonds, bauxite (aluminium ore), and manganese ore. They are found in the rainforest area, as the map on page 27 shows.
- It has some oil offshore (but not enough – it imports a lot more). It has far more natural gas offshore, which it began using in 2004.
- The hot wet climate in the south west is ideal for growing cocoa, for chocolate. So Ghana is the second largest cocoa producer in the world. (Its neighbour, Côte d'Ivoire, is first.)
- It has many protected areas in the rainforest and savanna, where you can see wildlife: elephants, buffalo, lions, hippos, chimps, monkeys, birds, butterflies and more. These are starting to attract tourists.

Ghana's people

Ghana has 60 different ethnic groups. They were brought together by the British, who carved the country from a mixture of kingdoms. (More about this later.)

As a result of Ghana's history, English is its official language. But there are four other main languages. In school, everything is taught through English.

Where do people live?

The map on the right shows Ghana's main towns and cities. 45% of the population live in towns and cities, and the rest in rural villages.

Many of these villages do not yet have electricity or a water supply, and many villagers live in great poverty.

What do people do for a living?

Ghana is an **agricultural economy**. 60% of its workers farm for a living. In the south west, as the map shows, people grow cocoa and oil palms. (Oil from oil palms is used for cooking, and to make soap and cosmetics.)

There is not much industry (manufacturing) in Ghana yet – but the government has big plans to change this. 15% of the workers are in industry.

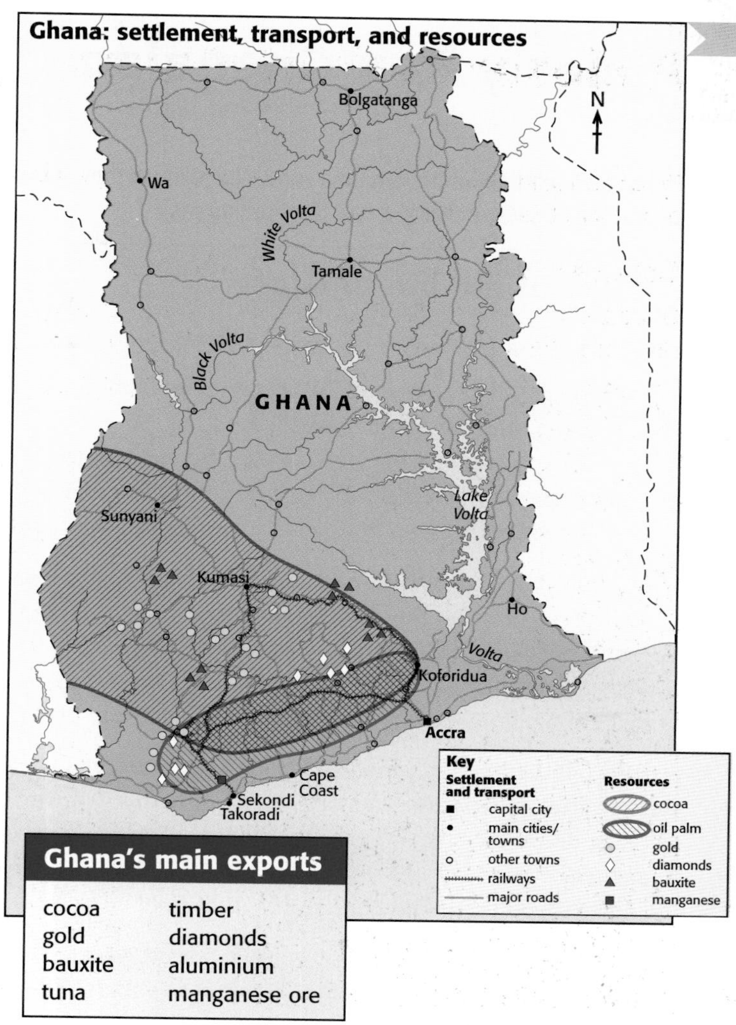

Ghana's main exports

cocoa	timber
gold	diamonds
bauxite	aluminium
tuna	manganese ore

Your turn

1 Using the maps on pages 26 and 128–129 to help you, explain why:
 a Ghana is hotter than the UK
 b X on the map on page 26 gets more rain than Y
 c it's much hotter at Z than at Y, in January.

2 a Ghana has lost three-quarters of its rainforest. This process is called *de*_______ (Glossary?)
 b Do you think it'd a good thing? Explain your answer. (Use anything you know already about rainforests!)

3 Study charts A–C on the right. Then write a report comparing Ghana and the UK, using these headings:
 Where people live
 What people do for a living
 The age structure of the population
Use terms like *more than, less than, twice as many as* in your answer. And try to come up with explanations for the differences you find. The glossary may help.

4 Ghana exports raw materials such as palm oil and cocoa. It has to import manufactured goods.
 a The government wants to set up lots more factories. Why do you think this is?
 b Come up with a list of factories it could set up – at least ten. (Think about its natural resources!)

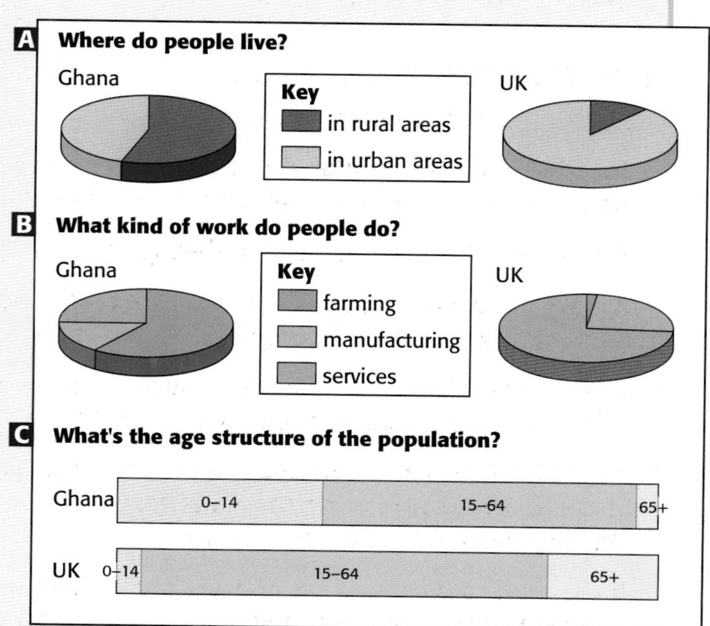

Poverty in a Ghanaian village

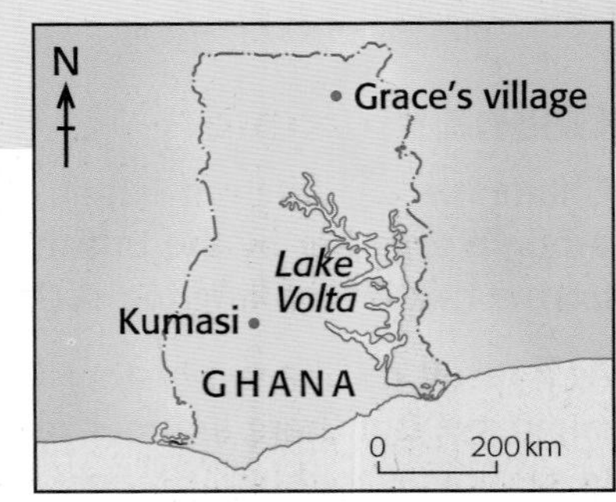

Here you'll read about poverty in a rural village in northern Ghana. (As in most LEDCs, poverty is worst in rural areas.)

A day in the life of Grace

So you want to know what it's like to be poor?

I lie here on my straw mat, staring up into the darkness. My baby lies beside me, snuffling in her sleep. And over there on the mud floor my four other living children, all curled up together. Out in the yard, in their graves, the two dead ones. My firstborn died when she was three, and the youngest boy last year. How I cried when I buried them.

I lie here thinking about my problems. First, my husband. A good man. He works hard, and is always thinking of ways to make our lives better. Two months ago he went to Kumasi to find work. 'We will buy a goat with the money' he said, 'and send the eldest boy to primary school.' But I have had no message from him. He could be ill, or in trouble.

And the farm. The rains were poor last season. Out in our tiny field the millet is dry and stunted. Enough to feed us for two months, perhaps. What then? In the darkness I can feel my savings, tied in the corner of my cloth. Nineteen thousand cedis. If any of the children fall ill, that won't even be enough for medicine.

I could sell something – but what? You could count our possessions in seconds. Three enamel bowls. Two metal plates. The cooking pot. The water bucket. The kerosene lamp made from a bottle. The wooden pestle for pounding the millet. One machete. One hoe. Two small knives. A fork. A torch with no bulb. Two mats. And a few bundles of worn clothing.

But today is a new day. Soon I will rise and slip out to the clump of bushes behind the huts, which is the village toilet. Like the other women I go while it is still dark, for privacy. And at daybreak I will set off to get water. The river is nearly dry now, so the water will be very muddy and dangerous. It killed my children. But what can I do?

It takes me over an hour to get to the river, and longer to get back with my heavy bucket. I will give the children a little water to drink. I will breastfeed the baby. Then I will go to the farm to tend the millet and pick what's ready. And all day long I will hope that someone from the village will come running with a message from my husband.

While I am away my eldest daughter will pound millet. The eldest boy will go looking for firewood – every day a little further. Towards dusk we will eat our one meal for the day: millet porridge. At 6 it will get dark, as usual. I want to save the little kerosene that's left. So we will go to bed early, as usual – and, as usual, still hungry.

So, this is poverty. Coping with it takes all my energy. But we will survive, and I will find a way to create a better future for my children.

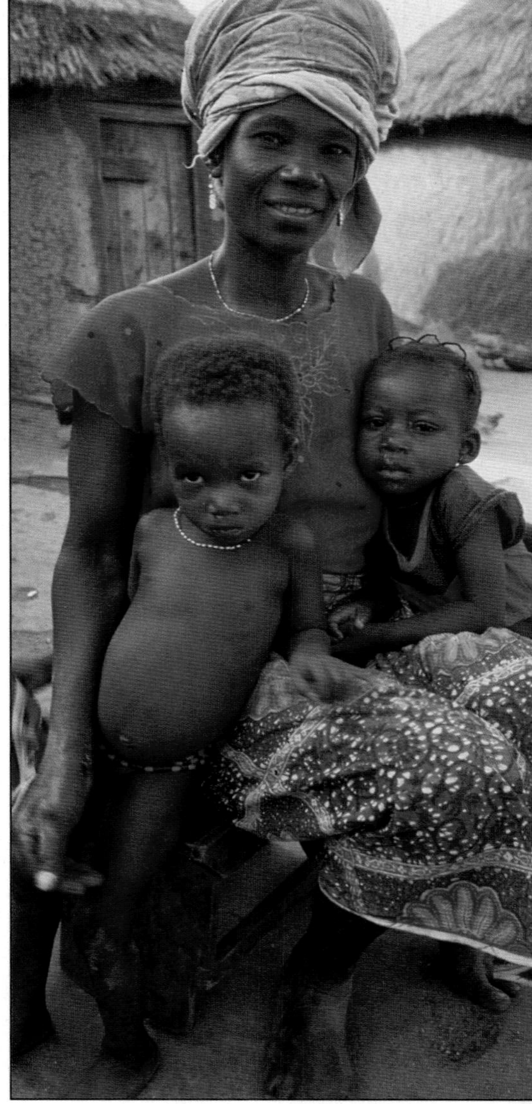

▲ *Grace with two of her children.*

Did you know?

- *A child dies every 10 seconds, somewhere in the world, from a disease carried by dirty water.*

Did you know?

- *Ghana's currency is the cedi.*
- *16 000 cedis equalled about £1, in 2005.*

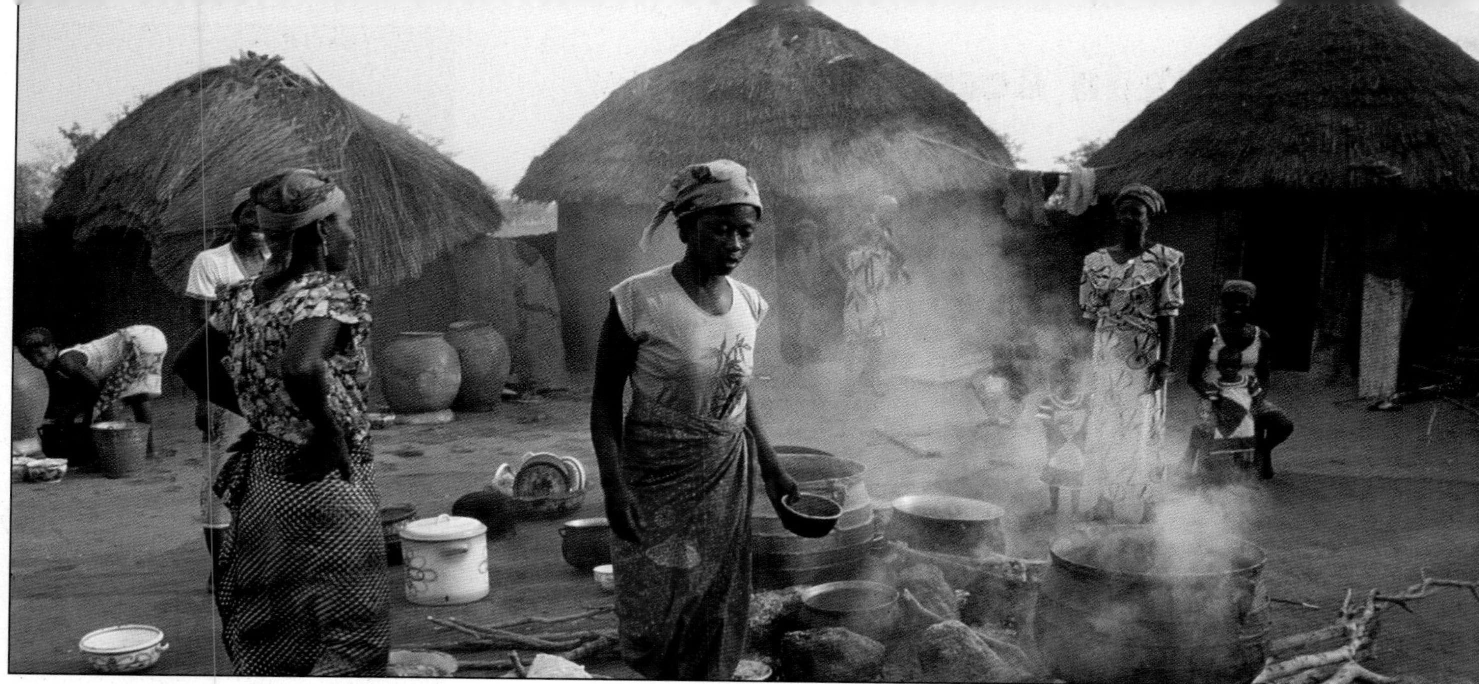

▲ *Grace's village. All her friends are poor, like her. They all work very hard.*

Your turn

1 a List the items Grace has, for her kitchen.
b Now list the things in your kitchen.

2

Time spent on tasks in Grace's household

	Task	*Minutes*
A	preparing dinner (pounding and boiling millet, making a sauce)	200
B	getting water (from the river)	170
C	sweeping (the yard and hut)	45
D	washing clothes (at the river)	200
E	washing up (one meal a day)	20
F	obtaining fuel (firewood)	120

a Make a table like this for these tasks in *your* household. (Change what's in the brackets.)
b Now draw a suitable graph to compare the times for these tasks in your household and Grace's.
c Did you have any problems in drawing the graph for b? If yes, explain why.
d For which task is the time difference greatest? Why?
e For which is it least? Why?
f In total, how much longer is spent on these six tasks in Grace's household than in yours? How might this affect Grace and her family?

3 Grace lives in great poverty. Draw a spider map to show what that means, for her. You could start like this.

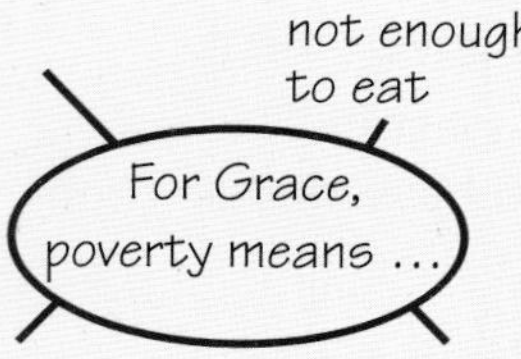

4 a Next, study the photo above, and note as many points as you can about life in Grace's village. For example note what the people are doing, and using. Which groups of people are missing? Don't forget to look in the background too. What are the houses like? Are there any electricity cables?
b Now use your notes to write a couple of paragraphs about life in the village. Make them interesting!

5 You'd like to help the people of Grace's village. You can provide money and equipment to help them to:

A install a village pump, giving clean safe water
B read and write (so Grace can write to her husband)
C fit solar cells (PV cells) to the hut roofs, so they can have electric lighting
D build a latrine (a concrete toilet where the waste drains away into the ground)

a Which do you think Grace would like first? Why? Write down all the benefits it would bring.
b Arrange the four projects in order of priority, from Grace's point of view.
c Who should have most say in deciding about the projects, you or the villagers? Give your reasons.

6 And now it's time to tell Grace about you.
a Write a page about a day in your life, and the kinds of tasks you have to do, and what you worry about. (Imagine that someone who can read will read it out to Grace and her children for you.)
b How do you think Grace and her children will feel about your life?

2.4 Contrasts in Accra

In this unit you'll learn about Accra, the capital city of Ghana.

How old? How big?

Accra began about 500 years ago, when people of the Ga tribe settled there. It grew quickly when the European traders arrived. The British made it the capital of Ghana in 1877.

About 2 million people live there – or about 10% of Ghana's population. And the number is growing daily. Many of the new arrivals are from rural areas, looking for work. Many are migrants from neighbouring countries. But most of the growth is due to a high birth rate.

What's it like there?

Accra is bustling, colourful, and friendly. The streets are full of tro-tros (minibuses) and taxis, horns blaring. There's music from every doorway.

You'll see people carrying big loads on their heads, women with babies on their backs, business people in smart suits, shoeshine boys, beggars, and children selling newspapers. You'll see posh buildings, broken-down shacks, pleasant open spaces, and smelly open drains.

▲ *A street scene in Central Accra.*

A map of Accra

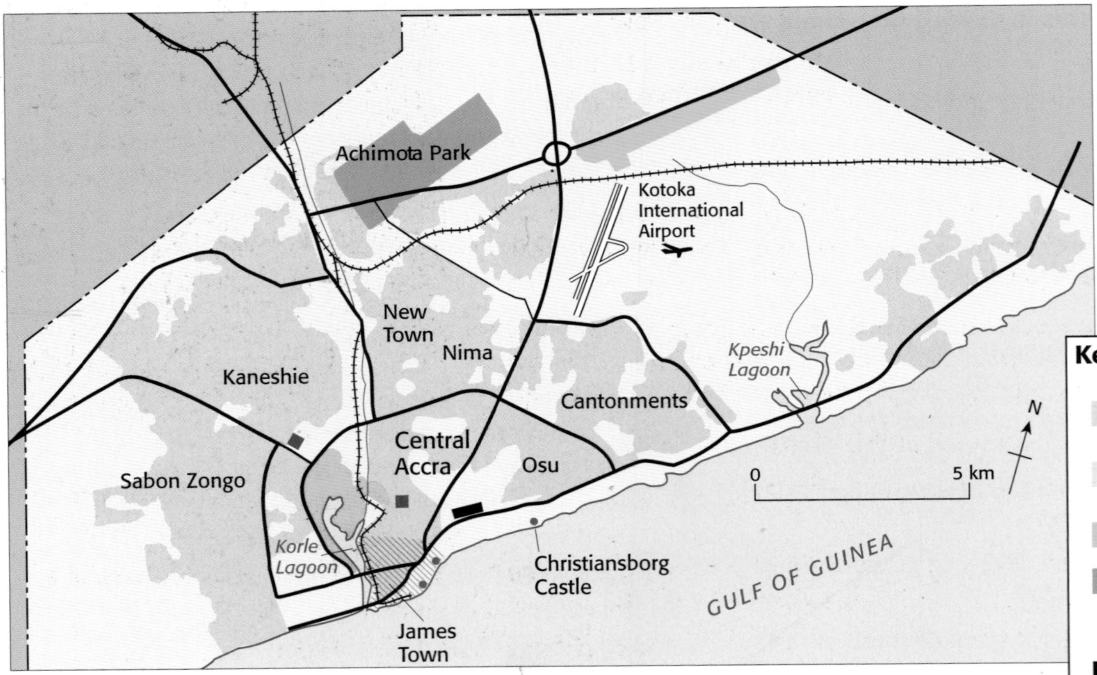

Achimota Park
Kotoka International Airport
New Town
Nima
Kaneshie
Cantonments
Kpeshi Lagoon
Central Accra
Osu
Sabon Zongo
Korle Lagoon
James Town
Christiansborg Castle
GULF OF GUINEA
0 — 5 km
N

GHANA
Accra

Key

- built-up area
- lightly populated, or open land
- industrial area
- forest
- main market
- government buildings
- forts built by Europeans
- major road
- railway
- boundary of Accra metropolitan area
- Accra around 1870

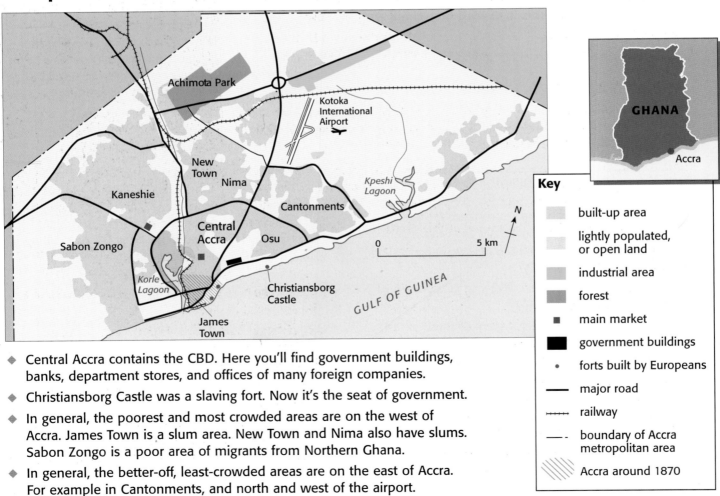

- Central Accra contains the CBD. Here you'll find government buildings, banks, department stores, and offices of many foreign companies.
- Christiansborg Castle was a slaving fort. Now it's the seat of government.
- In general, the poorest and most crowded areas are on the west of Accra. James Town is a slum area. New Town and Nima also have slums. Sabon Zongo is a poor area of migrants from Northern Ghana.
- In general, the better-off, least-crowded areas are on the east of Accra. For example in Cantonments, and north and west of the airport.

A city of contrasts

Accra is a city of contrasts. There are well-off areas of low-density housing, with big gardens, and many very poor and crowded areas.

A survey from 2005 suggests that, out of every 100 people in Accra:

- 77 are poor. They own very little, and live in slums. A third of them have little or no education.
- 17 are quite well off.
- 6 are well off, and some of these live in luxury.

▲ *You'll find homes like these in Cantonments, or around the airport.*

Day-to-day living

If you are wealthy, life in Accra is easy. Water on tap, cooks and gardeners and drivers at your service, and department stores for imported goods.

But for most people in the city, life is not so comfortable. For example:

- 60% of homes do not have running water. They have to use taps in the street. Or buy water (that might not be safe) from water sellers.
- 35% of homes have no toilet of any kind. People have to queue for public toilets, and often these are just pits. (Flush toilets are a luxury.)
- Around 10% of homes have no electricity.
- Less than 10% of homes get their rubbish collected. The rest have to take it to collection points. But a lot gets thrown into drains instead, or dumped on open land, where mountains of rubbish grow.

You might think this is terrible. But don't forget: conditions in London, Glasgow, and other British cities were not so different, 150 years ago.

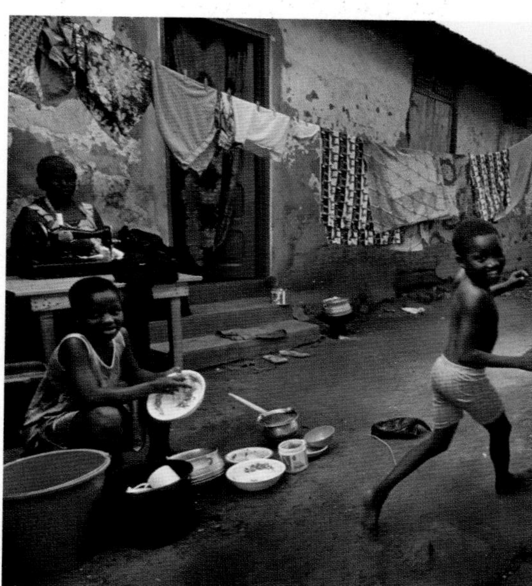

▲ *You'll see homes like these in the poorer parts of Accra.*

The challenges facing Accra

Accra's big problem is that it has grown very fast, with little control or planning. Water supply, sewage and other services have not kept up with its growth, because there was not enough money.

There are other problems too. Unemployment is high. Many children have to work for a living. Accra has around 11 000 homeless children, who live and sleep on the streets. In spite of all this, the level of crime is not high.

Accra is now working hard to solve its problems. And still smiling!

Your turn

1. The British made Accra the capital of Ghana. Using the maps on pages 30, 126, and 129, suggest some reasons why they chose this location.
2. The map of Accra shows features and patterns that you also find in British cities. See how many you can list.
3. There's inequality everywhere.
   a What signs of inequality are there where you live?
   b Do you think it is greater, or less, than the inequality in Accra? Say why you think so.
4. If you were Grace (page 28), would you rather stay in your village, or move to Accra? Give your reasons.
5. You are the new Mayor of Accra. You intend to solve at least some of its problems.
   a Make a table with headings like this:

Problems I will tackle	
Problem	*Action*

   b Write a list of the problems you will tackle, in order of priority.
   c Beside each problem, write at least one action you will take, to solve that problem.
   d And the big big question: where will you get the money? (The government does not have much.)

So why is Ghana an LEDC?

Here you'll learn some of the reasons why Ghana is a less developed country.

Why is Ghana an LEDC?

You saw that Ghana has many natural resources, including gold and diamonds. It's the world's second largest producer of cocoa. Its people work hard. But millions of them still live in deep poverty. Why?

There's a whole mixture of reasons. And some are historical.

A little history

The first Europeans to arrive at the coast of Ghana were the Portuguese, in 1471. They found different kingdoms – and plenty of gold! They began to trade for it, giving cloth, knives, beads, rum, and guns in exchange.

The news spread. Soon Dutch, Danish, German and British traders arrived too, in search of gold. The British called the land the **Gold Coast**.

By 1650, the **slave trade** was more important than gold – because the Europeans needed workers for their sugar and tobacco plantations in the Caribbean, and North and South America. They got thousands of slaves a year from the Gold Coast. Local tribes fought each other, to capture people to sell. This went on for over 150 years.

Little by little, Britain took control of all the trade, and then the country. By 1901 the Gold Coast was a British colony. Its kingdoms and tribes were forced together, to make a single unit.

The British shipped gold, metal ores, diamonds, ivory, pepper, timber, corn and cocoa from the Gold Coast. They paid very little for these. They built railways to carry them to the coast. They built some roads and schools and hospitals too. But they made the people pay for them through taxes.

In the end, the people had enough. They wanted freedom! At last, in 1957, the Gold Coast gained independence. It changed its name to Ghana. A free country – but with no factories, few services, and few skilled people to run it. (And that was just over 50 years ago.)

Did you know?

- Ghana exports over 300 000 tonnes of cocoa beans a year.
- Some end up in your chocolate.

Did you know?

- West African tribes had slavery long before the Europeans came.
- They sold criminals, and enemies, to traders from North Africa.

Did you know?

- Over 12 million slaves were shipped from Africa by European slave traders.

▲ The fort at Elmina from which many slaves were shipped. It was owned in turn by the Portuguese, Dutch and British.

▲ These slaves were shipped to North America, and are being sold to plantation owners in an auction.

Other reasons

Many other countries, that were colonies, have developed quite fast since independence. These are some reasons why Ghana has been slow:

- It has had much political unrest, in the years since independence. The army took control of the country from time to time.
- It started off with big plans for development projects. But there were few people with the skills to plan and manage these projects. So large amounts of money got wasted – or stolen by corrupt officials.
- Ghana borrowed the money for these projects. So it had to pay out lots of **interest** each year. That left less money for development.
- Ghana relies on its cocoa exports. But the price of cocoa has been falling over the years. So Ghana earns less and less per tonne.
- Farmers rely on the soil. But parts of the savanna in northern Ghana are turning into desert, where crops won't grow. This is caused by drought, chopping down trees, heavy grazing, and erosion of bare soil by wind and rain. It is called **desertification**.

  In the south, over three-quarters of the rainforest has been destroyed – mostly by logging companies, some by farmers for land to grow cocoa, and some for firewood. This is called **deforestation**. It gives people land to farm – but the exposed soil is soon useless.

  Ruined soil means fewer crops and animals. It means less food for farmers to feed their families, and to sell. So it means greater poverty.

▲ *A farm in the savanna in northern Ghana, at risk of desertification.*

Did you know?

- In 2002 Ghana paid out 200 million dollars to richer countries in interest on its loans.

Your turn

1 You have to draw a time line for Ghana.
 a On a large sheet of paper draw a vertical time line from 1450 up to 2000. Make it 30 cm long if you can. (Use two pages?)
 b On your line mark in events from the text **and** the event box below. (Small neat writing!) Add a title.

Year
1500
1450

2 Beside your time line shade the period in which:
 a West African slaves were bought by Europeans
 b the Gold Coast was partly or wholly a British colony.

3 Now underline the events that you think:
 a *helped* Ghana to develop, in one colour
 b *held back* its development, in another colour
 c *did a mixture of both*, in a third colour.

4 Add a key for your colours and shading, for 2 and 3.

5 Choose *one* event you underlined for 3c above, and explain why you underlined it.

6 *'Since independence, Ghana's development has been completely under its own control'.* From the work you have just done, do you think this statement is true? Give your reasons.

EVENTS

- 1878: a Ghanaian brings back cocoa plants from Fernado Po, an island off Africa
- 1928: a large harbour built at Takoradi
- 1980: economy almost collapses due to low cocoa price and other problems
- 1885: the first cocoa exported to Britain
- 1999: crisis in Asia and Russia causes world chocolate sales to fall
- 1830: the world's first chocolate bars made in England by J S Fry and Sons
- 1528: chocolate drink from the Aztecs introduced to Europe, by Spanish explorers
- 1502: first slave ship leaves West Africa
- 1807: Britain starts campaign to stop the slave trade
- 1618: first British trading settlement set up on the Gold Coast
- 1993: Ghana earns $222 million from selling rainforest timber
- 1898–1927: railways built by the British
- 1817: slavery abolished in Europe
- 1657: London's first drinking chocolate café opens
- 1965: the Akosombo dam completed, to provide Ghana with hydroelectricity
- 1874: Britain takes control of the south of the Gold Coast
- 1949: campaign for independence starts
- 1983: Ghana has to pay back loans of $1.5 billion to other countries

Bitter chocolate? Ghana's cocoa farmers

Here you'll learn about the importance of cocoa to Ghana, how the world market works, and how Fairtrade chocolate helps cocoa farmers.

Meet Kofi Boadu, cocoa farmer

This is Kofi Buadu and his son, from near Kumasi in Ghana. You have never met Kofi – but he may have played a small part in your life.

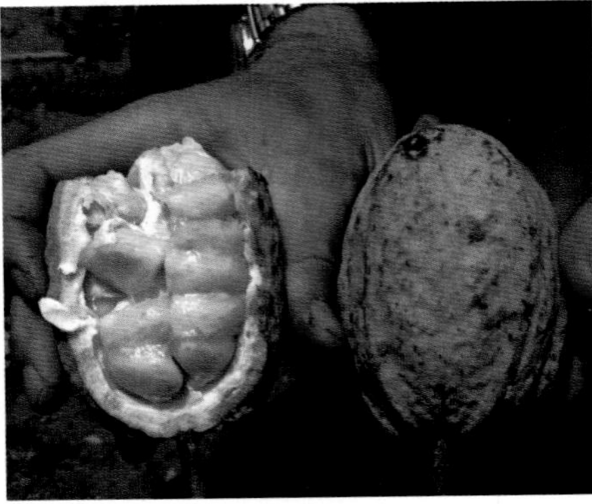

Because Kofi grows cacoa trees. The trees produce pods like this one, full of cocoa beans. The beans are dried, packed and sent …

… to the UK. And there they are used for making chocolate. And cocoa powder, for cakes and drinks. And cocoa butter, for body lotion.

An important crop for Ghana

Cocoa is very important to Ghana. It accounts for about 50% of exports. It is grown by about half a million cocoa farmers, like Kofi, on small family farms. They grow other things too. Like bananas, and vegetables such as yam and plantain, for the family. But cocoa is their **cash crop**.

Who grows cocoa?

Country *	Share of world production, 2005
Côte d'Ivoire	38%
Ghana	19%
Indonesia	13%
Nigeria	5%
Brazil	5%
Cameroon	5%
Ecuador	4%
Malaysia	1%
Others	10%

* All are on or near the Equator. (Cacoa trees need warmth and rain.)

What's the work like?

It's not easy. The trees need fertiliser. They are easy to damage. The pods ripen at different times through the year. Kofi has to watch out for the ripe ones, and cut them down carefully with a long clipper.

He cracks the pods open with a hammer. He takes out the beans, heaps them up, and covers them with a mat for a week or so. During this time they ferment, and turn brown. He spreads them in the sun to dry, turning them often. Then he takes them along to the cocoa bean buyer.

How much does he earn?

How much does Kofi earn? About 50p a day this year. It might be more next year – or less!

And certainly not enough to buy chocolate. Kofi and his children have never tasted it.

Why does he earn so little, when chocolate costs us quite a lot?

This chocolate bar has the answer. Suppose you pay £1 for it. Look where your money goes. Note who gets the biggest share. How much of the £1 does Kofi get?

If you pay £1…

7p goes to Kofi. He gets paid by the cocoa bean buyer, who works for the Ghanaian government's Cocoa Board.

7p goes to the Ghanaian government. It depends on this money to help it run the country.

40.5p goes to the big international company (TNC) that bought up thousands of tonnes of Ghana's cocoa beans this year, and turned them into chocolate and cocoa.

28p goes to the shop where you bought the chocolate bar.

17.5p goes to the British government, as a tax called VAT. It depends on this money to help it run the country.

The ups and downs of it

Suppose Kofi works extra hard next year. That does not mean he'll earn more! Because the world price for cocoa beans keeps changing.

When the cocoa-growing countries grow more cocoa beans than are needed, the world price falls. That's bad for Kofi. His family will have hardly enough to live on.

But if there's a shortage of cocoa beans, the price rises. So Kofi gets paid more. He might even earn enough to send his children to school.

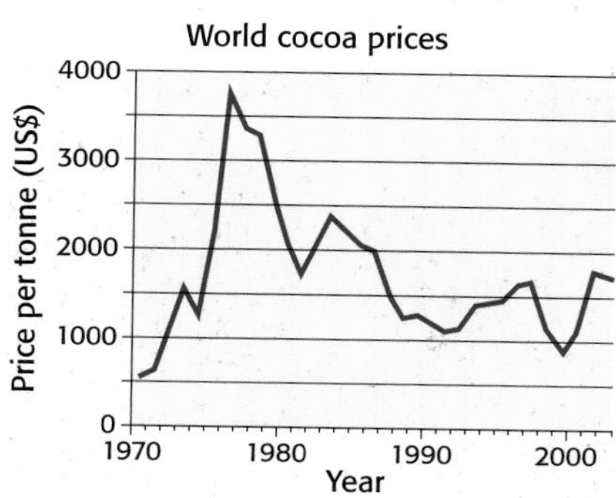

Sadly for Kofi, the *overall* price trend is now downwards. Because first, countries are growing more beans. And second, the big TNCs who buy them push the price down.

The big TNCs who buy the beans try for the lowest price. They don't think about Kofi, or how much he needs to earn, or how hard he's worked.

Another way to look at it

There's another way to buy cocoa beans: *Decide on a fair price to pay the farmers.*

It is called **fair trade**. This flowchart shows how it works.

The Fairtrade Foundation was set up by Oxfam and other charities.

The farmers use some of the money they earn for projects to help their villages. Like a primary school, or a new well.

If you buy ...

So if you buy chocolate with the Fairtrade logo, you know the cocoa farmers got a fair deal, and their villages benefit too.

Around 30 000 cocoa farmers in Ghana now belong to a group that works with Fairtrade companies. Perhaps Kofi should join them.

Fair trade for cocoa farmers

A chocolate company and a group of cocoa farmers decide to work together.

↓

They agree a price for the cocoa beans, that covers the cost of growing them, and the farmers' cost of living – plus some extra.

↓

The company pays some of the money in advance, so that the farmers won't run short.

↓

The Fairtrade Foundation has to check the deal, before the company can use the Fairtrade logo on its chocolate.

↓

In the shops, people who want to help the cocoa farmers will buy the chocolate – and don't mind that it costs a bit more.

Your turn

1 Look at Kofi's share of the price of a £1 chocolate bar.
   a Do you think it's fair? Give your reasons.
   b Can you suggest a fairer way to split the money?

2 What effect do you think this will have on the world price of cocoa beans? Explain your answer.
   a A civil war breaks out in Sierra Leone.
   b China decides it wants to make lots of chocolate.
   c A disease strikes Ghana's cacoa trees.
   d Doctors say chocolate is really bad for you.

3 Here are two opinions. For each, what would you say in response?

We should force the TNCs to pay a fair price for cocoa beans.

I love chocolate – but the cocoa farmers are not my problem.

Small is beautiful

> **Did you know?**
> ◆ About 1 100 000 000 people around the world do not have access to a supply of clean safe water.

In this unit you'll learn that development is not just about big expensive projects. Small local projects can greatly improve people's lives.

Ghana's water problem

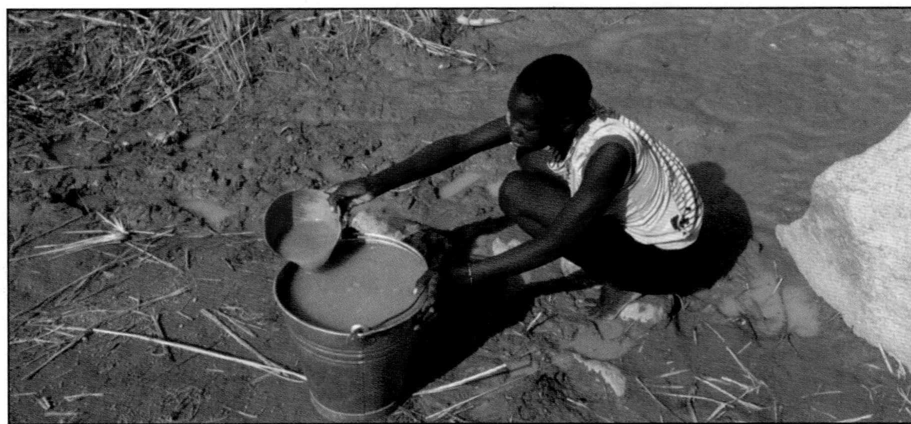

◀ *Like a drink of this?*

This is Lamisi. And this is her family's water supply, for drinking, cooking and washing. She has been here collecting water for over three hours already.

The water in the bucket looks very muddy. But far worse than the mud are the things you can't see: bacteria that cause diarrhoea, typhoid, and cholera; and tiny eggs that grow into worms inside you, leading to bilharzia and other diseases.

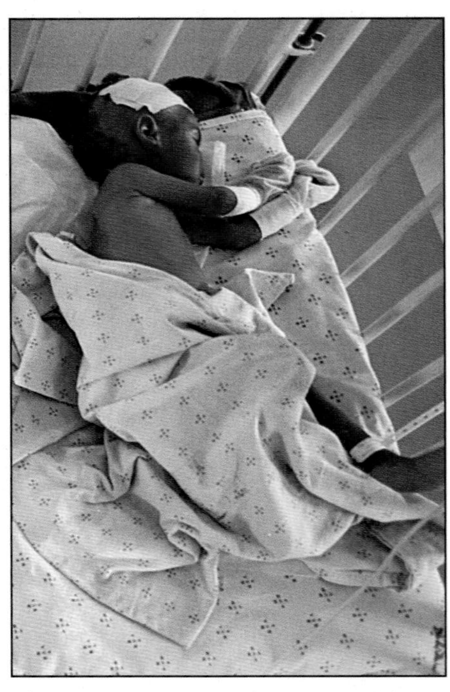

▲ *This baby has cholera, one of the many diseases caught from dirty water.*

Development little by little

Lamisi is not alone. Over 5 million Ghanaians have no access to clean safe water. One day, everyone in Ghana will have piped water. But people can't wait. So, right now, many villages are digging wells for themselves with help from a UK charity called WaterAid.
Everyone in the village gets involved:

WaterAid supplies the know-how, the materials for lining the well, and the pump.

↓

Villagers form a committee to decide where the well will be, and organise the work.

↓

Everyone in the village joins in to help clear the site, and dig, and carry soil away.

↓

Some villagers are trained to look after the well and carry out repairs.

Cost of a hand-dug well: about £1200.
Cost of Akosombo dam: over £130 million (in 1960).

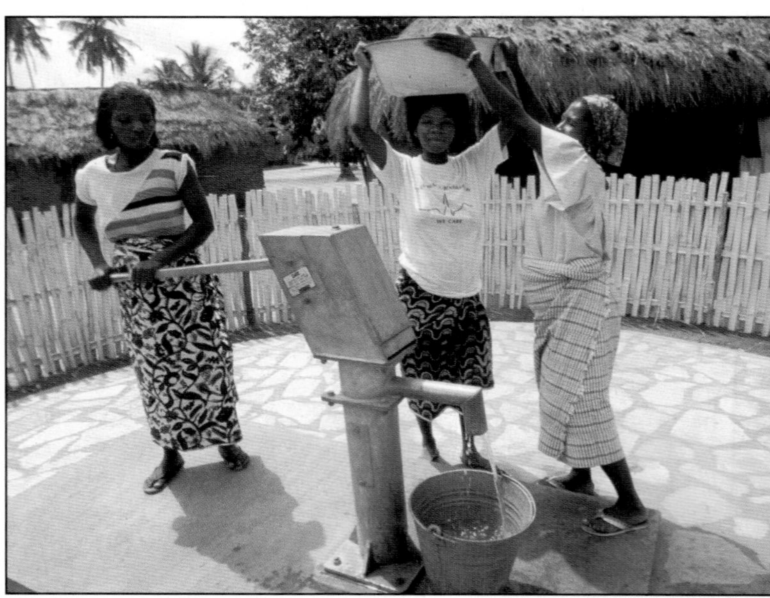

▲ *A new well. Everyone helped to build it, and everyone benefits.*

The difference a well makes

Wells don't bring just clean water! When Abena (below) and other villagers were asked how the wells had benefited them, this list shows what they said.

The changes we noticed

- A more young people have time to go to school
- B teachers happier to stay in the villages to teach
- C much less illness, so less spent on medicine
- D women potters can produce more pots
- E more people cooking food to sell
- F more people selling iced water
- G no more quarrels with neighbouring villages about water
- H people take more pride in the village
- I cooked foods look much better
- J visitors can be offered clean drinking water
- K clothing and homes kept cleaner
- L much less time taken to fetch water
- M less far to walk for water, so less tired

Your turn

1 This diagram shows a hand-dug well, and pump.

a Draw a larger simpler version of it.

b Then write the labels below in the correct places. (There are just *some* leader lines to help you.)

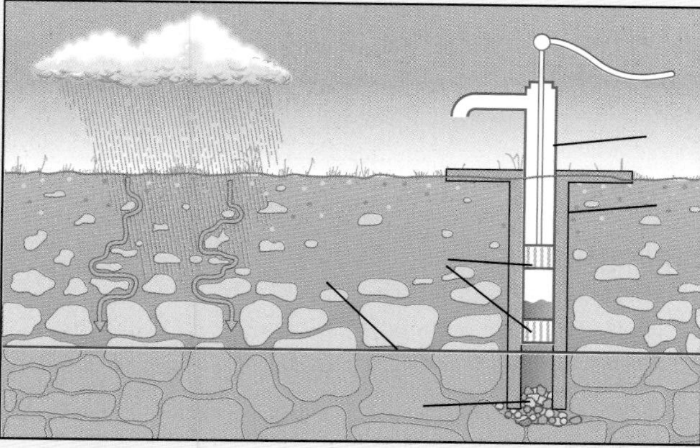

- rain soaks down to form groundwater
- the pump
- pushing the handle down draws water up the pipe
- the water table (the top of the groundwater)
- groundwater fills all the spaces in the rock
- hand-dug well lined with concrete and steel
- the water passes through valves in these plates
- soil and rock filter the water, helping to keep it clean

2 You are the chief of Lamisi's village. You want a hand-dug well for the village. But first, you must ask questions like these: *How will we pay for it? Who should be in charge of the project? How high is the water table here?*

a Make a large table with the headings shown on the right, and fill in questions to ask about the well. Write as many as you can. (The glossary may help.)

b Write in any answers you can, below your questions, in a different colour.

3 Now look at the list of changes **A – M** above.

a Draw a larger copy of this diagram.

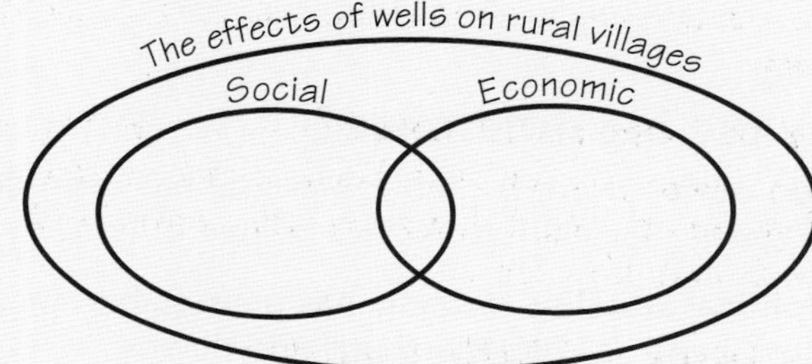

b Write letters **A – M** where you think they should go. (Glossary?) At least one where the loops overlap!

c Choose one change that you placed in the overlap and explain why it belongs there.

4 These are all aspects of *sustainable* development:

A Local people have a big say in the decision.

B It benefits the local people.

C It does not harm the environment.

Do you think the well in the photo on page 36 is a good example of sustainable development? Give it a score from 0–10, and explain your score.

5 a Look at the title of this unit. What does it mean?

b See if you can come up with a few more ideas for small projects that could make a big difference to Abena's village. (It's like the village on page 29.)

c i Choose the one you think the village would like most. How much do you think it would cost?

ii Plan a campaign to raise money for it in your school.

Questions about the well		
Environmental aspects	*Economic aspects*	*Social aspects*

The future for Ghana

In this unit you'll learn about what Ghana plans to do, to help itself develop.

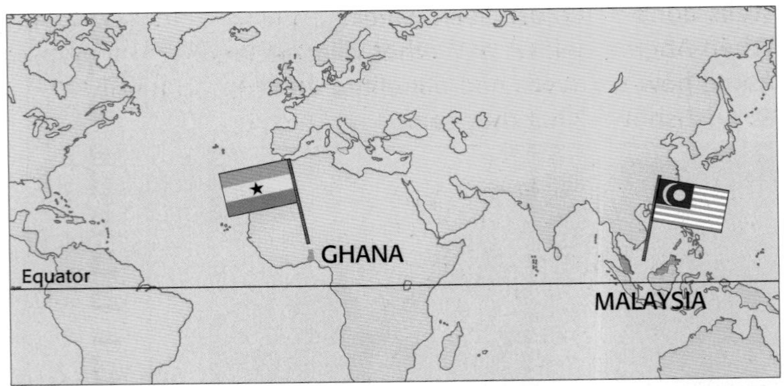

First, what about the past?

On 6 March, 2007, Ghana was 50 years old.

On Independence Day, 50 years earlier, it had been full of hope and excitement about the future. So how has it done since March 1957?

One way to answer this is to compare it with another country: Malaysia, which also gained independence from Britain in 1957.

Which of the two countries has done better? The table on the right will help you decide.

	Ghana	Malaysia
Population (millions)	21	24
GDP per capita in 1958 ($ US)	$170	$200
GDP per capita today ($US)	$290	$3900
Life expectancy (years)	57	73
Adult literacy rate (%)	58	89
Access to safe water (%)	75	99
CO_2 output per person (tonnes)	0.4	6.4

Why the big difference?

As you can see from the table, Malaysia has been developing a lot faster than Ghana. Several factors have helped it. Two key ones are:

- **Political stability.** Malaysia has been stable since independence. But Ghana has had many ups and downs.
- **Industry.** Like Ghana, Malaysia depended on a couple of primary products (rubber and tin). But after independence, it quickly began to set up industries. Ghana hoped to, but soon gave up.

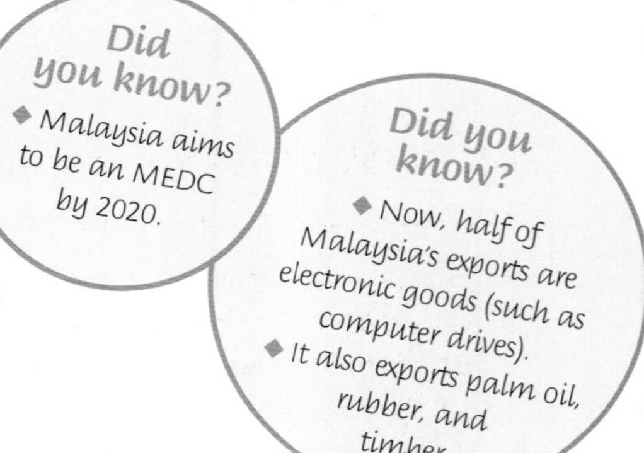

Did you know?
◆ Malaysia aims to be an MEDC by 2020.
Did you know?
◆ Now, half of Malaysia's exports are electronic goods (such as computer drives).
◆ It also exports palm oil, rubber, and timber.

So what has Ghana got going for it now?

Right now, Ghana is feeling very hopeful about the future, because:

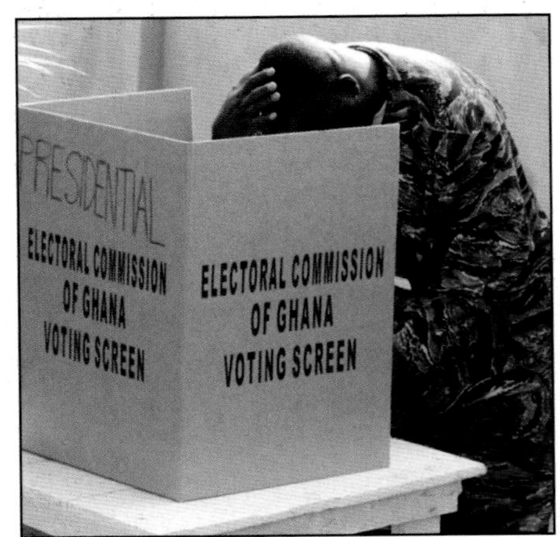

It has had several years of political stability – and this is likely to continue. Development is easier when a country is stable.

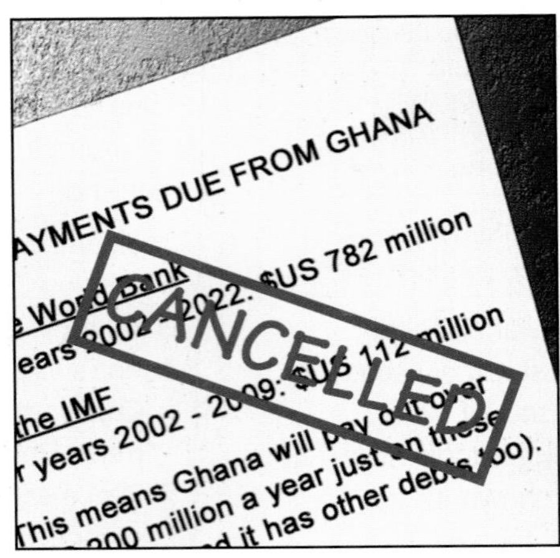

As you saw earlier, it had heavy debts, and spent a lot on interest payments. Now a large share of these debts has been cancelled.

With help from other countries, it is working hard to bring basic services to all its people: health clinics, schools, a water supply, and so on.

And so to the future

There are many projects going on in Ghana, to reduce poverty. For these projects, Ghana depends on large grants from other countries. But it also needs to *earn* itself more money. Here are some of the things its advisers tell the government:

Help farmers to farm better
60% of Ghana's workforce are in farming. Help them to grow more, by helping them with:
- irrigation
- loans to buy fertilisers
- training in better methods.

Help cocoa farmers diversify
Cocoa prices go up and down, so depending on it is a bit risky.
- Cocoa farmers should keep on growing cocoa.
- But help them grow other high value crops for export too (such as fruit and vegetables).

Get manufacturing!
You could focus first on:
- food processing. For example make cocoa powder, chocolate, and fruit juice for export.
- clothing. Many countries have started off with clothing factories.

Remember, you earn more from selling finished goods than from selling raw materials!

Expand the service sector
- Help tourism to develop. (It is growing, but slowly.)
- Could Ghana develop a call centre business too?

But what about fair trade?

Ghana's success also depends on world trade agreements. For example:

- Hundreds of Ghanaian farmers grow rice, for sale in local markets. But far cheaper rice is coming in from Europe, Asia and the USA, where rice farmers get **subsidies**. So Ghana's rice farmers are going out of business.
- In the same way, Ghana's chicken farmers can't compete against the frozen chicken coming in from Europe and the USA.

But in exchange for debt refief, Ghana is not allowed to stop these imports. Many people think that is unfair. They think poor countries should be allowed to use tariffs, to protect their farmers and fragile industries. Ghana (and other LEDCs) are protesting about it.

▲ *A factory in Ghana, making garden furniture for export to the UK.*

Your turn

1 Look at the table on page 38. (And the glossary too?)
   a The GDP per capita today is bigger for Malaysia than Ghana. What can you tell from that?
   b How many times bigger is it?
   c In which country did children have a better chance of going to school, ten years ago? Explain.
   d On average, how much longer do people in Malaysia live than people in Ghana? And why?
   e Malaysia produces more CO_2 per capita than Ghana does. What does this tell you? (Page 62?)

2 These pie charts show the economic structure of Malaysia and Ghana. The cream colour shows the service sector.
   a What does *economic structure* mean?
   b Which pie is for Ghana? Explain.

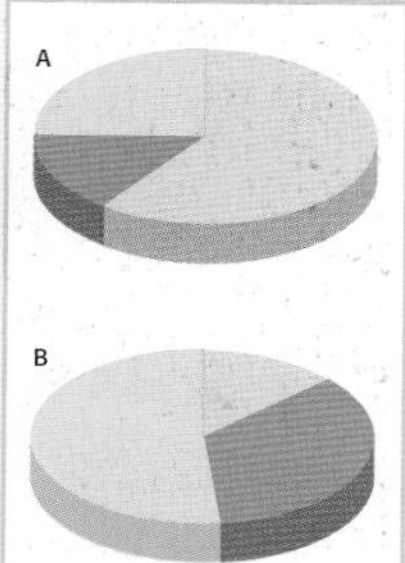

3 Explain *why* experts think it's important for Ghana to develop industry.

4 You are Ghana's Minister of Tourism. Write a plan for developing tourism in Ghana. You can give it as a set of bullet points. What aspects of Ghana will you focus on?

3 Ohio, Nippon!

Welcome to Japan! One of the world's most developed countries. Where you'll find …

▲ … an Emperor and Imperial Family …

▲ … picnics under the cherry blossom, in the spring …

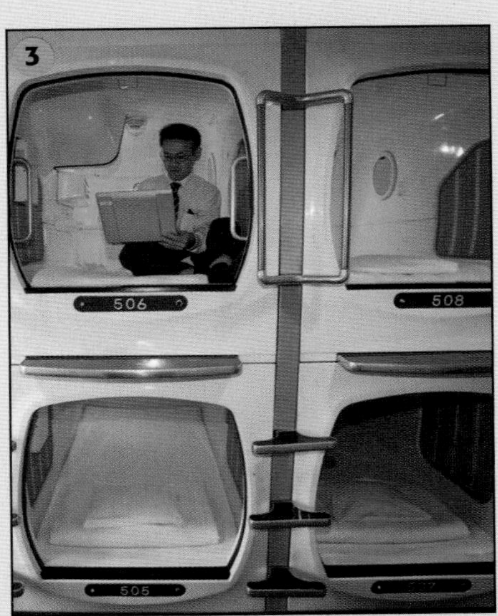

▲ … capsule hotels to curl up in …

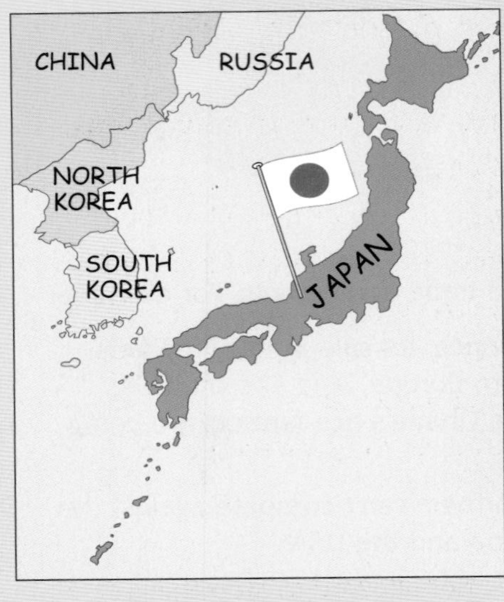

▲ … lively crowded city streets …

▲ … the world's fastest trains …

▲ …a culture rich in tradition …

▲ … and a great line in robots!

The big picture

This chapter is all about Japan. These are the big ideas behind the chapter:

- Japan is one of the world's most developed and wealthy countries.
- Like most countries, industry helped it to develop.
- Like every country, it faces challenges, and change.
- Because of its location, it suffers earthquakes, volcanic eruptions, and typhoons.
- Like every country, it depends on other countries – and they depend on it.

Japan at a glance

Area:	377 800 sq km (one and a half times the size of the UK)
Population:	127 million people (twice as many as the UK)
HDI rank:	about 7th in the world

Your goals for this chapter

By the end of this chapter you should be able to answer these questions:

- Where in the world is Japan, and who are its neighbours?
- What are its four main islands called? And the seas around it?
- How was Japan formed?
- What can I say about these aspects of Japan?

  its relief *its climate* *the factors that influence its climate*
- What natural resources does Japan have?
- Which parts of it are the most crowded? And the most empty? Why?
- What's happening to Japan's population?
- Where is Tokyo, on the map of Japan? And what's it like?
- Which other Japanese cities can I name, and place? (At least five!)
- How developed is Japan? What is my evidence?
- Which natural hazards does Japan have to cope with? And why?
- What are the challenges facing Japan's rural areas?
- In what ways are Japan and other countries interdependent?

Did you know?
- The Japanese for 'Hello' on the phone is 'Moshi Moshi'.

Did you know?
- Snowballing is a proper sport in Japan.
- Your team tries to capture the other team's flag, in the face of a blizzard of snowballs!

Did you know?
- The Japanese word for Japan is 'Nippon' - but pronounced 'Ni-hon'.

And then ...

When you finish this chapter you can come back to this page and see if you have met your goals!

Your chapter starter

What's the first thing that springs to mind, when you think of Japan?

What else do you know about it?

In what ways do you think it's like the UK?

In what ways is it different?

Do you have any links with Japan, of any kind? Think about it!

Just don't step on my tatami.

Japan: a country of islands and mountains

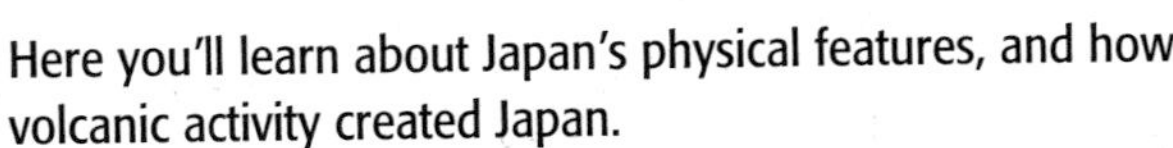

Here you'll learn about Japan's physical features, and how volcanic activity created Japan.

What's Japan like?

Japan is a really exciting place for geographers!

- It is made up of islands. Four main ones, and over 3000 smaller ones. The four main ones are named here. Most of the others are off this map, or too small to show up.
- Look how mountainous it is. About three quarters of Japan is covered by mountains. Its highest peak, **Mt Fuji** (3776m) is nearly three times as high as Ben Nevis (1344m).
- The **Kanto plain** is the largest area of flat land.
- Japan has over 75 active volcanoes. Mt Fuji is one! (But it has not erupted in over 300 years.)
- It has a great many rivers too. They flow very fast down the mountains.
- And finally, it has lots of trees. About 65% of Japan is clothed in forest.

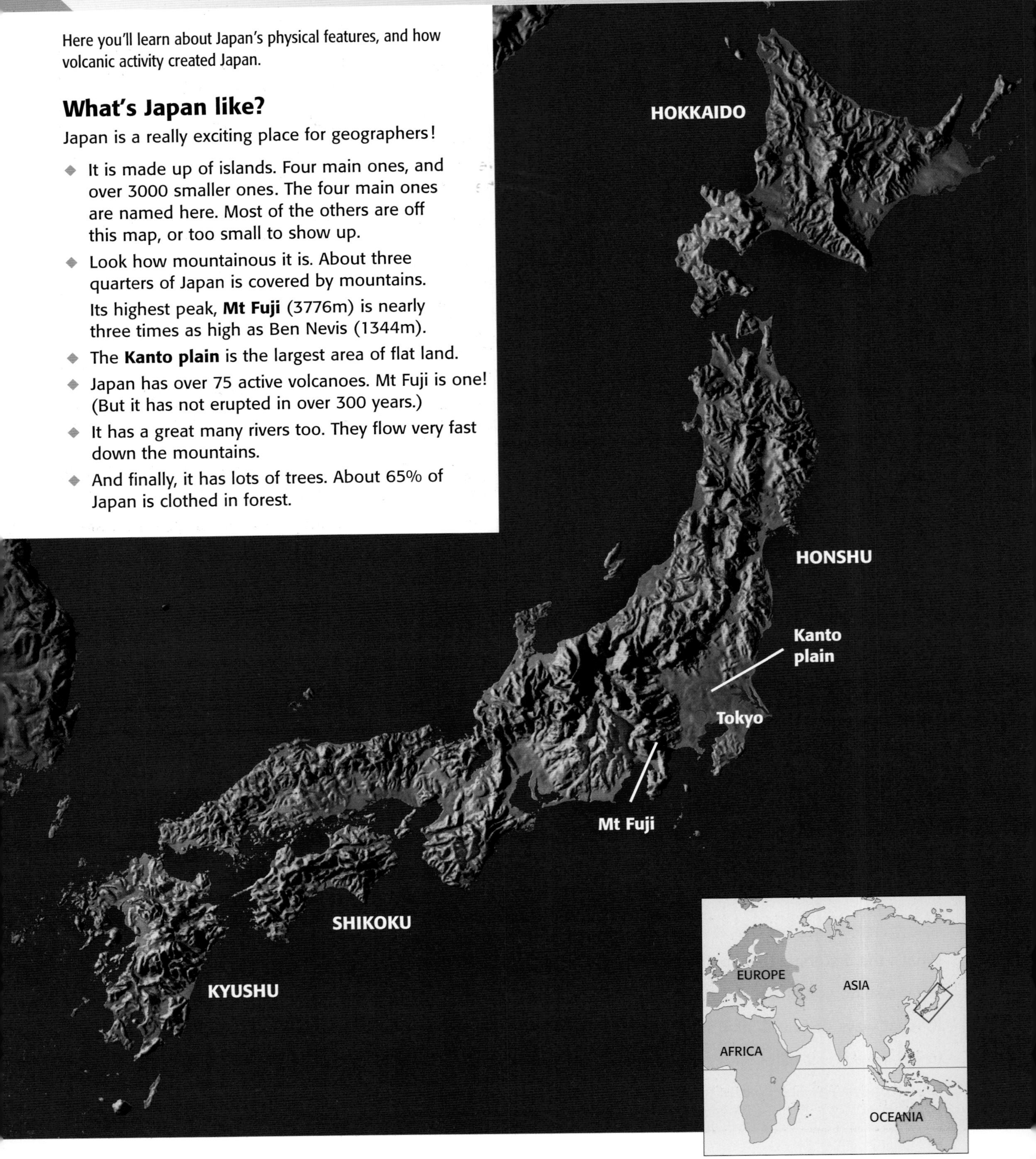

HOKKAIDO
HONSHU
Kanto plain
Tokyo
Mt Fuji
SHIKOKU
KYUSHU

EUROPE
ASIA
AFRICA
OCEANIA

Born of volcanoes ...

In fact, Japan was formed by volcanic activity. Like this ...

Inside the Earth, it's so hot that some rock is soft – and completely melted in places.

The outer part, that we live on, is hard – but cracked into over 50 slabs of different sizes. We call these slabs **plates**. (Page 95 shows the main ones.) The plates move around very slowly, dragged by currents in the soft rock below them. They push and jostle each other at their edges.

Three plates meet, and push into each other, beside Japan. Look at the map on the right. Their movements gave rise to Japan. Like this:

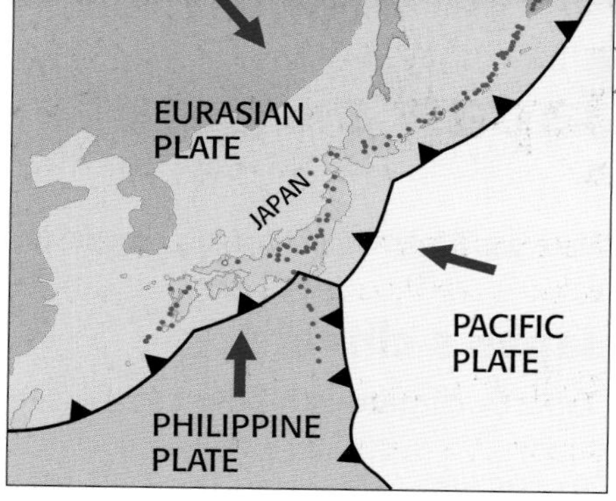

▲ *The three plates meeting. Blue arrows = direction of travel. Black arrow heads = edges sliding under. Red dots = volcanoes.*

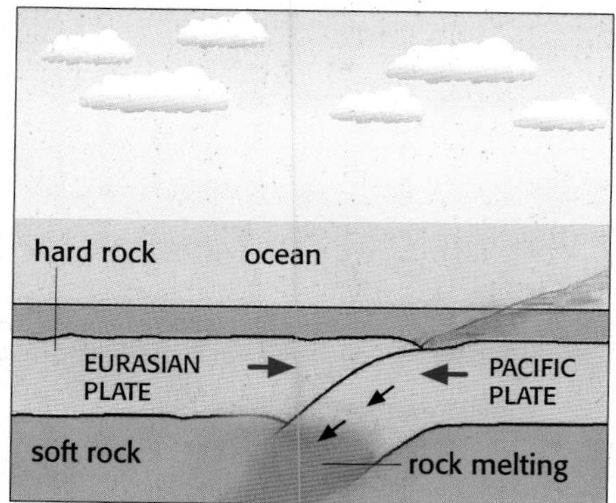

As they push, the plates slide under each other at some edges. (Look at the black arrows.) The rock that's pushed down gets hot, and melts.

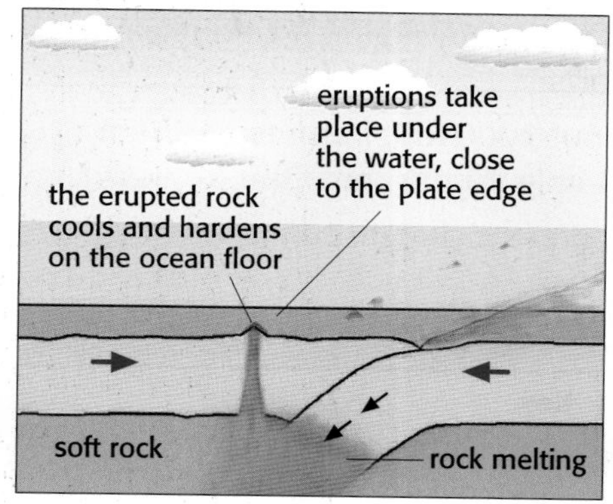

The melted rock rises, and erupts through the ocean floor, as a string of volcanoes. Over time these grow taller and taller, and eventually ...

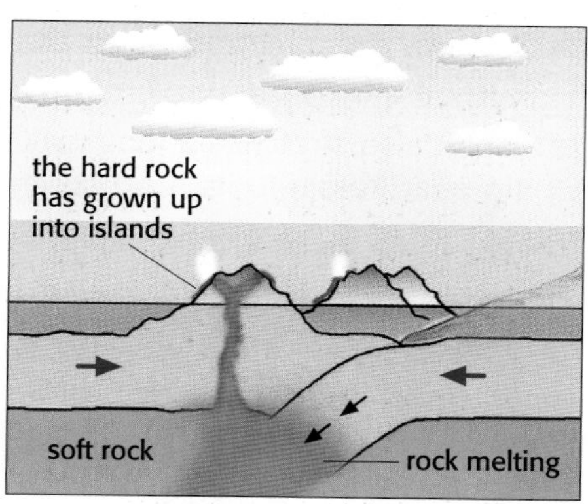

... they poke up through the water, giving the islands of Japan. (And the plates are still pushing, so Japan still has active volcanoes.)

... and shaken by earthquakes!

As the heavy plates push into each other, huge pressure builds up in the rock along and near their edges. From time to time, this rock shudders and shifts, causing earthquakes. So Japan has many earthquakes too.

Your turn

The maps on pages 127 and 128–129 will help here.

1 a Which continent is Japan on?
  b In which hemisphere is it?
  c Name four countries that are its nearest neighbours.
  d Roughly what is its longitude? East or west?
  e Within which latitudes does it lie?

2 Now copy this table, and fill in the names of Japan's four main islands, in the correct places.

Island	Area (sq km)
	18 800
	83 450
	36 720
	227 410

3 Humans arrived in Japan over 12 000 years ago. Where might they have chosen to settle first? Why?

4 Now, write a paragraph describing the shape, and relief, of Japan. (Glossary?)
Try to use all these terms in your answer: *flat rugged highest east islands plain indented smooth*

5 See if you can explain these facts:
  a Japan has no really long rivers.
  b There are a great many waterfalls in Japan.

6 Why does Japan have active volcanoes? Explain as if to a nine-year-old.

7 Now compare Japan and the UK, in terms of their physical geography. (You could draw up a table?)
  a In what ways are they alike? List these.
  b In what ways are they different? List these too.

Japan's climate and natural resources

Here you'll learn about Japan's climate, and Japan's shortage of natural resources.

> **Did you know?**
> - Japan is quite a lot wetter than Scotland.
> - Average precipitation in Japan is 1720 mm a year.
> - In Scotland it is 1440 mm.

Japan's climate

Japan's climate is influenced by several factors:

- For rain, you need moist air that rises. Thanks to all that water around it, and all those mountains, Japan gets lots of rain.
- In winter, cold north winds blow down from Russia, bringing snow.
- In summer, warm moist winds blow up from the tropics. They bring heavy rains in June and July.
- A warm ocean current skirts the south east of Japan. A cold ocean current affects the most northern parts.
- Japan also stretches a long way. About 2000 km, from its northern tip near Russia to its most southern little islands, near the tropics.

Thanks to all these factors, Japan has different climate zones:

- Hokkaido has long cold winters, and cool summers.
- Winter brings very heavy snow. In summer it rains, but less than in other parts of Japan.

- The east side of Japan gets cool winters, and warm to very warm summers.
- Winters can bring snow. Summers are rainy and humid.

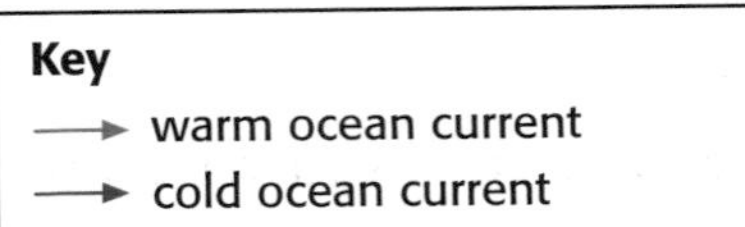

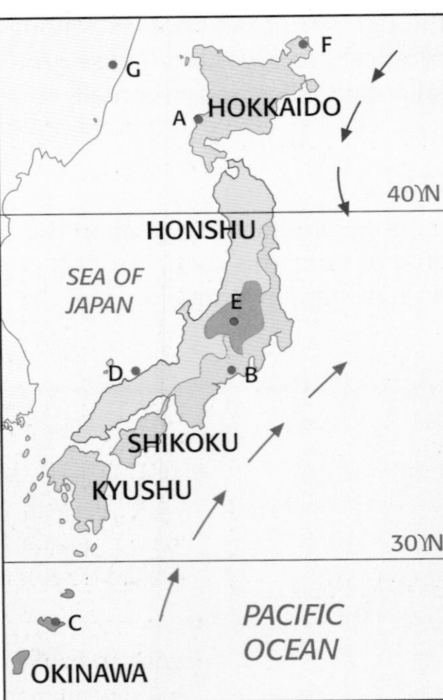

- The higher you go, the colder it is. So Japan's highest areas are cool or cold all year.
- For example, Mt Fuji has some snow for most of the year.

- The west side of Japan has milder winters than the east, and hot humid summers.
- The heaviest rain is in June and July.

- Okinawa island is quite near the tropics. So it has warm winters and hot summers.
- It has a lot of rain all year.

Typhoons

One feature of Japan's weather is hurricanes – or **typhoons** as they are called in that region.

These violent spinning storms start over warm tropical waters in the Pacific Ocean. When they hit land they bring torrential rain and raging winds. They also bring storm surges of sea water, that flood the coast.

At least three typhoons a year hit the main part of Japan. The southern islands, such as Okinawa, can get up to ten. The typhoon season is May to October, with August and September the peak months.

▲ *Typhoon Tokage in 2004: over Japan's southern islands, and heading north.*

Japan's natural resources

- The ocean is its main natural resource. It offers fish, and trade routes.
- The fast-flowing rivers are used for hydroelectricity.

But apart from these, Japan has very few natural resources.

- Because it's so mountainous, there is not even much farmland. Only about 13% of the land is used for farming. (It's over 70% in the UK.)
- It has no oil or natural gas, and has to import these.
- It does have some coal, but most of its mines are now shut.
- It has very few metal ores. So it has to import iron ore, aluminium ore and other essential metals.

But even though it has few natural resources, Japan is a highly developed and wealthy country, as you'll see in Unit 3.4.

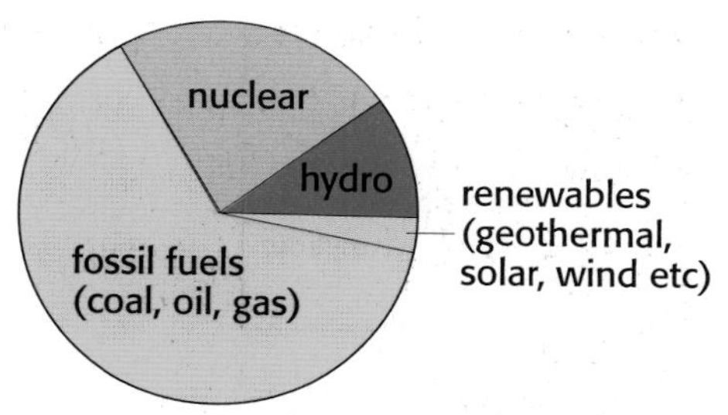

▲ *Japan's sources of electricity, in 2003.*

Your turn

1 Look at the climate graph on the right. It matches one of the places marked **A–C** on the climate map. Which place? Explain your choice.

2 Now look at the climate data in the table. It also matches one of the places **A– C**. Which one? Explain your choice.

3 Look at the climate map on page 44. (Page 42 will help too.) See if you can explain why:
  a Japan gets such a lot of rain.
  b It is always warmer at **B** than at **F**.
  c **B** has milder winters than **D**, at the same latitude.
  d **B** gets less snow than **A**.
  e It's usually hot and humid at **B** in July.
  f You can find snow at **E** even in May.

4 See if you can suggest a reason why:
  a Japan does not get typhoons in December.
  b **C** is at greater risk of flooding from typhoons than **G** is.

5 Do you think the UK is better off, or worse off, than Japan, for natural resources? Give some evidence!

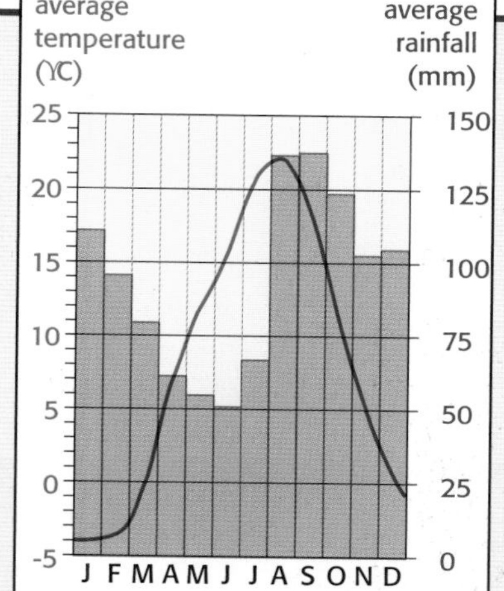

Month	Av temp (° C)	Av rainfall (mm)
J	17	114
F	17	125
M	19	160
A	21	181
M	24	234
J	27	212
J	29	178
A	28	247
S	27	200
O	25	182
N	22	124
D	18	101

6 Look at the pie chart above. About what % of its electricity does Japan get from:
  a fast-flowing rivers? b nuclear power stations?
  Choose your answer from this list:
  2% about 10% about 30% about 60% 88%

7 Japan has several nuclear power stations. They have to be extra careful about where they locate these, in Japan. See if you can explain why.

So... where is everyone?

Here you'll see how the population is distributed in Japan, and how its age structure is changing.

> **Did you know?**
> ◆ The city of Saitama (below) was born on May 1, 2001, when three smaller cities joined.

How the population is distributed

Over 127 million people live in Japan. But they are not spread evenly around the country. This map shows how the population is distributed.

Japan has 13 cities with over 1 million people. They are named on the map. The UK has only one city with over a million people. Which one?

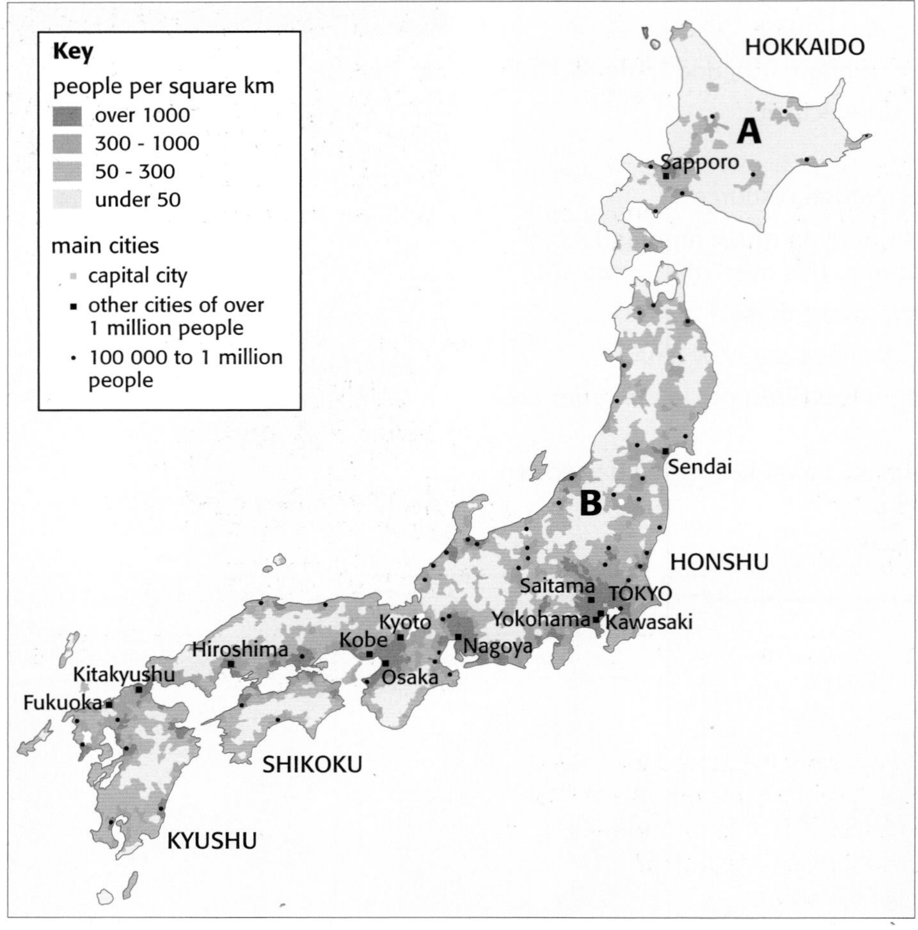

Japan's 'over a million' cities		
	Name	Population (millions)
1	Tokyo	8.13
2	Yokohama	3.43
3	Osaka	2.60
4	Nagoya	2.17
5	Sapporo	1.82
6	Kobe	1.49
7	Kyoto	1.48
8	Fukuoka	1.34
9	Kawasaki	1.25
10	Hiroshima	1.13
11	Saitama	1.02
12	Kitakyushu	1.01
13	Sendai	1.01

Some UK cities	
London	7.17
Birmingham	0.98
Leeds	0.72
Glasgow	0.58
Edinburgh	0.45

▲ *All these are the populations within the official city limits.*

▲ *The Tokyo skyline at night.*

◀ *Crowds at a zebra crossing, in Tokyo.*

Where have all the babies gone?

In 2005, something worrying happened in Japan. 1.08 million people died through the year, but only 1.07 million new babies were born. Japan's birthrate has been falling for years. In 2005, for the first time, the population actually began to shrink.

At the same time, Japanese people are living longer. Look at this table:

Year	Average number of children per woman	Life expectancy (years)	Average age of the population
1950	3.7	64	22
2005	1.4	81	41

Since there are fewer new babies each year, and people are living longer, the average age of the population is rising. The population is **ageing**.

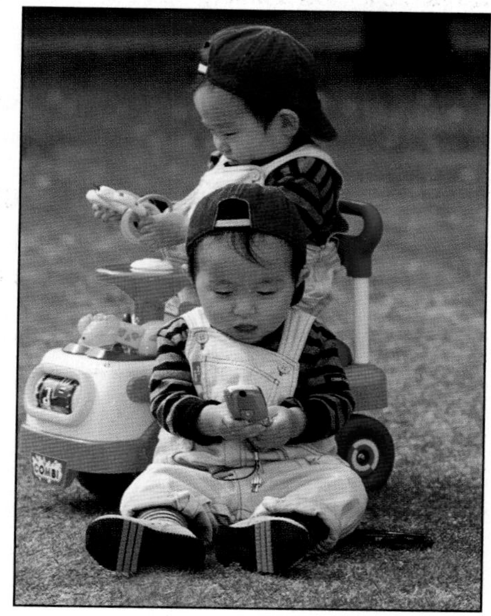

▲ *Fewer than there used to be ...*

Population pyramids for Japan

A **population pyramid** is a type of bar graph. It shows the population divided into males and females, in different age groups. Like this:

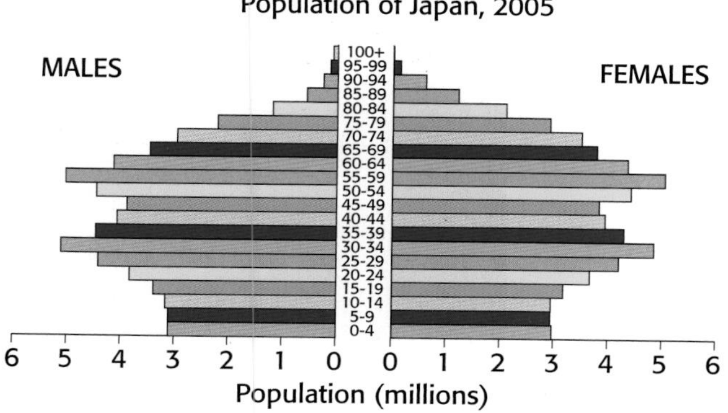

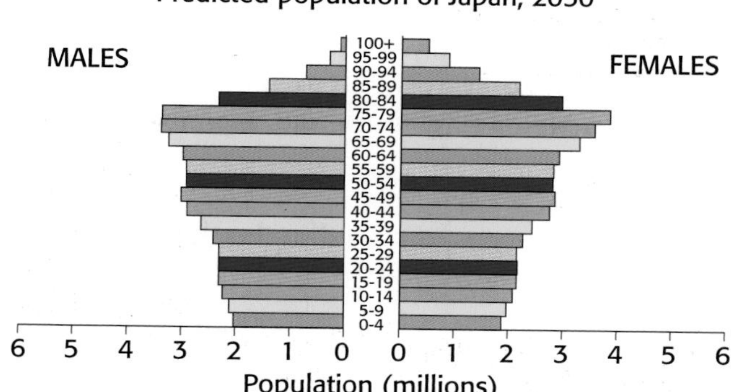

Look at the lowest bars in each graph. They show that there were just over 6 million under-fives in 2005. (About 3 million of these were little girls.) But experts predict that there will be only 4 million under-fives by 2050. Do you think that's good news, or bad news, for Japan?

Your turn

1 Look at the map on page 46. It shows how the population density changes around Japan.
- a What does *population density* mean? (Glossary.)
- b How is it worked out?
- c What can you say about the population density:
  i at **A**? ii at **B**? iii around Tokyo?

2 Overall, which parts of Japan are:
- a the most crowded? b the least crowded?

3 Compare the maps on pages 42 and 46.
- a Describe any patterns you notice.
- b Now see if you can *explain* these patterns.

4 a The *birth rate* in Japan is falling. What does the term in italics mean? (Glossary.)
- b If it keeps falling, what will happen in the end?

5 Using the population pyramids above, say roughly how many 15–19-year-olds:
- a there were in 2000 b there may be in 2050.

6 Repeat **5**, but this time for 75–79-year-olds.

7 If Japan's population keeps falling, what problems may arise? See how many you think up. (You could show them on a spider map.)

3.4 How is Japan doing?

Here you'll use development indicators to compare Japan with some other countries. You'll also look at its economic structure, and trade.

It's a highly developed country

Japan is one of the world's most developed countries. Look at this table:

Development indicators (2004)	Japan	UK	USA	Ghana
GDP per capita ($US PPP)	$29 250	$30 820	$39 680	$2240
Life expectancy (years)	82	78	77	57
Doctors per 100 000 people	198	230	256	15
Human development index (HDI)	0.949	0.940	0.948	0.532

How did it develop?

To understand about Japan's development, you need a little history!

Japan and World War II

In 1945, Japan was in tatters. For four years, it had been fighting in World War II, against the Allied Forces (mainly the USA and UK). Its cities had been bombed repeatedly. Then on 6 August 1945, a US plane dropped an atomic bomb on Hiroshima. Two days later, another fell on Nagasaki. After the terrible damage these did, Japan surrendered.

After the war

After the war, Japan was placed under the command of an American: General Douglas MacArthur.

The USA wanted Japan as an ally, not an enemy. So it helped Japan to rebuild itself, and develop new industries. It provided equipment and new technology, and trained people in new ways of working.

Within 20 years, thanks to its new industries, and hard work, and a high level of exports, Japan was flourishing. Its standard of living rose fast.

▲ *Inside a computer chip factory. Not a speck of dust allowed! Japan sells chips and electronic goods all over the world.*

What about today?

About 67 million people are employed in Japan today. What do they do? The pie chart below shows Japan's **economic structure**.

- The primary producers work in farming, fishing, and forestry.
- Nearly three out of every ten people work in the secondary sector, in manufacturing and construction. Many work in factories making cars or electronic goods.
- Those in the tertiary sector work in offices, banks, schools, hotels, transport and so on.
- Japan's quaternary sector – where people do hi-tech research – is very lively. (But the numbers are too small to show up in this pie chart.)

The structure of Japan's economy, 2006

primary (4%)
secondary (27%)
tertiary (69%)

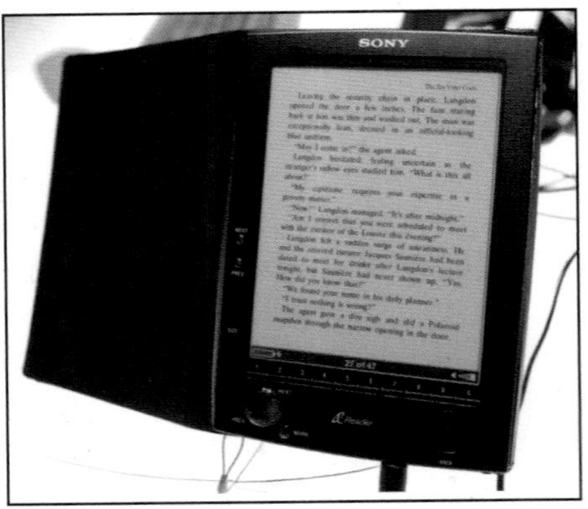

▲ *Another clever invention from Japan. One day, all your school books may be held on an e-reader like this one. No more heavy bags to carry …*

Japan's exports

Japan depends heavily on its exports.

As you saw, it has few natural resources. So it imports fuels, and metals, and metal ores, to make things. Then it sells the finished goods to other countries, at a profit.

It also has to import food, because its farmers produce only 40% of the food it needs.

This table shows just a few of Japan's exports and imports for 2005.

Overall, Japan earned £329 billion from exports that year, and spent £285 billion on imports. So was it winning, or losing?

Some of Japan's exports and imports, 2005

Exports	Earned (£ billions)	Imports	Spent (£ billions)
cars	44.9	oil	51.6
computer chips	22.0	foodstuffs	24.6
iron and steel	15.2	clothing	12.5
ships, boats	6.5	coal	7.6
cameras	2.6	iron ore	3.1

Did you know?
◆ Japan's largest company is Toyota, the car maker.

Did you know?
◆ Sony, a Japanese company, sold £35 billions' worth of goods in 2006.

Challenges facing Japan's economy

A country's economy can do well one year, and badly the next. Like every country, Japan's economy faces challenges.

- **Oil prices.** When these shoot up, as they do from time to time, that costs Japan a lot of money.
- **Competition.** China is developing new industries fast. It can make goods more cheaply than Japan can, because it has lower wages. One day, other countries may prefer to buy things made in China.
- **A falling population.** If it keeps falling, Japan could run short of workers to grow food, or to make the things it needs to sell.

Solutions to challenges facing Japan
energy costs
competition
aging population

▲ *This is for question 5 below.*

Your turn

1 Look at the table on page 48.
  a What does GDP per capita (PPP) mean? (Glossary?)
  b On average, were people wealthier in Japan or the UK, that year?
  c About how many times wealthier were people in Japan than in Ghana that year, on average?

2 a What does *life expectancy* mean?
  b Japan has the highest life expectancy in the world (but not the highest ratio of doctors). See if you can think up reasons for such long lives.

3 The *human development index* is a good indicator of how developed a country is.
  a What is the human development index?
  b Which country in the table scored best?

4 The pie chart on page 48 shows *economic structure*.
  a What does economic structure mean? (Glossary?)
  b Which does Japan have more of: farmers or factory workers?
  c The two pie charts on the right also show economic structure. One is for the UK, and one is for Ghana. Which is which? Explain your choice.

5 The bullets above show challenges facing Japan. **A–G** below are solutions. This is what you have to do:
  a Make a larger copy of the Venn diagram started on the right above.
  b Then write the letters **A–G** where you think they should go. If you think they belong to two loops (or even three) put them in the overlap.

A Set up factories in China.
B Develop more types of robot, to work in place of humans.
C Raise the age at which workers can retire.
D Set up two more nuclear power stations.
E Pay couples to have babies.
F Focus on making exciting new gadgets that are much smarter than other people's.
G Allow more foreign workers in. (Japan has very few.)

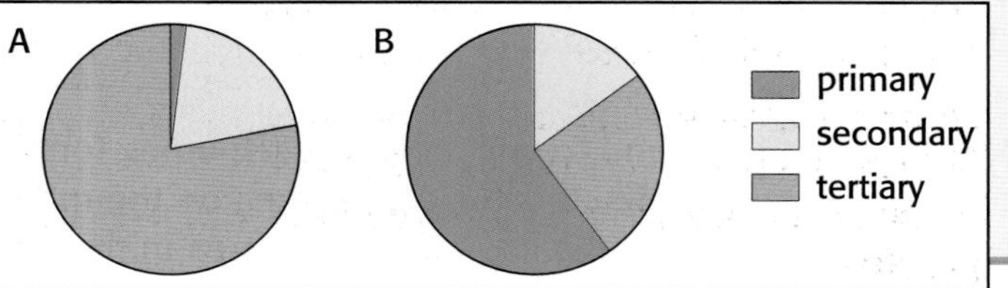

3.5 Tokyo: at the heart of a megapolis

In this unit you will learn about Tokyo: what it's like, and how it is changing.

A little history

Tokyo become the capital of Japan in 1868, when the Emperor moved there from Kyoto, the old capital.

In many ways, Tokyo is in a great spot for a capital city. Halfway down Japan. On a plain. On the coast. And with a natural harbour, open to the Pacific Ocean. But there's one big problem: it lies close to a fault in the Earth's crust, where the earthquake risk is high.

In 1923, a major earthquake hit Tokyo. Most of the houses were made of wood then. The earthquake struck at lunchtime, when people were cooking. Stoves fell over. Homes caught fire. High winds fanned the flames, and much of the city burned down.

After the disaster, people thought about moving the capital to somewhere safer. But instead it was rebuilt, with modern roads and railways. The new public buildings were built to cope with quakes.

And then came World War II. In 1945, Tokyo was bombed 102 times. Much of it lay in ruins. After the war, rebuilding began all over again.

Tokyo city

Greater Tokyo (includes Tokyo city)

▲ *Japan is divided into regions called prefectures. Together, four of them form Greater Tokyo.*

Tokyo grows… and grows… and grows

Tokyo, and the cities and towns around it, grew rapidly after the war. People came from all over Japan to find work.

As people moved in to Tokyo, new homes and factories were built at the edges of the city. It spread outwards, with little control. In time, it joined up to other growing towns and cities. Look at this map.

The pink line shows the edge of the original **Tokyo city**.
Population: 8.13 million.

The blue line shows the edge of the **Tokyo Metropolis**, which is the city plus a large area to its west.
Population: 12.5 million.

The orange line shows the edge of **Greater Tokyo**, which contains the metropolis plus a much larger area.
Population: 35 million – or over a quarter of Japan's population!

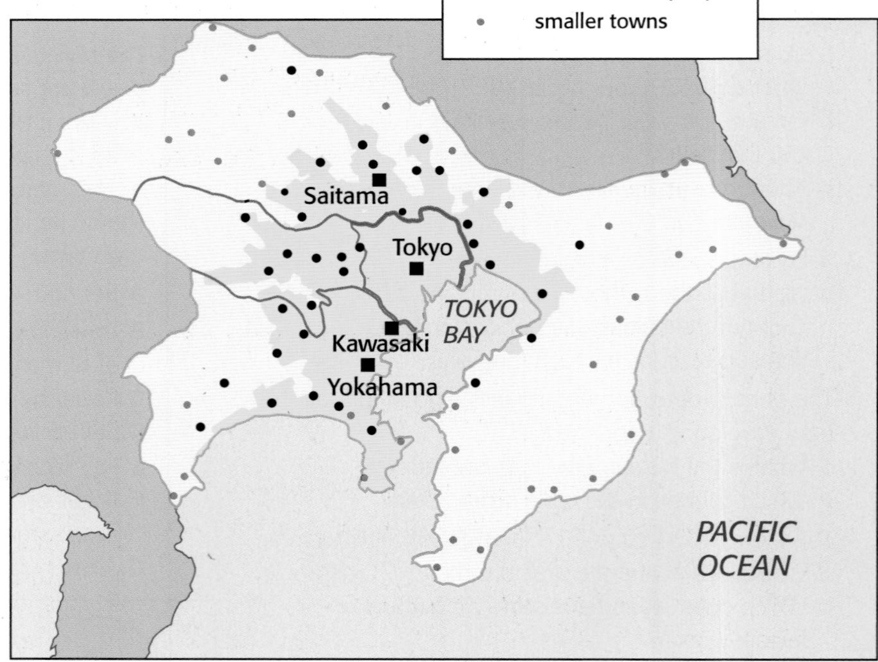

Greater Tokyo contains four cities of over 1 million people, many more of 100 000 to 1 million people, and many smaller settlements.

Many of these cities and towns run into each other, forming a huge built-up area called a **megapolis.** It is the yellow area on the map.
The Tokyo megapolis is the largest built-up area in the world.

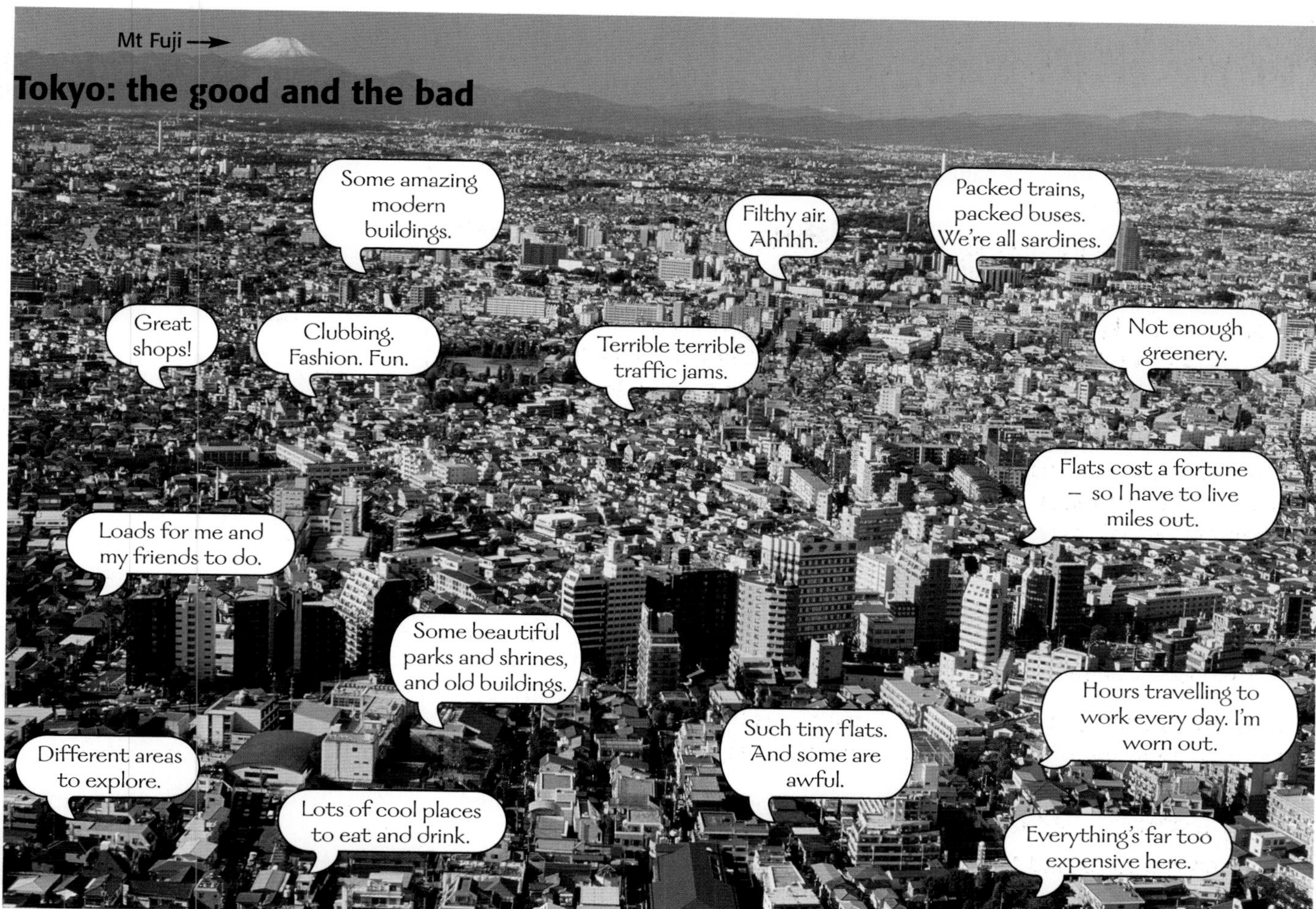

Improvement on the way

Like every big city, Tokyo has good and bad points. Some people say it has more bad points than good ones, and needs to be sorted. And that's what's happening. A massive redevelopment has begun – not just in the city but the whole metropolis. It will go on till at least 2015.

The list on the right shows just some of the things they intend to do, to make Tokyo an attractive city for the 21st century.

To do

- Redevelop the city's waterfront, to make it a great place to work and live.
- Build new homes near workplaces, so people don't have to travel so far.
- Improve old housing.
- Improve roads, to cut congestion.
- Create lakes, and open green areas.
- Widen the narrow city streets.

Your turn

1 What do these terms mean? (Glossary?)
  a metropolis b megapolis

2 Using the data on the right, draw a line graph to show how the population of the Tokyo metropolis has grown.

3 Look at your graph from 2.
  a When did the population fall sharply? Why?
  b When did it rise fastest? Why?
  c What happened to it between 2000 and 2005? Suggest a reason.
  d How will it have changed by 2050? Why?

Population of the Tokyo metropolis (millions)

Year	Population	Year	Population	Year	Population
1900	2.0	1940	7.4	1980	11.6
1910	2.5	1950	3.5	1990	11.8
1920	3.7	1960	10.2	2000	12.4
1930	6.3	1970	11.4	2005	12.3

4 Make up a conversation between two neighbours in Tokyo. One is excited about the plans for improving Tokyo. The other worries about earthquakes.

5 You live at the area marked **X** on the photo above. Do you think it's a good thing that a megapolis was allowed to develop? Write a blog for your website, giving your point of view.

Living with danger

Here you'll learn more about the natural hazards the people of Japan have to live with.

More on those plate movements

As you saw on page 43, the Earth's plates move around, very slowly. At their edges, they jostle and grind against each other. If one gets pushed under, you get eruptions. And any sudden rock movement causes earthquakes.

But earthquakes don't happen just at the edges. As the plates push, huge pressure builds up in the rock. Even quite a distance away, the rock can develop big cracks or **faults**, where earthquakes are likely to occur.

Japan's earthquakes

Japan lies where three plates meet. So there are many faults running across the country. And that means the risk of earthquakes is high.

- In fact Japan has around 1500 earthquakes a year. (Most are tiny.)
- The last big earthquake to hit Tokyo was in 1923. It killed over 140 000 people. Tokyo expects a big earthquake about once every 70 years, so another could happen at any time.
- The last big one to hit Japan was the Kobe earthquake in 1995. It killed around 5300 people, and did £ billions of damage.

Japan's volcanoes

As you saw earlier, Japan was formed by volcanic activity. And since plates are still being pushed under, it still has active volcanoes.

- Japan has over 75 active volcanoes.
- The most famous is Mt Fuji, which is classed as active, even though it has not erupted since 1707.
- Japan's worst volcano disaster was in 1792, when Mt Unzen erupted. It caused landslides, and a tsunami that killed over 15 000 people. It then went back to sleep – but erupted again in 1991, killing 43 people.

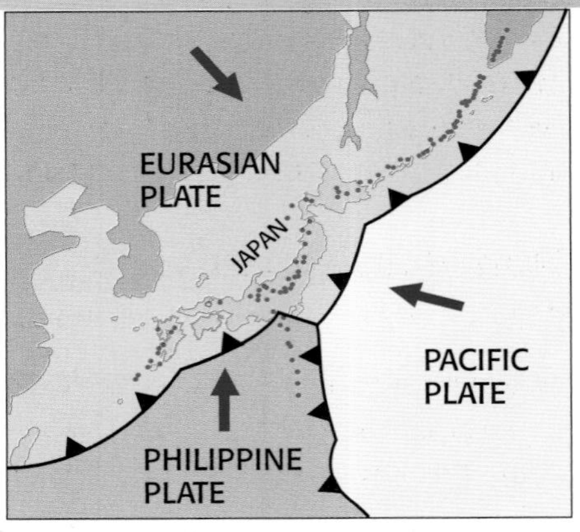

▲ *Japan, where three plates meet.*

▲ *A six-storey bank in Kobe, after the Kobe earthquake.*

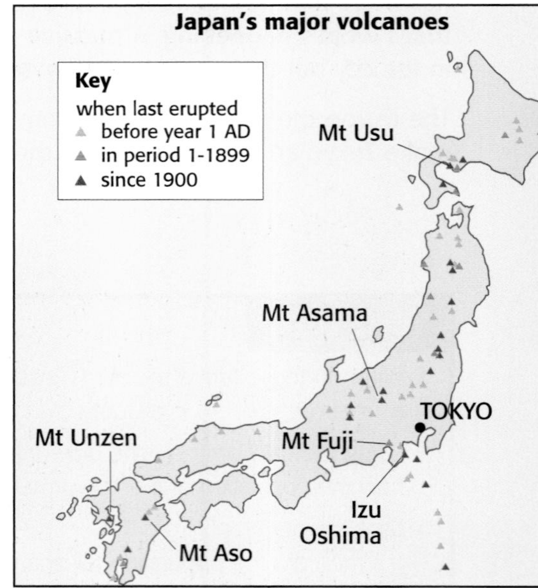

▲ *Japan's active volcanoes. The most famous ones are named.*

◀ *Mt Unzen, and homes it destroyed.*

In the path of typhoons

As you saw, Japan is also at risk from a third natural hazard: **typhoons**. In 2004, typhoon Tokage killed 83 people and injured many others. Nearly 20 000 had to flee from their homes. The typhoon tossed trees and trucks around. The flooding caused hundreds of landslides.

How does Japan cope?

With all those natural hazards, Japan has to stay alert.

- Weather forecasters can track typhoons, with the help of satellites. They can say where and when they'll hit land. So people have time to get somewhere safe.
- Volcanoes give out signs that an eruption is on the way. Like smelly gas, and showers of tiny earthquakes. Scientists monitor Japan's volcanoes closely, and can warn people to move to safety.
- But earthquakes are different. We can't predict them yet – so there is no warning. That's why they are such a big headache for Japan.

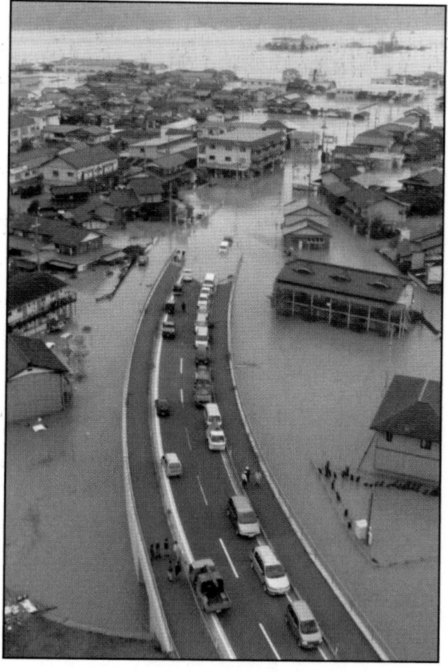

▲ *The town of Toyooka on Honshu, after typhoon Tokage had passed by.*

Earthquakes don't kill ...

Earthquakes do not kill people. The killers are buildings and bridges and other structures, that crack and collapse when they're shaken. And gas pipes that explode. Ripped electric cables. Houses that burn. And panic.

- So Japan works hard to design and build structures that can cope with shaking, without cracking up.
- Japanese students have earthquake drill at school.
- People have emergency knapsacks ready, in case of an earthquake, with things like drinking water, candles, and matches.
- The plans for Tokyo include making narrow streets wider, and creating more open green spaces. This is not just to make Tokyo more pleasant. The open spaces will also be to gather in, after an earthquake. Wider streets will help rescuers reach victims.

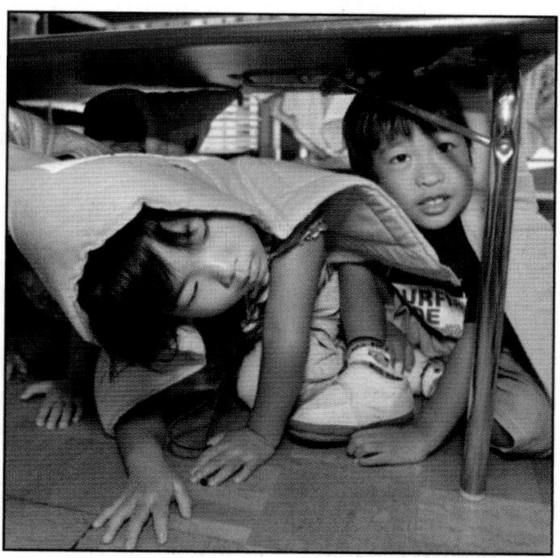

▲ *Earthquake drill in a primary school in Tokyo.*

Your turn

1 Japan faces earthquakes, eruptions, and typhoons.
   - **a** Using what you know already, put those hazards in order, the one you think the most dangerous first. Give reasons for the order you choose.
   - **b** Which of the three hazards could Japan get rid of?
   - **c** Which do you think costs it most money? Why?

2 In Japan, you should pack an emergency earthquake kit and leave it in a handy place, near the front door. Look at the list of things to put in it.
   - **a** Why not a torch, instead of candles?
   - **b** Why dried biscuits, not fresh ones?
   - **c** List the things in what *you* think is their order of importance, most important first.

3 In the work they are doing on Tokyo, they intend to bury all electrical cables underground in plastic piping. Why is that a good idea?

4 Given all those hazards that Japan faces, why doesn't everyone just leave the country?

Emergency kit

2 T-shirts
a packet of dried biscuits
a litre of water
a roll of toilet paper
a small sharp knife
safety pins
plastic knife, fork and spoon
plastic bowl with lid
a pen
2 candles and a box of matches
3 – 5 metres of strong string
some cash

3.7 The challenges facing rural Japan

Here you'll find out why the population is falling in Japan's rural areas, and about the problems the small farmers face.

How times have changed

A hundred years ago, most people in Japan lived in the countryside. Most had small farms, and rice was their main crop.

But, as in the UK and other developed countries, there have been huge changes over the years. Look at this graph.

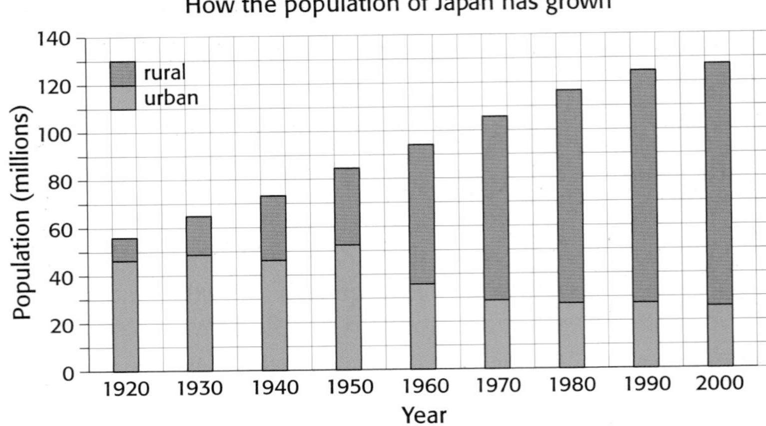

As you can see, while the population of Japan has grown a lot, the population in rural areas has shrunk.

Why has this happened?

While Japan developed rapidly after World War II, and grew prosperous, people flocked from rural areas to the cities, to work. It's still happening today … and it is creating problems!

Why don't you stay on the farm, son?

And you can get a job down the road too, like your dad.

But I can get a really good job in Tokyo, mum. And there's lots to do there.

Now there are only four children in the village school.

I remember when there used to be thirty.

Who'll run the post-ofice when the young ones all go?

Who'll collect the rubbish?

Look, we're 75. We're getting too old for farming.

But who'll look after the rice fields? The children

I can't wait to get out of here. It's so boring!

Let's go.

Nothing to do but farming or building work.

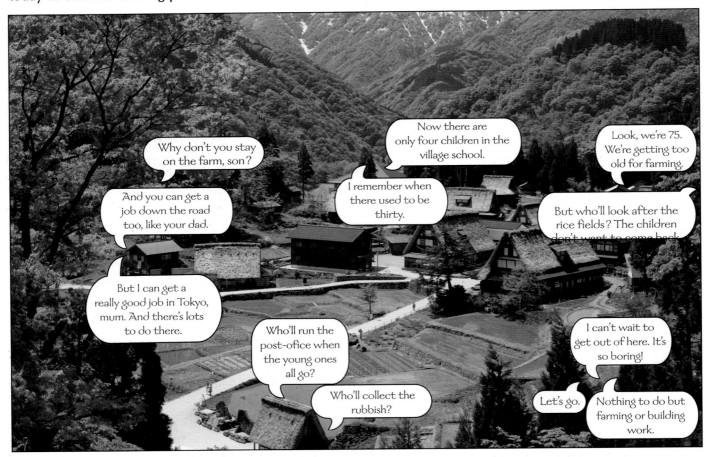

Japan's falling birthrate, plus young people leaving rural areas, means that:

- many of Japan's rural areas are being **depopulated**
- the older people are being left behind
- the average age of Japan's farmers is rising. It is now over 60.

And another problem ...

There's another problem too.

Japan always aimed to grow a high % of its own food, so as not depend too much on imported food.

So for years the government looked after the farmers by paying them big **subsidies** for rice, and setting high taxes or **tariffs** on imported crops.

Since most farms are small, the farmers often had other jobs too, in rural factories and nearby towns. So, overall, they had a good income.

But the government is being forced to drop tariffs and subsidies, as part of world trade agreements. So what will it do about the farmers?

The answers, on the right, are causing conflict.

We'll still give farmers money to help them out ...

... but only if the farms are at least 4 hectares ...

... because Japan needs bigger farms, with full-time farmers.

So we'd like small farmers to join and work together ...

... and we're happy if people buy up small farms to make huge ones.

After all, farming is a business like any other.

▲ *The parliament building in Tokyo. Japan's parliament is called the Diet.*

One drastic solution

All around Japan, small rural hamlets and villages are facing the problems of an ageing population, depopulation, and anxiety about farming. In one hamlet, they have come up with a drastic solution ...

The end of the road for Ogama

Sixty years ago, the hamlet of Ogama had around 240 people. Today, only 8 are left. The youngest is 61. All around them in their valley lie the ruins of houses. The forest is creeping back into empty fields, where rice once grew.

Kazuo Miyasaka is the head man. Ten years ago, he could foresee the problems. He started thinking about how to revive the place. He thought about a golf course – but there wasn't enough flat land. In the end, he got in touch with a waste disposal company in Tokyo. He asked if they wanted to buy the valley and turn it into a waste dump. The company said yes.

Kazuo put the plan to his neighbours. They could take the money, and pack up everything, and move to a town close by, with shops and a hospital. At first they were shocked and upset at the idea. But after months of anguish, they agreed.

So now, if the local council approves, the valley will be buried under 150 metres of industrial ash. Ogama will no longer exist.

Adapted from news reports, 2006.

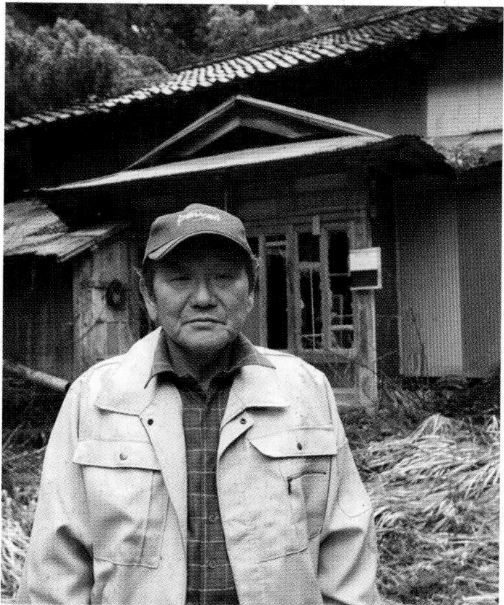

▲ *Mr Miyasaka, outside one of the abandoned homes in Ogama.*

Your turn

1 a What do these terms mean?
   i rural   ii depopulation
   b See if you can give an opposite term for each.

2 Look at the graph for Japan's population, on page 54.
   a i About what was the population in 1920?
     ii About what fraction of this was rural?
   b i About what was the population in 2000?
     ii About what fraction of this was rural?

3 Do you think it would *really* be a bad thing for Japan:
   a if everyone left the countryside? Explain.
   b if it had to import all its food? Explain.

4 By dropping subsidies and tariffs on rice, Japan annoys its farmers, and pleases farmers in Thailand. Explain.

5 You are Mr Taniguchi from Ogama. You are 76. Write to your son in Nagasaki telling him what's happening to Ogama, and how you feel about it.

3.8 Japan's place in the world

Did you know?
- The Japanese unit of currency is the yen.
- £1 = about Y220.

In this unit you'll learn how Japan depends on other countries – and vice versa.

We're interdependent !

Every country depends to some extent on other countries. Countries are **interdependent**. Look at Japan …

TRADE

Exports
Japan sells goods and services to other countries every year. (It earned £329 billion in 2005.)

Imports
Japan buys goods and services from other countries every year. (It spent £285 billion in 2005.)

FOREIGN INVESTMENT

Tax breaks!
Market share.
Lower wages.

Hundreds of Japanese companies have set up branches in other countries. And many foreign companies have set up in Japan.

AID

So how can we help you?

Japan gives aid to other countries, in the form of grants or loans at very low interest rates. Over £5 billion in 2004.

Did you know?
- In 1633, Japan closed its doors to the world for 220 years …
- … because it feared being colonised by Europeans.

JAPAN

Did you know?
Karaoke started in Japan – but has spread all over the world.

TOURISM

Oh, Tokyo!
Hey! Fuji-san!

At least 6 million tourists visit Japan each year, for its culture, scenery, and food …

Golf!
Galleries!

… and over 17 million Japanese go off to visit other countries.

PEACEKEEPING

We're going WHERE?

Japanese soldiers have begun going to other countries to help keep peace, and solve problems. For example, to Iraq.

TREATIES

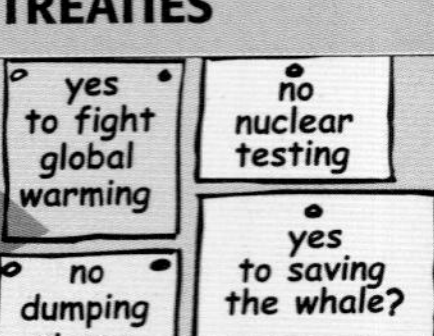

Japan has signed many **treaties** or agreements with other countries to help make the world more peaceful and safe.

Japan's TNCs

One big way that Japan interacts with other countries is through its **TNCs**. A TNC, or **transnational corporation**, is a company that has branches in different countries.

Japan has a large number of very successful TNCs. Think of Sony, Honda, Toyota, Nintendo. In fact, of the 500 largest TNCs in the world, around a quarter are Japanese. Around 40 Japanese TNCs have branches in Scotland. For example Epson. Fujitsu, Nikon, Oki.

You can find out more about TNCs in Chapter 5.

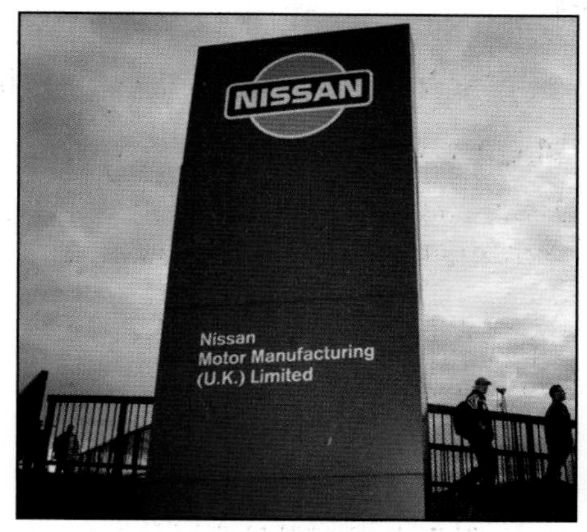

▲ *Nissan's car plant in Sunderland, north east England.*

Japan's army

Japan's army is different from other armies. After World War II, Japan promised never to use force against other countries again. So its army can defend Japan – but can't go to war in other countries. Its soldiers can go to another country only to help rebuild it (as in Iraq), or keep the peace.

Did you know?

In 2005 the UK ...
- *bought £8.3 billion of goods from Japan, and*
- *sold £3.7 billion of goods to Japan.*

Did you know?

- *Japan is called the Land of the Rising Sun - because it lies so far east.*

Did you know?

- *Japanese people work really hard.*
- *On average they take only half the holidays they're entitled to.*

Your turn

1 Countries are *interdependent*. What does that mean?

2 List five ways in which Japan depends on other countries. ('To buy its goods' is one.)

3 a What is a *TNC*?
  b Why would a company want to set up in other countries?
  c Why might a Japanese company want to set up in:
    i China? ii Scotland?
  d Do you think this would benefit Japan? See if you can give some reasons.

4 Like other more developed countries, Japan gives aid to poorer countries. Look at this table:

Country	Population (millions)	Aid given in 2004 ($US million)	Aid given per person
USA	299	19 700	?
Japan	127	8900	?
UK	60	7800	?

  a Which of the three countries gives the most aid?
  b Which gives the most aid *per person*?

5 There is one big way that a country affects every other country: by producing carbon dioxide from burning coal, oil and gas. (For example, to make electricity.) CO_2 causes global warming. Look at this table:

CO_2 output per person, 2004	
Japan	6.7 tonnes
UK	9.4tonnes
USA	19.8 tonnes

Which country produces most CO_2 per person? Suggest a reason for that.

6 Japan does not attract as many tourists as it could. You are the Minister of Tourism.
Write a report for the Prime Minister of Japan saying
  a why Japan has a lot to offer tourists
  b why it's a good idea to attract more tourists
  c what steps you will take to attract more tourists.

7 In 1633, Japan closed its doors to the world, and kept itself isolated for 220 years. Suppose it were to do that again, next year. What would the effect on Japan be? Give your answer in any form you like. For example as a spider map, or strip cartoon, or diary entry, or essay .

4 Energy: a key resource

The big picture

Resources are things we need to live, or can use to earn a living. This chapter looks at one important resource: energy. These are the big ideas behind the chapter:

- We use energy to cook, light our homes, drive cars, and so on.
- The fossil fuels are stores of energy. We burn them to release it.
- We use a lot of energy in one convenient form: electricity. We burn the fossil fuels to make this.
- But our use of fossil fuels is linked to global warming. And global warming may spell disaster, for most countries.
- We need to switch to 'clean' sources of energy, for making electricity.

Your goals for this chapter

By the end of this chapter you should be able to answer these questions:

- What do these terms mean, and what examples of each can I give?
  fossil fuel *a renewable source of energy*
  a non-renewable source of energy
- Why do we like electricity so much, as a form of energy?
- How is electricity usually made?
- Why are fossil fuels so important – and why is oil the most important?
- The fossil fuels are a cause of global warming. Why?
- How is global warming likely to affect our planet? Give at least five examples.
- What can be done to tackle global warming? And what can *I* do?
- The UK has several natural and renewable energy sources, that it can use to make electricity. How many can I name? (Try for five?)
- How does solar power work?
- What special advantages does solar power have, for poorer countries?

And then …

When you finish this chapter you can come back to this page and see if you have met your goals!

Did you know?

- *Heat, light, sound, movement, electricity, chemical energy – they are all forms of energy.*

Did you know?

- *Around 2 billion people in the world (or 1 in 3 of us) don't have electricity.*
- *They depend on firewood, kerosene, or animal dung, for cooking, heating and lighting.*

Did you know?

- *Many young people like you in poorer countries spend long hours every day searching for firewood.*

Did you know?

- *If the world grows 6° hotter than it was in 2006, almost all life will die off.*

Your chapter starter

Look at the photo on page 58.

What is that structure? And what can you see below it?

Why did they put that structure there?

About how tall would you say it is?

Has it got anything to do with you?

Sources of energy

Here you'll review the energy sources we use, and identify which ones are renewable.

We need energy!

You probably know from science class that energy can take many forms – heat, light, sound, electricity, movement, chemical energy. And it can change from one form to another.

We need energy for heating and lighting our homes, moving cars along, watching TV. We usually use **fuels** to provide it.

The fuels we use

The main fuels used around the world are these:

- the fossil fuels – oil, gas and coal (and things like petrol, from oil)
- nuclear fuel
- wood, and waste material such as household rubbish.

We usually burn fuels to release their chemical energy – mainly as heat. But we do not burn nuclear fuel. It contains unstable atoms. We can make these break down by shooting tiny particles called **neutrons** at them. When they break down, they give out a huge amount of energy.

▲ *The electric Mr Faraday. He discovered how to make electricity, using a magnet, in 1831.*

Electricity: energy made easy

There's one form of energy we all use every day: electricity. How is it made? Easy! Just move a magnet inside a coil of wire.

In a power station they use a large magnet called an **electromagnet**. They use steam to make the magnet spin, and a **fuel** to make the steam.

1 First they boil water to make steam. They heat the water:

- by burning a fuel – oil, gas, coal, wood, or even rubbish!
- or using the heat given out by nuclear fuel.

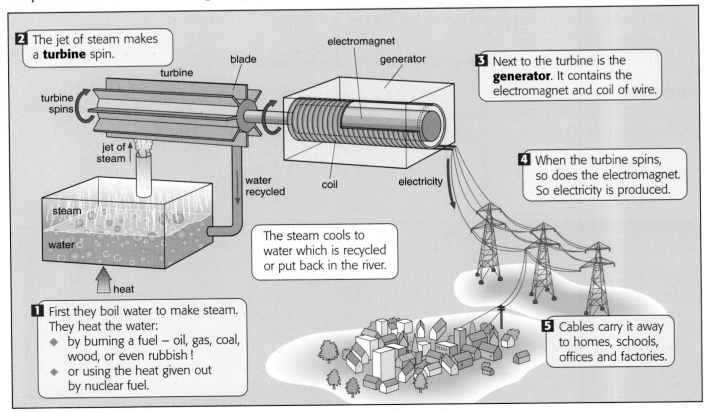

2 The jet of steam makes a **turbine** spin.

3 Next to the turbine is the **generator**. It contains the electromagnet and coil of wire.

4 When the turbine spins, so does the electromagnet. So electricity is produced.

5 Cables carry it away to homes, schools, offices and factories.

The steam cools to water which is recycled or put back in the river.

heat
water
steam
jet of steam
turbine spins
turbine
blade
water recycled
electromagnet
generator
coil
electricity

It doesn't have to be steam

The key to making electricity is to spin that turbine – in any way you can! You don't have to use steam. You could use a river, or the wind, or the sea.

In a **hydroelectric** station, fast-flowing **water** spins the turbines.

On a **windfarm**, the wind spins them, by blowing against blades.

In the sea, **waves** and the **tide** can be used to make a turbine spin.

The electricity can then be fed into the **National Grid**. It's the network of cables that carries electricity around the UK. (See the map on page 124.)

Renewable or not?

Coal, oil and gas are called **fossil fuels** because they are the remains of plants and sea animals that lived millions of years ago. Somewhere on the Earth, some are still forming. But we are using them up millions of times faster than they can form. So we will run out of them one day. That's why we call them a **non-renewable resource**.

It's the same with nuclear fuels. The Earth contains only a certain amount of them. Once we have dug them all up – that's it, folks!

But wood is different. We can keep growing new trees. So wood is a **renewable** resource. What about the wind? Is it?

When will we run out?
This is what some experts think:

At our present rate of use we could run out of ...	in about ...
oil	40 years
gas	60 years
coal	250 years

Your turn

1 Draw a flow chart to show how electricity is generated in a power station, using gas as a fuel.

2 We spend billions turning other fuels into electricity.
  a Why do we like electricity so much?
  b What advantages does it have over: i oil? ii gas?

3 Make a copy of this table. Then complete it by putting ticks in the correct places.

Sources of energy	A fossil fuel?	Used to make electricity?	A renewable resource?
gas			
oil			
coal			
wood			
nuclear fuel			
river			
the wind			
waves			
the tide			

4 Look at this pie chart for 2005.

Sources of UK electricity, 2005

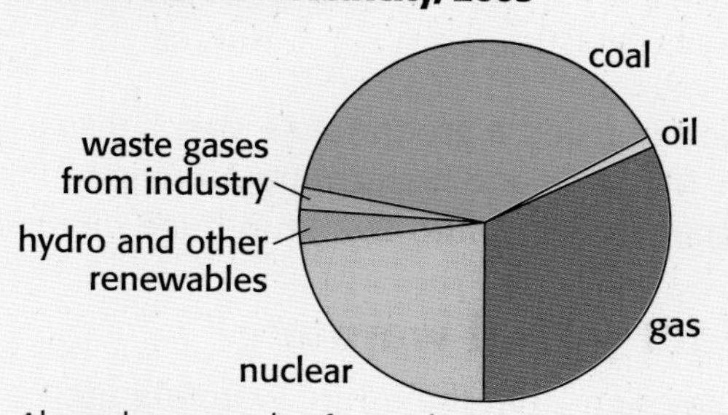

About how much of our electricity came from:
  a nuclear fuel? b oil? c coal?
  d fossil fuels? e hydro and other renewables?

Choose your answers from this list:
over two thirds just under a quarter one thirtieth a bit more than one third one sixtieth

5 Which energy sources are used to make electricity, in Scotland? And which are renewable? (Try page 124?)

4.2 The trouble with fossil fuels

Here you will learn what global warming is, and why it is happening.

▲ *A power station: pumping out steam and carbon dioxide.*

The world depends on the fossil fuels

The world depends on the fossil fuels – coal, oil and gas – for most of its energy needs. And it depends most of all on oil.

- We burn the fossil fuels in power stations to make electricity.
- We burn them in factory furnaces for heat, and in homes for cooking and heating.
- We burn petrol, diesel, kerosene and fuel oil (all from oil) in engines, to move cars, trucks, planes and ships.

The trouble is … global warming

Wherever the fossil fuels burn, they give off **carbon dioxide**, or CO_2. And this gas is linked to **global warming**. The Earth is warming up!

1 The sun warms the Earth.

2 The Earth reflects some heat away …

the Earth's atmosphere

3 … but this can't all escape into space. Some is trapped by gases such as carbon dioxide.

There is always a small % of carbon dioxide in the atmosphere. It traps heat – luckily. Without gases like it, we'd freeze to death when we turn from the sun at night.

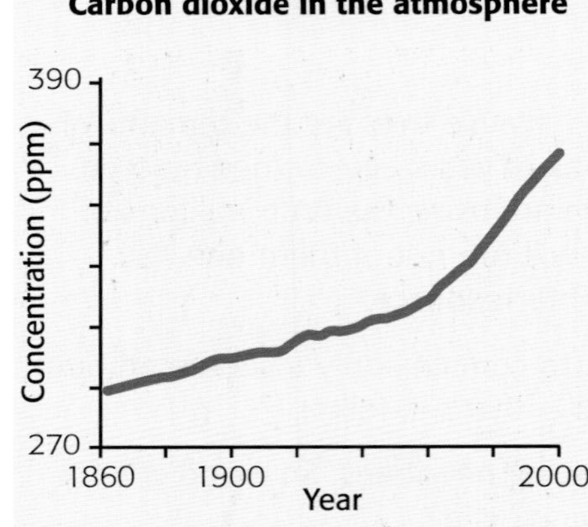

But the level of carbon dioxide is rising, because of all the fossil fuel we burn. (It started at the Industrial Revolution, when we began to burn lots of coal.)

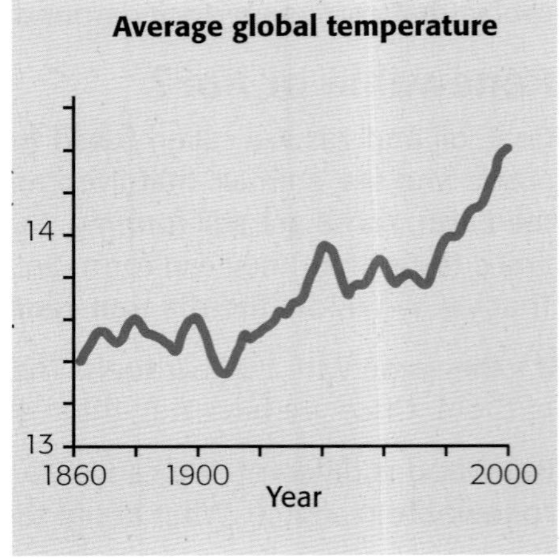

The more carbon dioxide in the atmosphere, the more heat gets trapped. So the Earth is getting warmer, as this graph shows. And that could lead to disaster.

Carbon dioxide is called a **greenhouse gas**, because it traps heat. It is not the only one. Methane and water vapour are greenhouse gases too. But it's the one we pump into the air in huge quantities.

Evidence for global warming

There are many signs that things are warming up:

- The ice is melting fast around the Arctic and Antarctica.
- There is less and less ice and snow on high mountains (like the Alps).
- The water temperature in the oceans is rising, even 3 km down.
- The water level is rising too. It rose about 17 cm in the 20th century – and it could rise 80 cm or more this century.
  Some of this rise is due to the water from the melting polar ice.
  And some is because water expands as it warms.

▲ *Where's my ice going?*

How will it affect us?

The warming of the Earth affects the patterns of wind and rain too. So climates are changing. And this is what scientists predict:

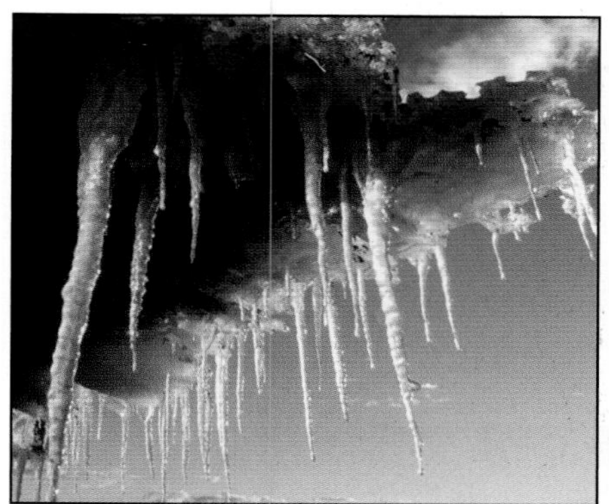

The ice at the poles and on high mountains will continue to melt. In the tundra around the Arctic, the permafrost will thaw.

Sea levels will continue to rise. The sea will drown low-lying coast – in the UK as well as in low flat countries like Bangladesh.

Storms, floods, heat waves and other extreme events will get more frequent, and more severe (including in the UK).

But it will get too hot and dry for crops in many places. This could lead to famines, and millions of refugees, and wars over water.

Much of the tourist industry will collapse. Mediterranean countries will be too hot in summer. Ski resorts will lose their snow.

Fish, birds, and other animals will move, as places get too warm for them. But animal and plant species that can't adapt will die off. Forever.

Every living thing on the Earth will be affected by these changes. And that includes you.

If the Earth's average temperature rises 6 °C more than it was in 2000, most living things will die out. But if we act now we can prevent such a total disaster. Find out more in the next unit.

Did you know?

- In the next 16 days, we will produce more carbon dioxide per person in the UK than a person in Ghana will produce in a year.

Your turn

1. Carbon dioxide is a natural gas. (We breathe it out.) But it could doom us. Why?
2. Traffic in your town is helping to make the Arctic ice melt. How?
3. The UK government could ban the use of fossil fuels. But that's not likely to happen any time soon. Suggest some reasons why.
4. Global warming will have *social*, *economic* and *environmental* consequences.
   a. Explain the terms in italics. (Glossary?)
   b. Then give one example of each type of consequence, using the information on this page.
5. See if you can name three animals that will die out if all the world's ice melts.

4.3 What can we do about global warming?

Find out here what the world needs to do, to try to control global warming. And think about how *you* can help.

How hot will it get?

Global warming is happening. We can't stop it. But how hot will it get? That depends on us!

Scientists have developed computer models to try to predict what will happen.

These maps show two different outcomes. **A** is the best we can hope for. **B** is very bad news.

Key
Rise in average temperature (in °C), compared with the present

0 0.5 1 1.5 2 2.5 3 3.5 4 4.5 5 5.5 6 6.5 7 7.5

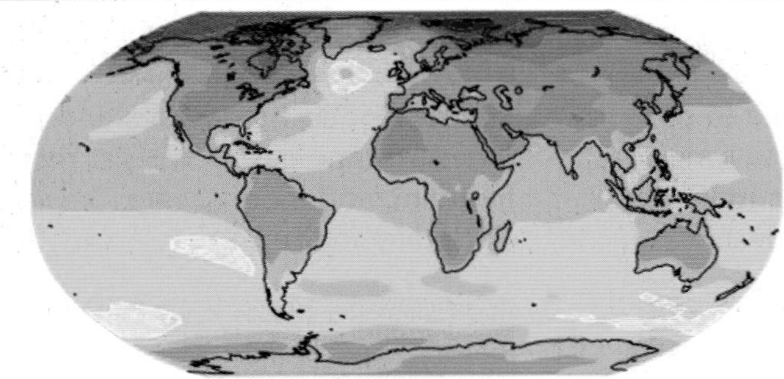

A It's likely to be this much hotter by 2095, even if:

- we start saving energy now
- countries switch to 'clean' energy quickly
- countries work *together* to solve the world's energy, economic, and social problems
- the world population rises until 2050, but then falls.

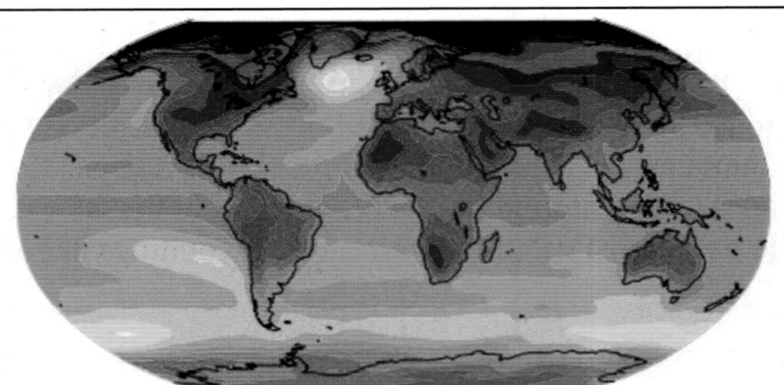

B But it's likely to be this much hotter by 2095, if:

- our energy consumption keeps rising fast
- countries switch to 'clean' energy slowly, bit by bit, here and there
- countries think only about themselves
- the world population keeps rising.

Which scenario do *you* think we should choose?

Saving, and switching

The more energy we save, the less fossil fuel we burn – so the less carbon dioxide we produce. So saving energy is a start. But it's not enough. We must switch to 'clean' energy sources, that don't produce carbon dioxide.

Here are some of the things we must think about:

1 Get electricity from clean renewable sources. But which ones?

2 Stop heat loss through roofs, walls, and windows. Insulate!

3 Improve public transport, to cut car use.

4 Switch off lights. Turn down the heating.

5 Don't waste hot water. (Or any water.)

6 Buy low-energy things: light bulbs, fridges, washing machines.

7 Solar panels on all roofs?

8 What about cars? Tax big cars more? Ban all cars?

9 Switch from petrol engines to hydrogen fuel cells?

10 Buy most of our food from local farmers?

11 Put bigger taxes on air travel?

12 Fly less?

13 Let more people work from home?

14 Cut packaging on food and other things we buy.

15 Recycle more.

Working together

Carbon dioxide from one country affects *every* country. So countries must work together to cut their output. But getting them to agree is not easy!

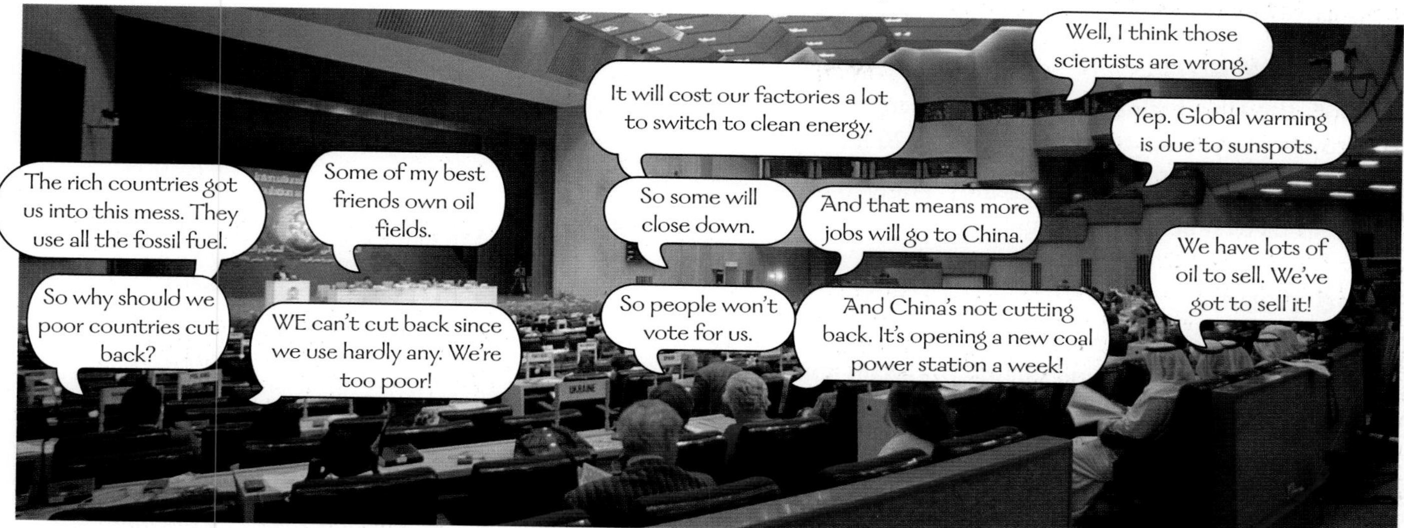

But 169 countries *have* signed a treaty called the **Kyoto Protocol**. In this:

- The more developed countries have agreed to targets and a timetable, for cutting output of carbon dioxide (and other greenhouse gases).
- The less developed countries don't have to make cuts. Because first, they don't produce much CO_2 per person, as this bar chart shows. And second, they need more industry, to help them develop. Which means burning *more* fossil fuel.
- If a country can't meet its target for cuts, it can help with a 'clean energy' scheme in a less developed country, to make up for it.

China and India don't have to make cuts yet. But both are very large, and industrialising fast. They may have to accept limits quite soon.

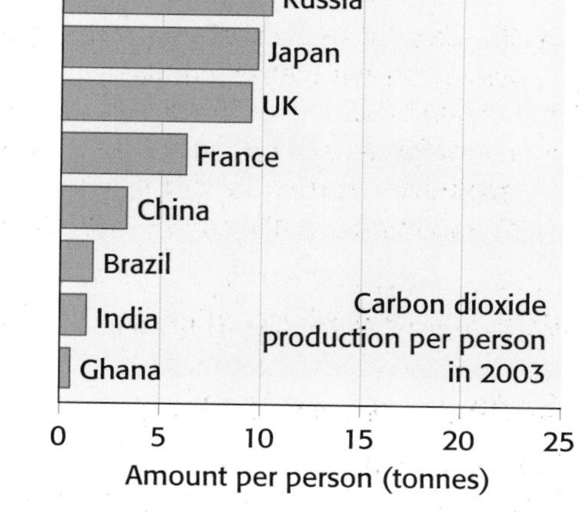

Roll on the renewables

So the pressure is now on, in the UK and other countries, to switch from fossil fuels to clean renewable sources of energy. In the next unit we'll look at some clean sources for electricity, here in the UK.

Your turn

1 Look at the maps on page 64.
  a The average annual temperature in England is about 10 °C. About what will it be in 2095:
    i in scenario **A**? ii in scenario **B**?
  b Mali, in Africa, is a hot dry country. (See page 129.) Its average annual temperature is about 30 °C. About what will it be in 2095:
    i in scenario **A**? ii in scenario **B**?

2 Look at the suggestions on the photo on page 64. Explain why these would help to cut CO_2 emissions:
  a 1 b 10 c 13 d 14 e 17

3 From the suggestions on page 64, pick out two that you think depend mainly on: a the government b businesses c individuals and families

4 Look at the graph above.
  a Ghana produces very little CO_2 per person, compared with countries like the UK. Why is this?
  b Do you think it's fair *not* to make Ghana cut back on CO_2 emissions? Give your reasons.
  c Now look at the third bullet point above. What do you think of that idea? How could it help Ghana?

5 And finally, you. The best way *you* can help to cut down on CO_2 emissions is to save electricity, gas and petrol. Write a serious list of ways you can do that.

Energy from wind and sea

Here you'll learn about three of the energy sources the UK is planning to use, for 'clean' electricity: the wind, the waves and the tide.

Get renewable!

In 2005, the UK obtained 4.6% of its electricity from renewable sources. The government aims to increase this to 20% by the year 2020.

We are lucky. We have three free and renewable resources around us, that can help us to reach those targets: the wind, the waves and the tide.

Wind power

The UK is the windiest country in Europe, thanks to its location. So experts say that the wind will be our main source of renewable energy. In fact the wind alone could provide 20% of our electricity needs by 2020.

A **windfarm** is just a collection of tall towers with turbines at the top, and big blades to catch the wind. Look at the two photos below. The diagram on the right shows how they work.

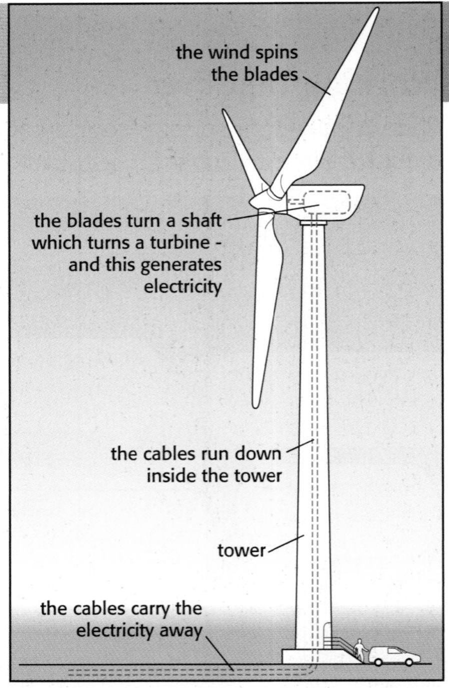

▲ *A wind turbine. If it's in the sea, the cables run along the sea floor.*

▲ *An onshore windfarm in North Yorkshire.*

▲ *An offshore windfarm off the north coast of Wales.*

The number of windfarms is growing fast. At the start of 2007, we had 136 windfarms, of which 5 were offshore. But 330 more were being built, or being planned. Of those, 21 were offshore.

Scotland: best for wind power

In low wind, the blades of a wind turbine stop turning. In very high winds the turbine is shut down, because it could be dangerous. So windfarms are best in areas with quite strong but steady winds.

Look at this wind speed map. It shows that Scotland has large areas with quite strong wind speeds (in yellow). Many of these areas have a low population density. So Scotland has some of the best windfarm sites in the UK.

By the start of 2007 Scotland had 39 windfarms. But of the new ones being built, or in planning, 129 are in Scotland. So Scotland is making a big contribution.

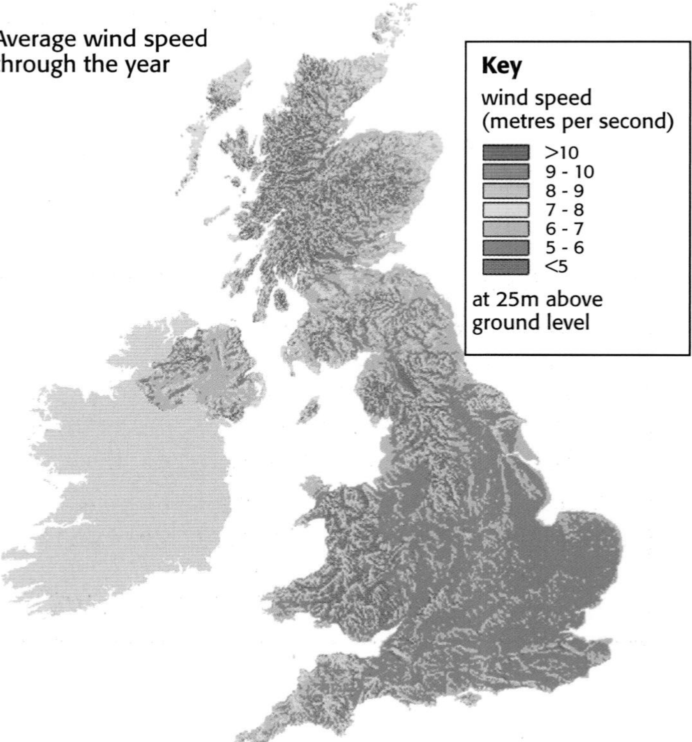

Solar power in the UK

The UK is not the world's sunniest place. But even on a cloudy day, enough sunlight gets through to provide solar power.

Now PV cells are being made into roof tiles, and built into glass for windows – so your home could provide a lot of its own electricity.

Experts think that solar power will be providing more of the UK's electricity by 2020, and that its share will keep on growing.

A solar-powered home in Oxford. ▶

Your turn

1 What is a photovoltaic cell? Describe in your own words what it does.

2 Say whether these statements about solar power are true or false. (The photos may help.)
 A Every home could make its own electricity.
 B You must live near a city to use solar power.
 C Solar power is used only in rich countries.
 D It is not sunny enough in the UK for solar power.
 E Sunlight is a renewable source of energy.
 F Solar power depends on fossil fuels.
 G Solar power makes global warming worse.

3 a What are the advantages of solar power, in your opinion? List them in order of importance.
 b Now give any disadvantages you can think of.

4 Look at the map below. What does it show?

5 a Which gets the strongest sunshine: Greenland, Ireland or Saudi Arabia? Why? (Pages128–129?)
 b Which of them would be best for solar power?

6 Overall, which of the *continents* shown on the map would be best for solar power?

7 a Solar power has special advantages for poorer countries. Explain why.
 b The map on page 14 shows wealth around the world. Name three poorer countries that have very strong sunlight they could use for energy.

8 Now match each place in the photos on page 70 to the correct dot on this map. Start like this:
 ① =

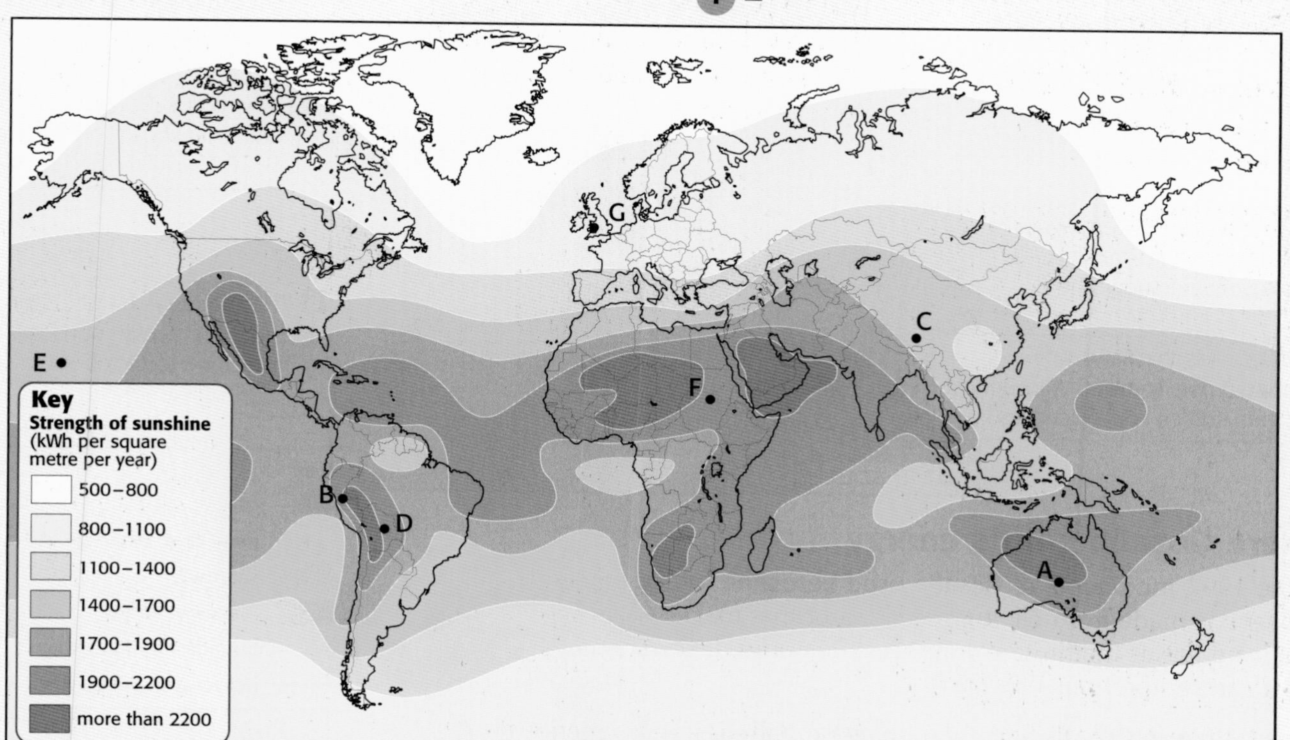

Going solar in Gosaba

Here you'll learn how solar power improved life in a rural village in India.

Where's Gosaba ?

This is Debu. He is 15. He lives in Gosaba, on a small island in an area called Sundarbans in India.

His home is the one on the far right above. It has a thatched roof and two rooms.

Did you know?

- The Indian government promises that everyone in India will have electricity by 2012.

CHINA
NEPAL
BHUTAN
BANGLADESH
INDIA
Bay of Bengal

This sketch map shows Sundarbans, with Gosaba marked in.

1 Sundarbans is a **delta** area (like its neighbour Bangladesh). It has 102 islands. This map shows just some of them.

2 Over millions of years, water flowing out from two great rivers, the Ganges and Brahmaputra, deposited sediment in the area.

3 It built up to form the islands – and the water just ran round them.

4 Now the region is teeming with rivers, stream, and canals. Only some rivers are shown here.

5 It also has thick swampy **mangrove forests**. With Bengal tigers, turtles and crocodiles!

6 The climate is hot and humid. There are heavy monsoon rains from June to October.

7 About 200 000 people live in the area shown on this map. 15 000 live on Debu's island.

8 Most people live on tiny farms in small hamlets – like Debu. His father also earns some money from fishing.

9 The only way to get to most of the islands is by boat.

Kolkata (Calcutta)
INDIA
Gosaba
BANGLADESH
Bay of Bengal
NOT TO SCALE

Key
- city
- main town or village of island
- sea/river
- mangrove forest
- boundary of Sundarbans
- border with Bangladesh

Where Gosaba got its energy

Before 1997, the people of Gosaba used **kerosene** for lighting and cooking. Kerosene is made from oil. It gives out soot that makes walls and ceilings black, and fumes that irritate your eyes and lungs. It gives a dim light. And it can set the house on fire!

Some homes in Gosaba had TV, running on batteries. But batteries don't last long, and cost a lot. Which means less money for other things.

Solar power arrives

In 1997, some homes and other buildings in Gosaba got solar power, as a trial. Debu's home was one.

The governments of India and the USA paid for most of the project. But the users also had to pay a little – £23 a year for 5 years.

Solar power has made a big difference to Debu and his family.

In fact the whole project was so successful that other parts of the Sundarbans are going solar too. The target is 31 of the 53 inhabited islands by 2008.

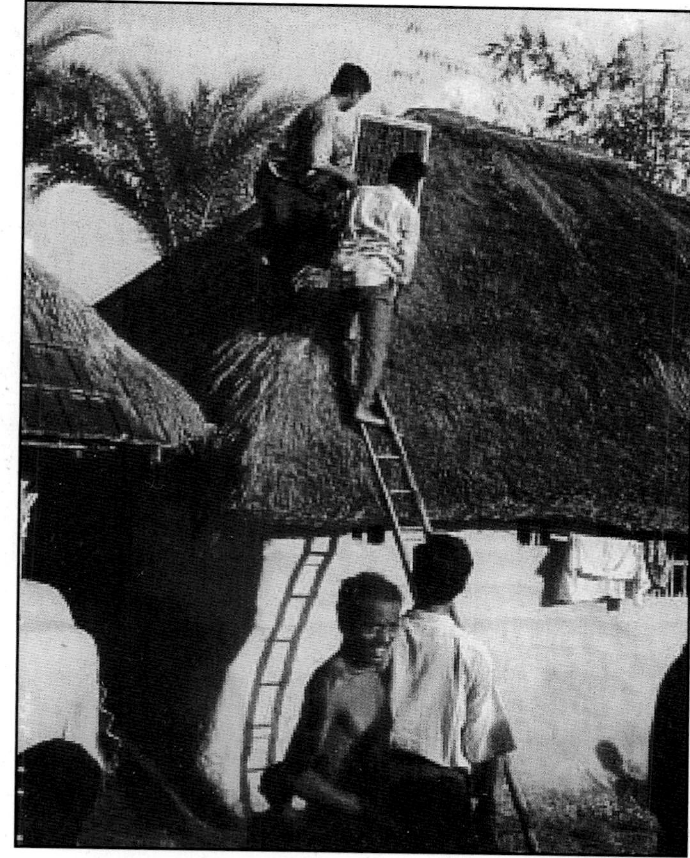

▲ *Up go the PV cells on Debu's roof …*

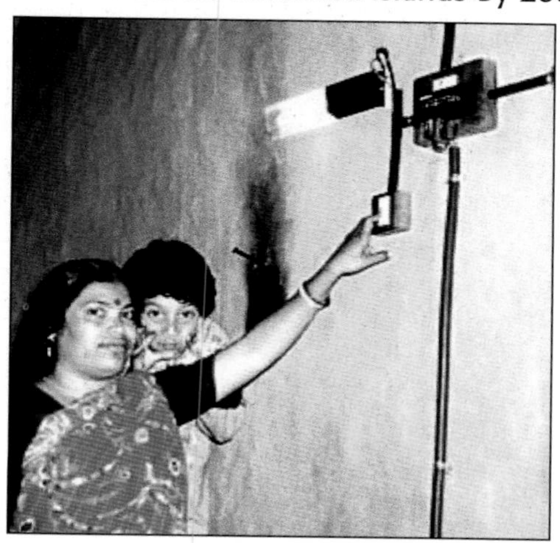

◀ *… and on go the lights!*

Your turn

1 **a** In which country is this area of Sundarbans?
 b In which continent is it?
 c Which country is it next to?

2 Explain why:
 a there are so many islands in Sundarbans
 b floods are a problem there.

3 India has a National Grid for electricity, like the UK. Cables carry electricity from power stations to different places. But India will never be able to extend its grid to Gosaba. Suggest reasons for this.

4 Before solar power, Debu's family had just two kerosene lamps like this one. They lit them every evening when it got dark, around 6. What problems can kerosene lamps cause?

5 **a** The table on the right shows the results of a survey in Gosaba. Which was the most common reason people gave, for liking solar power?
 b Why do you think this reason is so important to them?

6 Display the results of the survey in any way you like. For example you could draw a pictogram or bar graph. Make it look interesting!

7 It is 1997. You are Debu. Write to your cousin Kali in Kolkata telling her about solar power, and how it has affected your family.

8 *'Solar power in Gosaba is a great example of sustainable development.'* Do you agree? Explain.

Impact of solar power on people in Gosaba

Benefit	% who mentioned this
Better light	80
No fumes to irritate the eyes	85
Less coughing	10
Can earn more now since can work longer hours	25
Easier to serve food now	12
Easier to use than kerosene	64
Helps children to study	88
Can watch more TV news	44
Can watch more TV serials and films	78

5 Global fashion

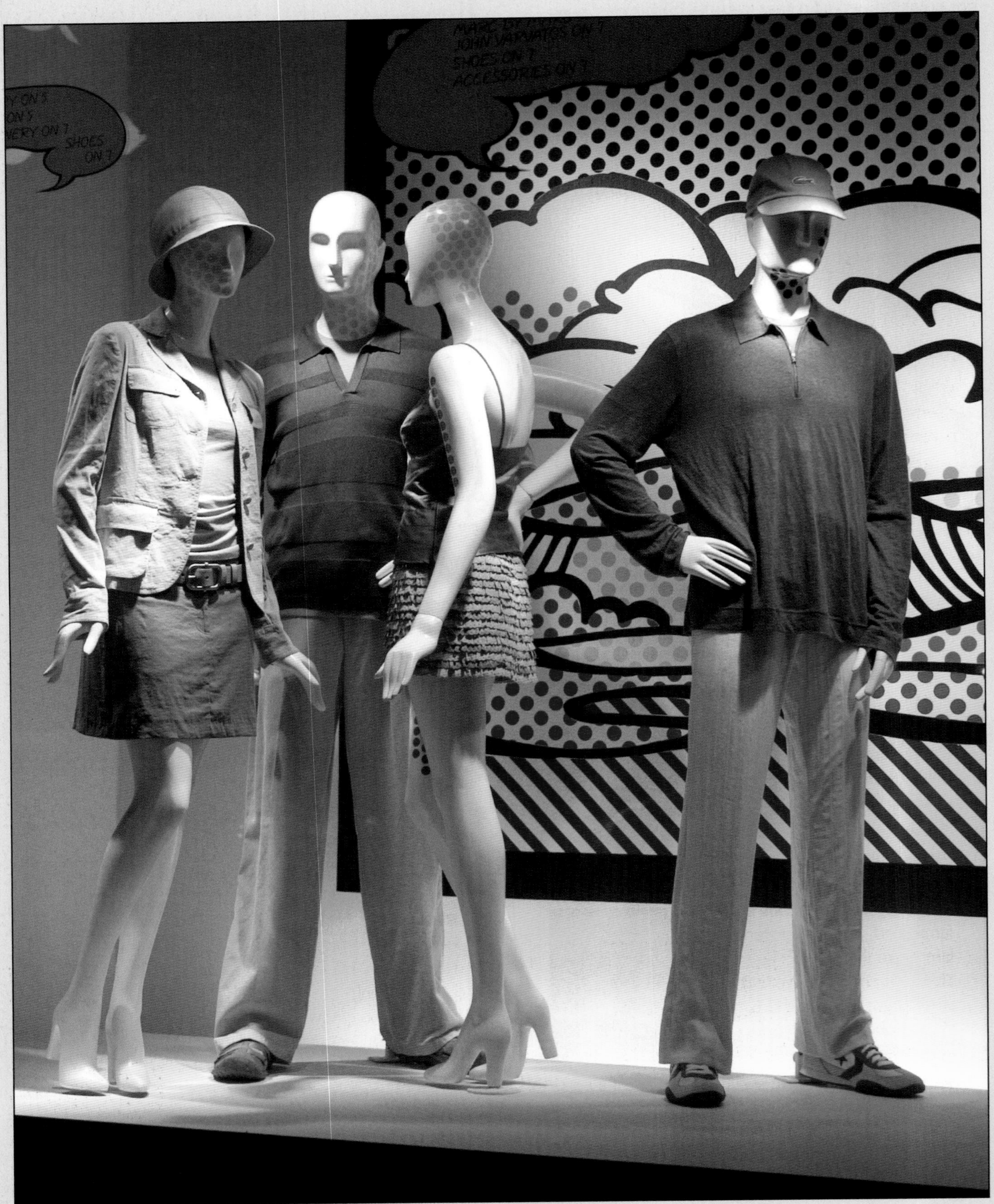

The big picture

This chapter is about **global fashion**, and **globalisation**. These are the big ideas behind the chapter:

- We are linked to real people all over the world, through the things we buy. Clothing is a good example.
- Most of the clothes we buy are made in poorer countries, where wages are a lot lower than here.
- Their manufacture is usually arranged by large companies from richer countries, who want to make as much profit as possible.
- The people who make the clothes get only a very small fraction of what you pay for them, and some have to work in very poor conditions.
- Jobs are continually moving from richer countries like the UK to countries with low wages.

Country	Hourly wage in clothing factory (US $)
USA	9.35
UK	9.50
Mexico	1.75
Malaysia	1.36
China	0.86
India	0.71
Sri Lanka	0.57
Indonesia	0.24
Pakistan	0.23

Did you know?

- Companies like Nike and Quiksilver don't really make clothes.
- They get companies in poorer countries to make them.

Your goals for this chapter

By the end of this chapter you should be able to answer these questions:

- What do these terms mean?
  transnational corporation (or TNC) *globalisation* *GDP* *revenue* *profit* *sweatshop* *exploitation*
- In what ways does globalisation affect my life?
- Why do companies like to go global, if they can?
- Why are some TNCs more powerful than many countries?
- Why do companies like Nike and Quiksilver like to get things made in poorer countries, and in other people's factories?
- What kinds of conditions might you find in sweatshops?
- What is the role of the World Trade Organisation (WTO)?
- What are some benefits of globalisation? (Give at least three.)
- What are some disadvantages of globalisation? (Give at least three.)

Did you know?

- China is the world's top exporter of clothing.

And then …

When you finish the chapter, come back to this page and see if you have met your goals!

Did you know?

- The business of clothing humans is worth around 400 billion dollars a year.

Your chapter starter

Look at the clothes on page 74.

What do you think of them?

Who do you think made them?

Do you think they got paid much?

Why do clothes shops take a lot of trouble with their windows?

5.1 Arthur's global jeans

Here you'll see how an ordinary pair of jeans can involve many countries.

Cool or what?

Arthur, trying on his latest birthday present. Not cool – but well-travelled!

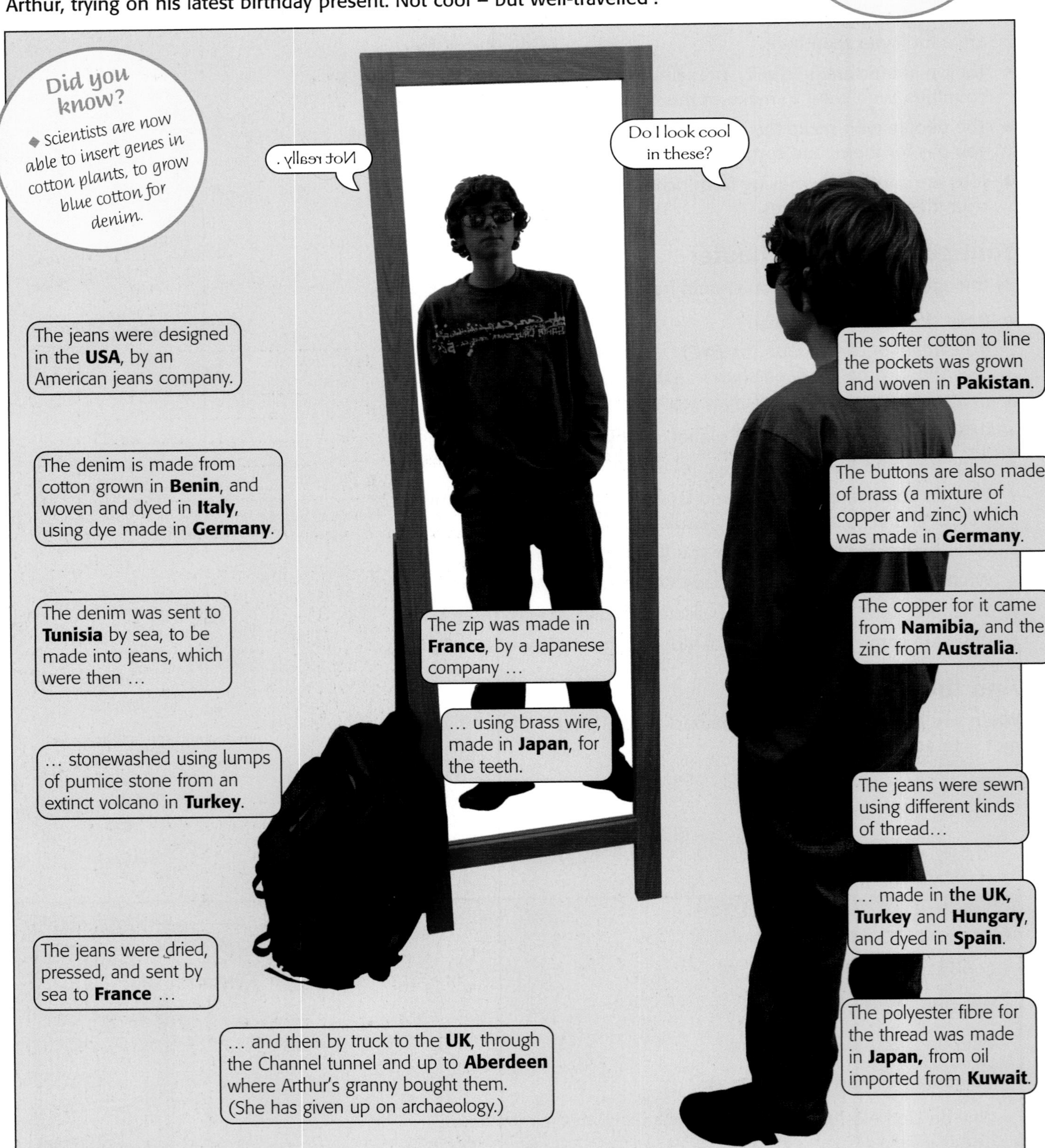

Did you know?
◆ Scientists are now able to insert genes in cotton plants, to grow blue cotton for denim.
Not really.
Do I look cool in these?
The jeans were designed in the **USA**, by an American jeans company.
The denim is made from cotton grown in **Benin**, and woven and dyed in **Italy**, using dye made in **Germany**.
The denim was sent to **Tunisia** by sea, to be made into jeans, which were then ...
... stonewashed using lumps of pumice stone from an extinct volcano in **Turkey**.
The jeans were dried, pressed, and sent by sea to **France** ...
... and then by truck to the **UK**, through the Channel tunnel and up to **Aberdeen** where Arthur's granny bought them. (She has given up on archaeology.)
The zip was made in **France**, by a Japanese company ...
... using brass wire, made in **Japan**, for the teeth.
The softer cotton to line the pockets was grown and woven in **Pakistan**.
The buttons are also made of brass (a mixture of copper and zinc) which was made in **Germany**.
The copper for it came from **Namibia,** and the zinc from **Australia**.
The jeans were sewn using different kinds of thread...
... made in **the UK, Turkey** and **Hungary**, and dyed in **Spain**.
The polyester fibre for the thread was made in **Japan,** from oil imported from **Kuwait**.

Getting Arthur's jeans together

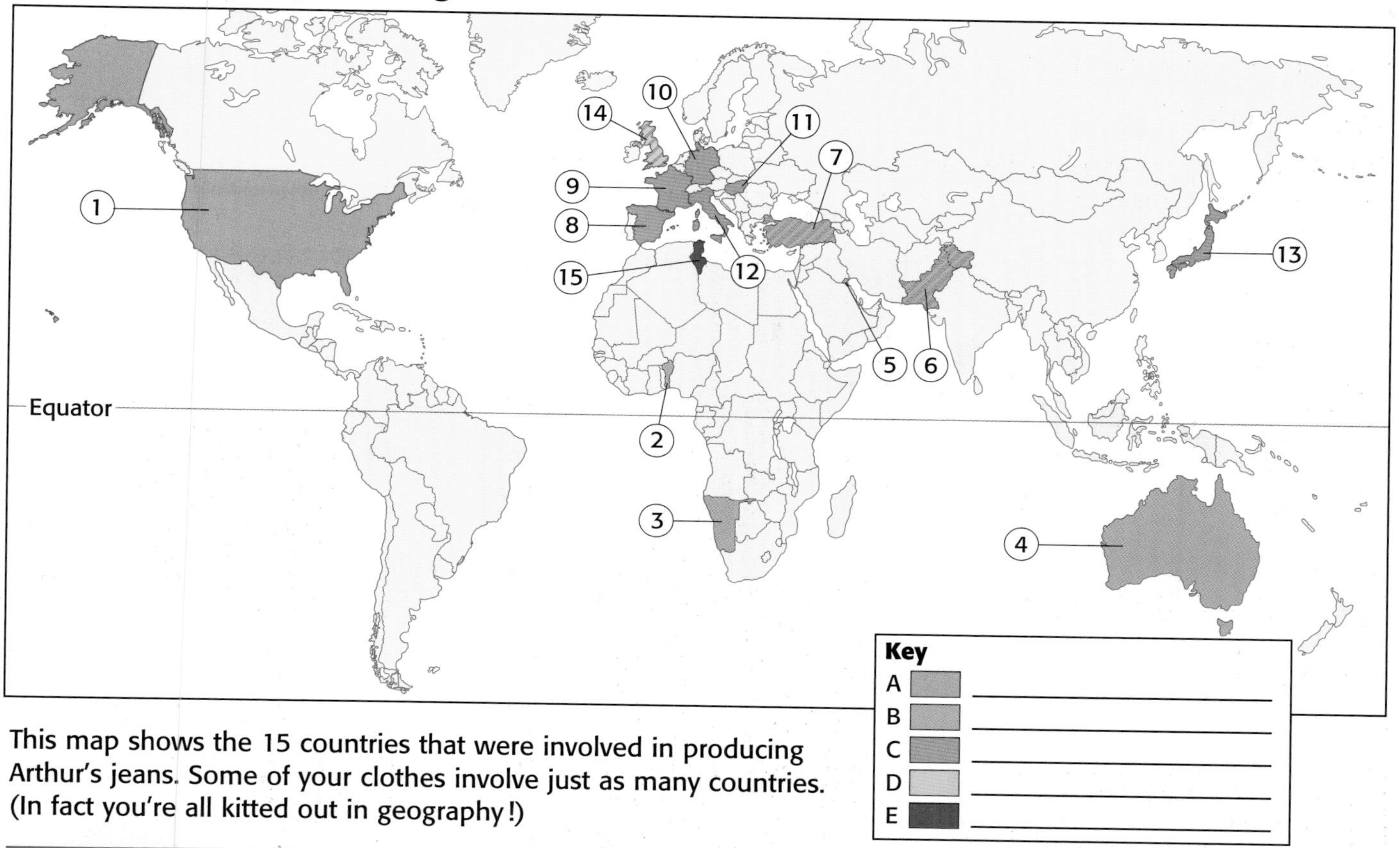

Equator

Key
A ____
B ____
C ____
D ____
E ____

This map shows the 15 countries that were involved in producing Arthur's jeans. Some of your clothes involve just as many countries. (In fact you're all kitted out in geography!)

Your turn

1 Which *continents* contributed to Arthur's jeans?

2 Name the countries marked 1 – 15 on the map above. Pages 128–129 will help. Answer like this: ① = ____ Then, after each country, write what it contributed to the jeans. (For example, *zip*.)

3 The map key is not complete. Complete it by matching the letters to the terms in italics below.
Give your answer like this: A = ____________
manufacture and processing of materials
source of a raw material
making and finishing the jeans
design and brand name
country where jeans sold
The glossary may help, if you're stuck.

4 Some countries on the map (for example the UK) have stripes of a second colour. Explain why.

5 The table on the right shows wages in clothing factories. Use it and the map above to see if you can explain why:
a the American company didn't get the jeans made in the USA
b the denim was sent 1000 km from Italy to Tunisia, to be sewn into jeans.

Where your money goes when you buy a pair of jeans

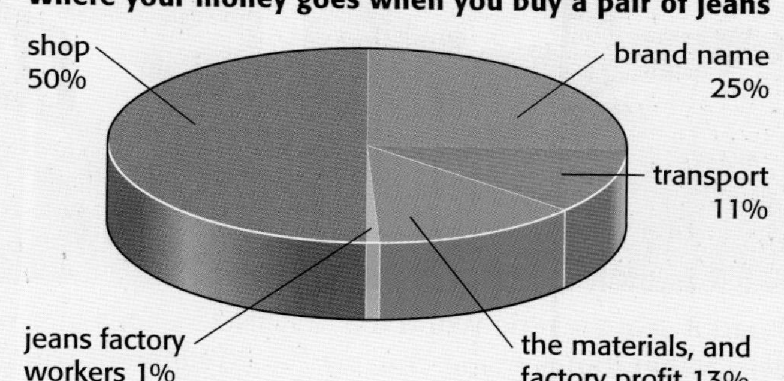

6 a Look at the pie chart. Arthur's granny paid £40 for the jeans for Arthur. Of this, how much went to:
i the shop where she bought them?
ii the American company whose label they carry?
iii the worker(s) who sewed them?

b Does what you found in **a** seem fair to you? Explain.

7 Do you think Arthur's jeans had any impact on the environment? Give reasons for your answer.

Hourly wages for clothing factory workers

Country	Average pay per hour (£)
USA	6.64
UK	6.55
Italy	6.49
Tunisia	0.99

5.2 Behind the swoosh

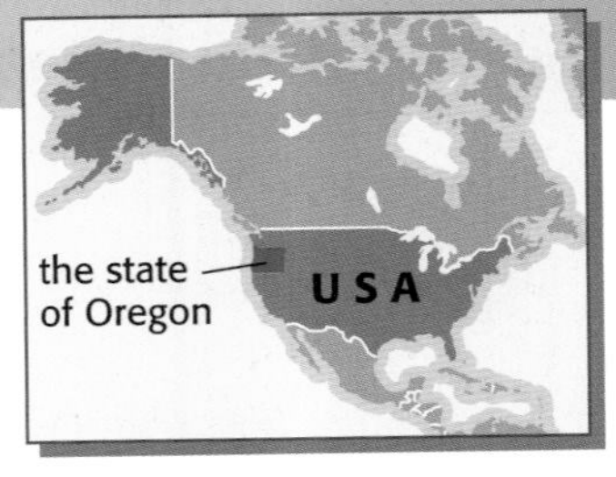

In this unit you'll see how Nike has spread around the world.

The Nike operation

Arthur's jeans (page 76) were just ordinary. But what about labels like Nike? Where are their clothes made?

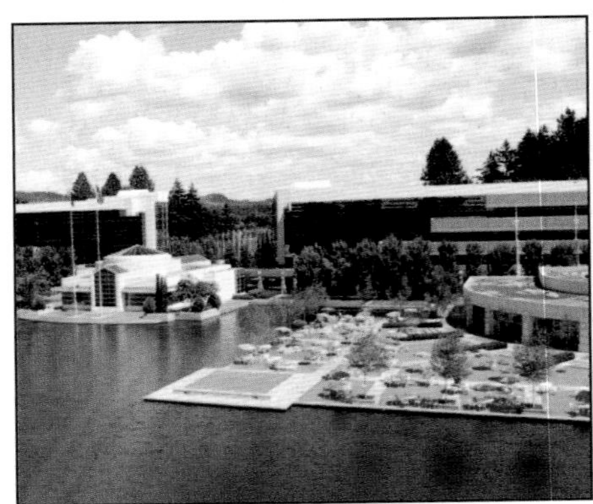

Nike is based in Oregon in the USA. This is the headquarters from which the business is controlled.

The people who run Nike are anxious to make as much money as possible. So Nike keeps on …

… bringing out new designs for its clothing and trainers. But it does not *make* these things itself.

Instead it searches the world for places to get things made cheaply, in other people's factories.

Nike goods are made in nearly 40 different countries, mostly by young women like these.

While they are working really hard, so is Nike – getting people like you to buy things with the swoosh on.

Nike spends over 1.7 billion dollars a year on advertising, in around 160 different countries.

It pays top athletes millions to wear Nike products, as another way to advertise.

It supplies its goods to over 51 000 shops round the world. (It owns just a fraction of these shops itself.)

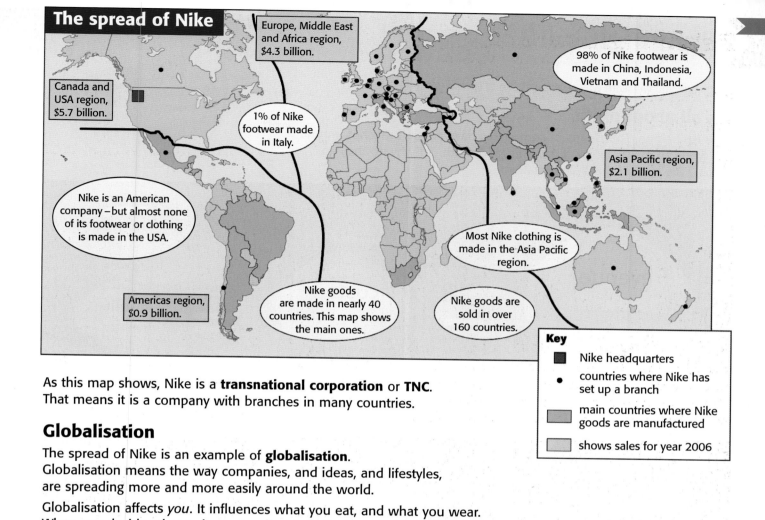

The spread of Nike

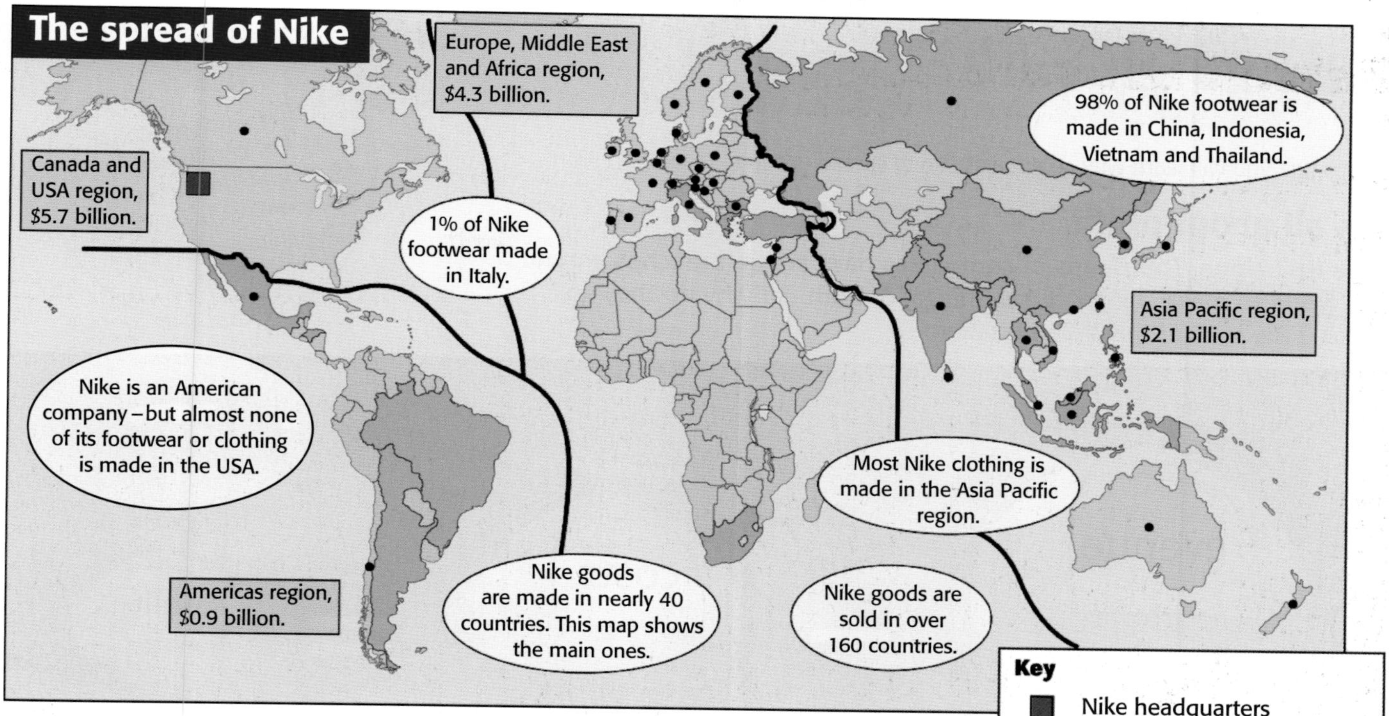

Europe, Middle East and Africa region, $4.3 billion.

98% of Nike footwear is made in China, Indonesia, Vietnam and Thailand.

Canada and USA region, $5.7 billion.

1% of Nike footwear made in Italy.

Asia Pacific region, $2.1 billion.

Nike is an American company – but almost none of its footwear or clothing is made in the USA.

Most Nike clothing is made in the Asia Pacific region.

Americas region, $0.9 billion.

Nike goods are made in nearly 40 countries. This map shows the main ones.

Nike goods are sold in over 160 countries.

Key

- Nike headquarters
- countries where Nike has set up a branch
- main countries where Nike goods are manufactured
- shows sales for year 2006

As this map shows, Nike is a **transnational corporation** or **TNC**. That means it is a company with branches in many countries.

Globalisation

The spread of Nike is an example of **globalisation**. Globalisation means the way companies, and ideas, and lifestyles, are spreading more and more easily around the world.

Globalisation affects *you*. It influences what you eat, and what you wear. When you decide what to buy, you affect people thousands of miles away.

Your turn

1 What kinds of goods does Nike sell? Write a list, and give prices if you can.

2 Using the map on pages 128 – 129 to help you, name:
  a six countries where Nike has a branch *and* gets goods made
  b two countries where Nike goods are made but Nike does not (yet) have a branch
  c eight other countries where Nike has a branch.

3 Nike is a *transnational corporation* or TNC. Its growth is an example of *globalisation*. Explain each of the two terms in italics.

4 Now compare the Nike map with the one on page 14.
  a Look at the GDP per capita for the countries where *most* Nike goods are made. What do you notice?
  b Suggest a reason why Nike chooses these countries.
  c On which *continent* does Nike *sell* most goods? Is this continent rich or poor?
  d Suggest a reason why Nike does not (yet) get goods made in countries like Ghana.

5 The spread of Nike is an example of globalisation. See if you can give at least *four* other examples. (Companies? TV programmes? Examples from sport or politics?)

6 Each of these helps the process of globalisation. For each, write a short paragraph to explain why.

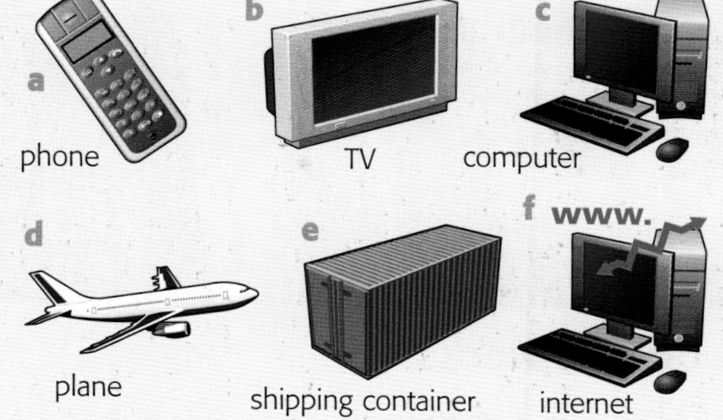

7 Now give six examples of how globalisation affects you. (Think about what you wear, and eat, and do in your free time.) Present your answer in an interesting way!

Why go global?

In this unit you will learn why companies like to spread around the world.

Did you know?
- Nike employs around 28 000 people directly.
- Around 1 million others are involved in making, supplying and selling its goods.

It's all about profit

Nike isn't alone. Thousands of companies have set up branches around the world to make things, or sell things, or both. So why do they go global? Because of this little equation:

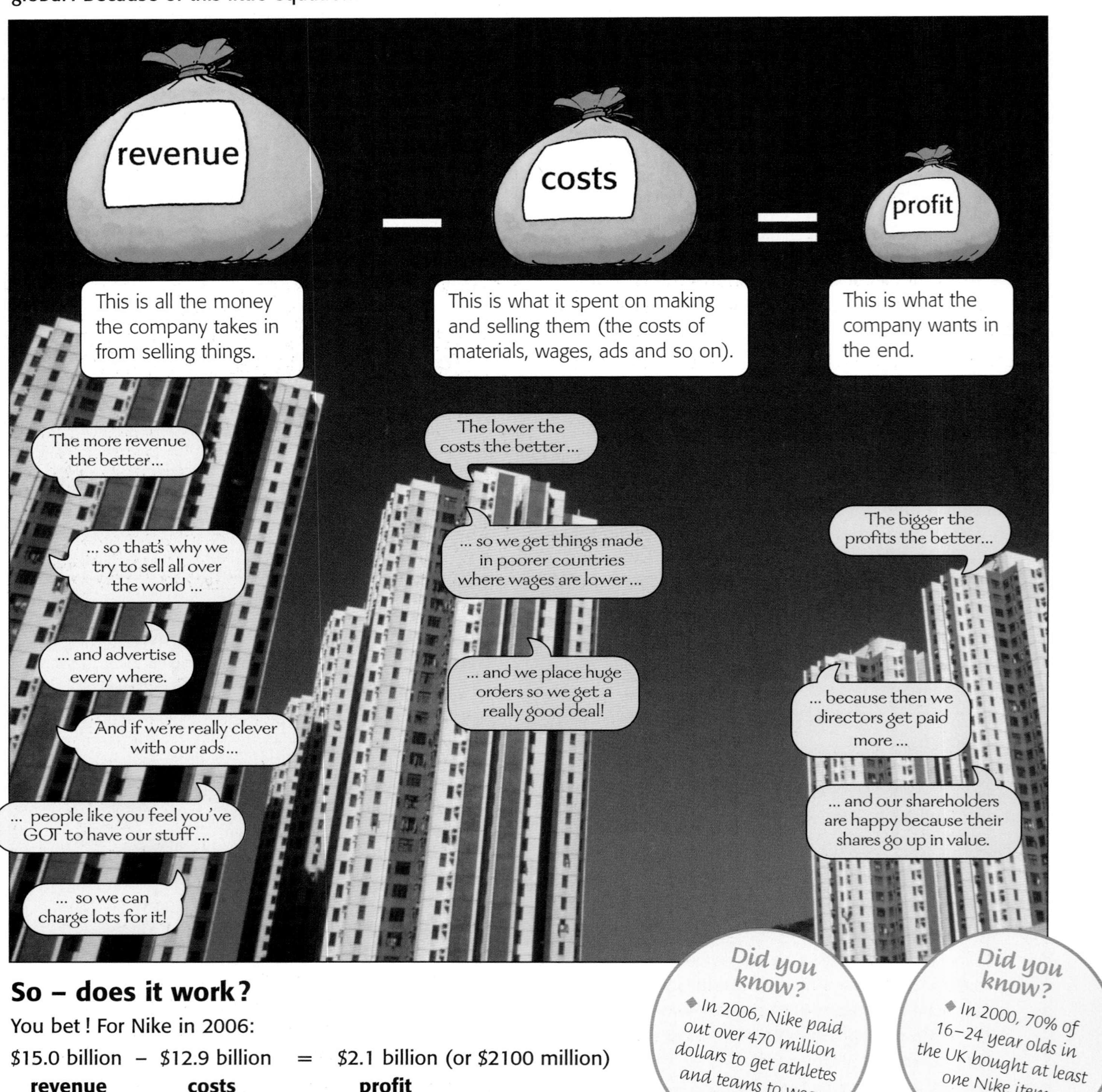

revenue
–
costs
=
profit
This is all the money the company takes in from selling things.
This is what it spent on making and selling them (the costs of materials, wages, ads and so on).
This is what the company wants in the end.
The more revenue the better...
... so that's why we try to sell all over the world ...
... and advertise every where.
And if we're really clever with our ads...
... people like you feel you've GOT to have our stuff...
... so we can charge lots for it!
The lower the costs the better...
... so we get things made in poorer countries where wages are lower...
... and we place huge orders so we get a really good deal!
The bigger the profits the better...
... because then we directors get paid more ...
... and our shareholders are happy because their shares go up in value.

So – does it work?

You bet! For Nike in 2006:

$15.0 billion	–	$12.9 billion	=	$2.1 billion (or $2100 million)
revenue		**costs**		**profit**

The US government then took $750 million of this profit as a tax.

Did you know?
- In 2006, Nike paid out over 470 million dollars to get athletes and teams to wear the swoosh.

Did you know?
- In 2000, 70% of 16–24 year olds in the UK bought at least one Nike item.

Some other TNCs

Nike is very small compared with some TNCs, as this first table shows. Wal-Mart, a supermarket chain, had over 20 times more revenue that year.

Revenues for 10 TNCs (in 2004)

TNC	Its business	Based in	Revenue ($ billions)
Exxon Mobil	oil/petrol	USA	298
Wal-Mart	supermarkets	USA	256
BP	oil/petrol	UK	204
Toyota	cars	Japan	159
Nestlé	foods	Switzerland	67
Microsoft	software	USA	37
Coca-Cola	you know what	USA	22
McDonald's	you know what	USA	19
GAP	clothing	USA	16
Nike	sports goods	USA	12

GDP for 10 countries (in 2004)

Country	GDP (or total wealth produced) $ billions PPP
USA	11 651
India	3390
UK	1845
Belgium	324
Bangladesh	260
Switzerland	244
Nigeria	149
Tunisia	77
Jamaica	11
Ghana	9

Now look at the second table. It shows the GDP for ten countries, for the same year. Note that each of the TNCs earned more than some of those countries !

In fact, for that year, McDonald's revenue was greater than the GDP of 65 of the world's countries. It even beat the *combined* GDP of 20 countries !

Did you know?
◆ Wal-Mart owns Asda in the UK.

▶ *Who has over 30 000 restaurants in over 120 countries?*

Your turn

1 Copy and complete, using terms from the brackets.
The more _____ a company sells and the _____ its _______ the higher its _______ will be.
(*money profits losses costs goods lower*)

2 Like every company, Nike aims to increase its profits.

a Make a *large* copy of the Venn diagram on the right. (Use a full page.)

b On your diagram, write in **A–H** below, *in full*, in the correct loops. (Small neat writing!) If you think one belongs in both loops, write it where they overlap.

A It gets 40% of its trainers made in China.
B It runs a website.
C It sponsors top school sports teams.
D It closed its trainer factories in the USA.
E It now owns no trainer or clothing factories.
F It employs sports scientists.
G It brings out new styles regularly.
H It opened a branch office in Australia.

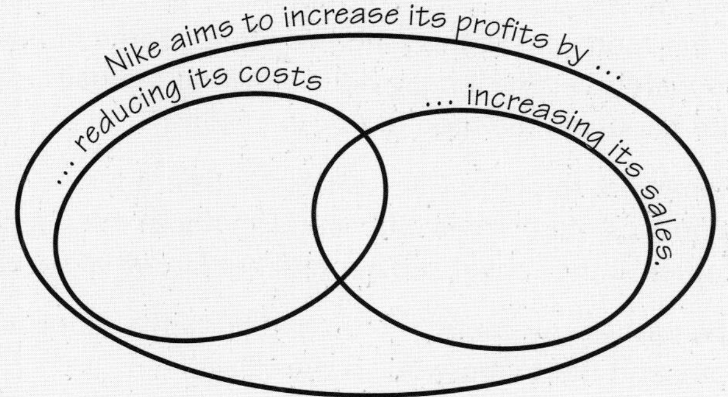

... reducing its costs
... increasing its sales.

3 Now look at the tables at the top of the page.

a What is *GDP*? Give your answer as a sentence.

b Make *one* list showing the 20 companies and countries, in order of revenue / GDP. (USA first.)

c On your list, underline the countries in one colour and the companies in another. Add a key and a title.

4 Which do you think has more real power in the world, Exxon Mobil or Ghana? Explain your answer.

A fashion victim?

Here you'll see how some of our clothes are made by exploiting people in poorer countries.

It's just the fashion

Nike is not the only company to get clothing made cheaply in poorer countries. Look at the list on the right. But who actually sews the clothes? It could be someone like Rosa in Manila.

Rosa's day

Rosa can hardly keep her eyes open. But she must must must concentrate. Otherwise she'll pierce her fingers. Or sew crookedly. If she does that, the supervisor will yell at her again.

She's tired because she worked overtime last night. Until 2 am. She didn't want to, but if you refuse they sack you on the spot. Everyone is forced to do overtime now for the big Christmas orders.

She dragged herself in again this morning, at 7 am. To sew non-stop, all day long, the side seams for sports joggers. Snatch a pair from the trolley beside you, slap them on the machine, race down each leg as fast as you can, throw them back on the trolley, grab another pair. On and on and on. By 8 her shoulders were aching. By 9 the heat was already stifling. And still an hour to go till the toilet break, when she can escape from the clatter of 500 machines for 10 minutes.

She thinks sadly about her family and village, like she does every morning. She left home just after her 16th birthday, 5 months ago. She was so excited about the job. They promised she'd earn enough to send some home. But the 280 pesos she gets (£4) for a 12-hour day is hardly enough to live on, when they take out rent and lunch.

Overtime again tonight. At 2 am she will leave the sewing section and drag herself past the guards, down the path by the barbed wire fence, to the room she shares with five others. Three bunk beds. No chairs. No wardrobe. She'll hang her clothes on the nails in the wall and climb into her bunk, too tired to talk to anyone.

More work tomorrow. It's usually six days a week, but in this busy period it's often seven. She wonders about the people who buy the clothes. If they could see her and her life, what would they think?

She wishes she could give up and go home. But she can't. She must earn, and there's no work in the village.

Adapted from newspaper articles.

Just one of many ...

Over half the clothing in UK shops is sewn in LEDCs by girls like Rosa. Many are from rural areas, with little education.

Not all the clothes factories are bad. Many are more modern than UK factories. But there are many **sweatshops**, like Rosa's, where young women work in poor conditions, for very low pay. If the factory has no orders, they get no pay at all. They can be sacked without any notice.

Large % of clothing made in LEDCs *

Calvin Klein	Levi Strauss
Ralph Lauren	Tommy Hilfiger
Quiksilver	Next
The Gap	Topshop
Principles	M & S
Warehouse	Miss Selfridge

* *This is not a complete list!*

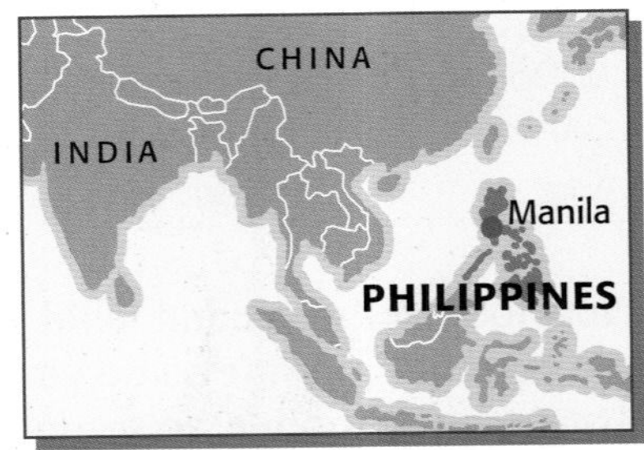

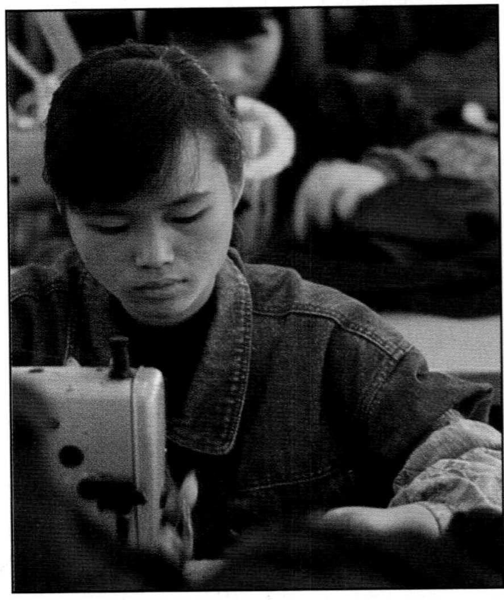

▲ *No rest for Rosa till she gets back ...*

▼ *... to the hut that's now her home.*

How does it happen?

How does it happen that people like Rosa have to work in these conditions? Again we take Nike as example – but it could be anyone:

Nike designs a new range of clothing. Next, it has to be made!

It's too low...
... but if I say no, he'll go somewhere else.
Can't you do it for this much?

2
Somewhere cheap...
... that will do a good job and give no trouble...
... but where we have a lot of control.

An executive goes to find a factory in an LEDC, where wages are low.

The factory owner takes on the work – and aims to make a profit.

4
Just do it ...
... or you're out. Okay?

So he forces his workers to work very quickly, for very little pay.

5
We better just do it ...
... since we don't have any choice.

The workers are not happy, but they need the jobs.

6
Mum, money. Please!
JUST IN
You're driving me mad.

The clothing gets finished on time. People like it. It sells really well.

Shoppers have found out about sweatshops, and many have protested. Nike and other clothing companies now say they inspect all the factories they use, to make sure the workers are treated okay. But many thousands like Rosa are still being exploited – all in the name of fashion.

Did you know?

◆ The head of Nike earns over 3000 times more per hour than Rosa does.

Your turn

1 Rosa usually works a 6-day week, 12 hours a day.
  - a How much does she earn: i per hour? ii per week?
  - b Does she get to keep all this pay?

2 Make a list of the working conditions in Rosa's factory. You can put them in order, with what you think is the worst thing first. (Is the low pay the worst thing?)

3 Now look at the chain above. What would happen if:
  - a the factory owner refused to work for Nike's terms?
  - b the factory owner increased his workers' pay?
  - c the workers went on strike?
  - d the customers didn't like the new clothing?
  - e the government of the LEDC passed a law that factories there must pay higher wages?
  - f customers refused to buy from Nike because of the sweatshops?
  - g Nike forced the factories to pay their workers more?

4 Do *you* think Rosa is being exploited? (Glossary.) If so, who is exploiting her? Explain your answer.

5 Look again at the chain. Of all the people in it, who do you think:
  - a has got *most* power to change things?
  - b has got *least* power to change things?

6 Here are two different opinions. Write down what you will say to each person in reply.

The factories don't belong to Nike – so the workers are not their problem.
I like Nike things – so why should I care where they're made?

5.5 Global actions, local effects

Dunfermline

In this unit you'll see how globalisation can lead to job losses too.

The other side of the story

On page 83 you saw how globalisation provides jobs for people like Rosa. Now let's look at the other side of the story.

Annie's job takes flight

This is Annie at her machine. Or rather, it was Annie at her machine. But now the machine has gone, and Annie has lost her job.

Annie lives in Dunfermline. She used to work for Castleblair, the Scottish clothing manufacturer, making clothing for women and children for UK stores – mainly Marks & Spencer. But now the factory has closed.

Why did the factory close ?

'The company was struggling to make a profit', said a company official. 'In fact we were losing £80 000 a week. We couldn't keep going.'

'We were under pressure from two sides. First, we were competing with cheap clothes coming in from China and other countries. So we were getting fewer and fewer orders. And then, when stores did give us orders, they pushed down the prices. They would only pay us £8 for something they used to pay £10 for.'

The Dunfermline factory employed 247 people. Jobs have also gone at the company's factory in Glenrothes, which employed 235.

Tears – and fears

'We knew orders were down', said Annie. 'But we kept hoping. Then the managers called us in, in April, to talk about redundancies. Some of the women were in tears. We'd worked hard. But in the end that didn't matter. And now I'm afraid I won't find another job around here.'

Regret

'We regret we had to close this factory', said the official. 'It has been part of Dunfermline since 1916. The workers have been hard-working and loyal. But it all boils down to one thing. Shoppers want cheap clothes !'

However, job losses in one place means more jobs in another. Castleblair will now make more clothes in the factory it owns in Turkey.

Other jobs under threat too

More and more UK clothing brands and stores are switching from using UK factories. For example, M&S had always tried to 'buy British'. Now it gets most of its clothing made overseas, so that it can cut costs, and sell to its customers more cheaply.

And it's not just clothing. Scotland has lost 30 000 manufacturing jobs in the last two years, as companies opt for cheaper labour in places like China and Eastern Europe.

(Adapted from news reports, July 2004)

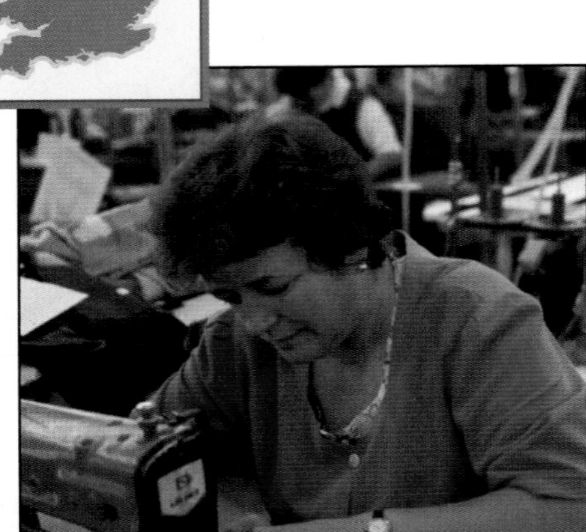

▲ *Annie at her machine.*

▲ *The Castleblair factory in Dunfermline.*

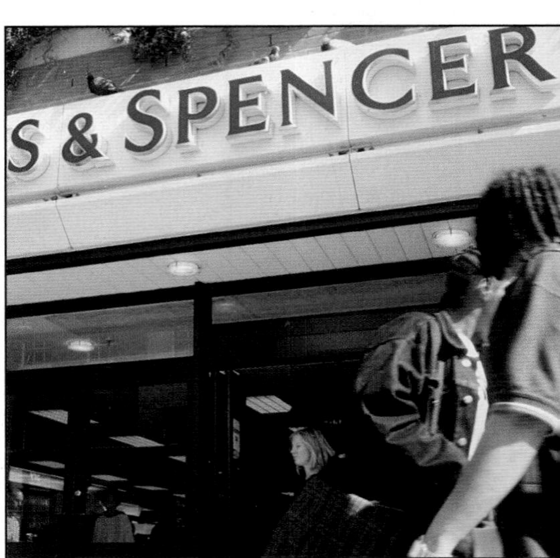

▲ *Like all High Street chain stores, Marks & Spencer now gets most of its clothing made overseas.*

Your turn

1 Why did Annie lose her job? The flowchart below will explain. But first you need to do some work on it!

No, the M&S one costs too much.
Arthur's aunt in Liverpool
People like Arthur's aunt shopped less in M&S.
Head of M&S
So profits fell for M&S.
Head of Castleblair
So profits fell for Castleblair, since M&S ordered less.
So Annie ...
So Rubina ...
Annie in Scotland
Rubina in Turkey

a Make your own copy of the flowchart and drawings. (Just draw stick people.)
b Complete the sentences in the flowchart boxes.
c Arthur's aunt has a thought bubble. Draw bubbles for the others and fill them in, with thoughts about their part in the chain.

2 a Who will have gained, when Castleblair moved production from Scotland to Turkey? Think of as many groups as you can.
b Who will have lost out, when Castleblair moved? (Was it *only* Annie and the other factory workers?)
c Do you agree that Annie was a victim of globalisation? Explain your answer.

Cut the workers' pay.
Open the factory just three days a week.
Find new customers and don't depend so much on M&S.
Charge M&S even less.
DO NOT DISTURB

3 Above are ideas a Castleblair manager had, for saving the Dunfermline factory. Choose TWO. Say if you think they were good ideas, and give your reasons.

4 Textiles (cloth) and clothing were important industries in Scotland, and the rest of the UK, for centuries. Now look at this graph:

People employed in manufacturing textiles and clothing, in the UK
Number employed (thousands)
700
600
500
400
300
200
100
0
1998 1990
1995
2000
2005
Year

a Is it true that the textile and clothing industries are *in decline* in the UK? (Glossary?) Give evidence.
b Try to give reasons for the trend the chart shows.

5 The table below shows exports and imports of clothing, for the UK (in millions of dollars).

UK exports and imports of clothing ($ millions)					
Year	1996	1998	2000	2002	2004
Exports	3319	2929	2717	2481	2719
Imports	6208	7125	8766	10 075	10 859

a Show the export and import data, both on the same graph. (Use any suitable type of graph.)
b Describe any overall trends you notice.
c Give reasons to explain these trends.
d If these trends continue, predict what the clothing industry will be like in the UK by the year 2020.

6 Think up ideas to save the UK clothing industry. (You can't prevent imports.) For example, could it focus on 'specialist' clothing? (Bullet proof? Heat proof? Luxury?) Think about help for young designers too. Put your ideas in a memo to the Prime Minister.

So is globalisation a good thing?

In this unit you'll look at arguments in favour of globalisation.

It's going on everywhere

There is globalisation in all kinds of business, not just clothing. TNCs are spreading everywhere. Is this a good thing?

1 The TNCs think so. (They would!)

Well, we're the people who make globalisation happen.
We go where workers are cheap...
... or markets are large ...
... and watch our profits grow!

2 Many governments in LEDCs think so.

And we need some TNCs (like oil companies), to help us exploit our resources.
We welcome TNCs...
... because they give our people jobs...
... and we hope the wages will help our economy.

3 Many governments in MEDCs think so.

We like to see our companies doing business overseas.
And we're happy when foreign TNCs set up here ...
It spreads our country's influence...
... because it means jobs for people ...
...and either way, we collect taxes on the profits!

4 Many workers all over the world think so.

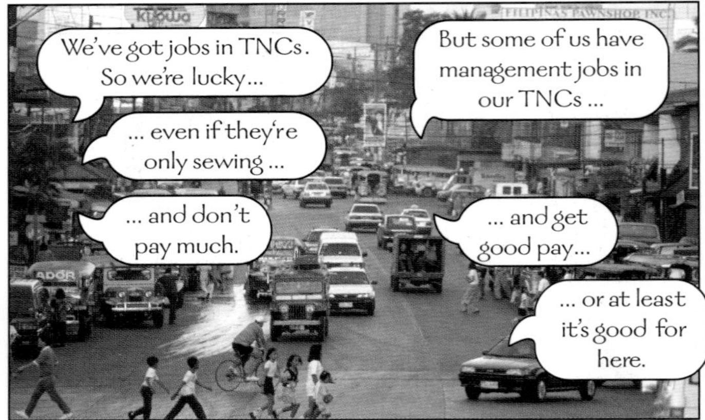

We've got jobs in TNCs. So we're lucky...
But some of us have management jobs in our TNCs ...
... even if they're only sewing ...
... and don't pay much.
... and get good pay...
... or at least it's good for here.

5 Many economists think so.

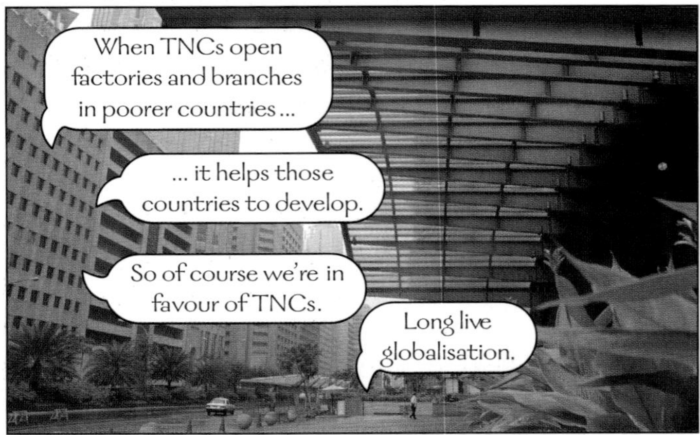

When TNCs open factories and branches in poorer countries ...
... it helps those countries to develop.
So of course we're in favour of TNCs.
Long live globalisation.

6 And the World Trade Organisation thinks so too.

If companies can move around freely...
... and export and import freely...
... it breaks down the barriers between nations...
... AND it gives shoppers such a good choice!

So, many people are in favour of globalisation and think we all benefit. But as you'll see in the next unit, many people disagree!

More about the World Trade Organisation

The World Trade Organisation or **WTO** was formed to promote world trade. It is based in Geneva in Switzerland. 150 countries are members.

The WTO aims to remove barriers to trade between countries, so that companies can trade freely everywhere.

In the past, when countries fell out over trade they often went to war. The WTO aims to prevent this. For example, if Europe tries to stop a crop being imported from the USA, the WTO will try to settle the dispute peacefully.

Any country that joins the WTO must sign an agreement to obey its trade rules.

Everyone here yet? Getting ready for a WTO meeting. ▶

Your turn

1 For each of these people, write down what you think is the *main* argument in favour of globalisation:

the Manchester United football team
the president of McDonald's
the government of Vietnam, which lets TNCs get clothes sewn there, tax free
the president of Ghana, who has signed a deal with a UK mining company
NEW!
FRIDGE
Joe, unemployed in Glasgow, where a foreign TNC is about to set up a factory
Arthur's aunt, buying a new fridge in Liverpool

2 This is Priya. She works in a call centre in Bangalore in India, for a British phone company.

Priya's job is to call and remind you, if you haven't paid your phone bill. She gets paid about £4000 a year. (The average wage in India is about £2000 a year, PPP.)

a Is this an example of globalisation? Explain.

b What do you think the phone company would say, in favour of globalisation?

c What do you think Priya would say, in favour of it?

d When it is 5 pm here it is 10.30 pm in Bangalore. What does that tell you about Priya's working hours?

3 The UK is a member of the WTO.

a What is the WTO? Give its full name in your answer.

b Write down two aims of the WTO.

c Write a short section for the WTO website saying why globalisation is a good thing. (120 words max.)

5.7 Against globalisation

In this unit you'll look at arguments against globalisation.

Does it do more harm than good?

Lots of people are in favour of globalisation, and the spread of TNCs – and lots are against!

1 Many politicians around the world are against.

Some TNCs are far richer and more powerful than many governments ...
... so they just walk in and do what they want.
No one can control them!
And they move on the minute they find a better deal elsewhere.

2 So are some workers in LEDCs.

TNCs don't care about people ...
... only about profit.
They just use us for cheap labour.
And most of the jobs they bring are badly paid ...
... like sticking soles on these trainers.
So we're not learning skills that will help us in future.

3 So are some workers in MEDCs ...

Well, globalisation is why we lost our jobs.
Factories are moving to countries where wages are lower ...
... so we're left unemployed.

4 ... and many environmentalists everywhere.

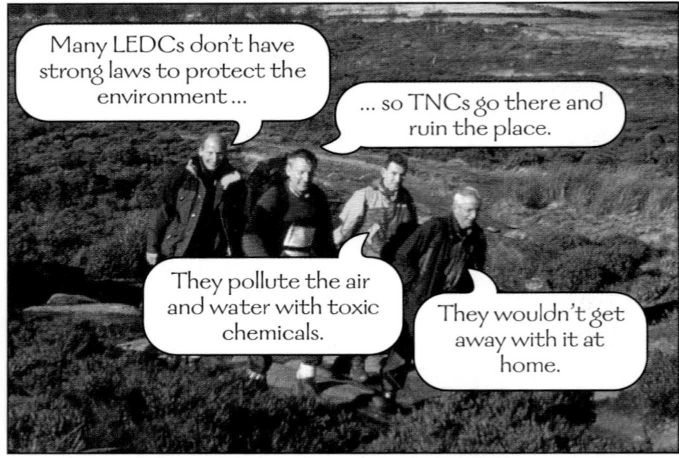

Many LEDCs don't have strong laws to protect the environment ...
... so TNCs go there and ruin the place.
They pollute the air and water with toxic chemicals.
They wouldn't get away with it at home.

5 Some economists are not too happy either.

TNCs move most of their profits back home ...
... so they don't really help the countries where they have branches.
What LEDCs really need is their own industries.
But they don't have
uch chance to

... with all this competition from TNCs

6 Many people feel their culture is being eroded.

Baseball caps and jeans every where ...
... and fast food and fizzy drinks ...
... and TV shows that undermine our values.
So now our children think our culture is inferior.
Well I think you're cool, mom.

Protest goes global too

Many people worry about the effect of globalisation on the world's poorer countries. And especially about free trade.

They think free trade will mainly benefit the richer countries, who can afford to set up TNCs in any poor country they want. And also that the richer countries have too much power, in the WTO.

So protest has gone global too. When world leaders meet to discuss world trade these days, protesters from all over the world gather in their thousands.

Protest in Scotland

In July 2005, the leaders of the G8 nations met to discuss poverty in Africa, world trade, and other issues, at the Gleneagles Hotel in Auchterarder, in Scotland.

In the days before the meeting, over 200 000 people took part in protest marches. And over 10 000 police officers were on hand, to prevent trouble!

(The G8 are the world's 7 richest industrial nations – the USA, Japan, France, Germany, Britain, Italy and Canada – plus Russia.)

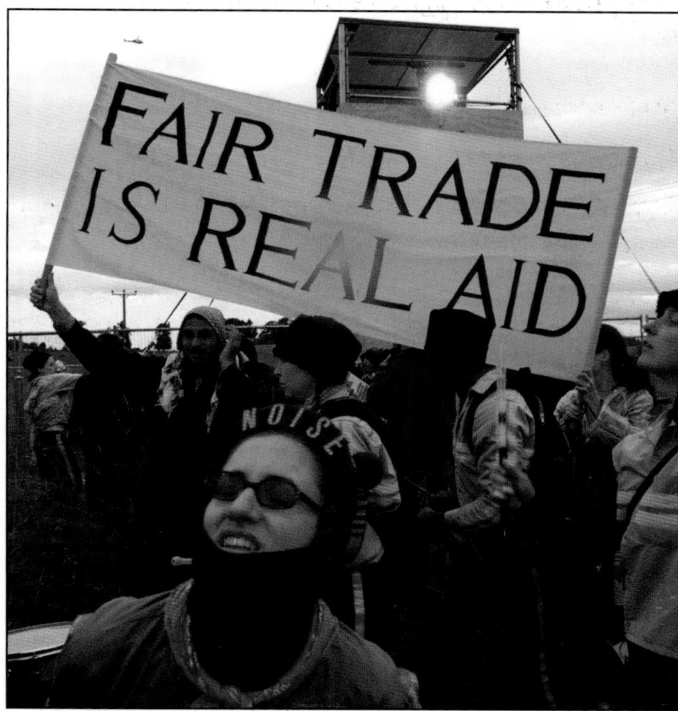

▲ *Protesting on behalf of the world's poorer countries, during the G8 summit meeting in Scotland. (You can read more about trade issues on pages 18–21.)*

Your turn

1 Page 88 shows things people say against globalisation. Using these to help you, write:
  - a a *social* argument against globalisation
  - b an *economic* argument against it
  - c an *environmental* argument against it.

  Give each as a short paragraph.

2 Globalisation is a complex issue.
  - a From pages 86 and 88, pick out two arguments that are *exactly* opposite.
  - b Now see if you can find *at least two more* pairs of opposite arguments. Write them down.

3 Look at the photo above, taken at a demonstration in Scotland, during the G8 summit.
  - a Why do you think people choose G8 summit meetings, as a good time to protest about world trade?
  - b See if you can name three groups of people who are likely to take part in such a protest. Explain your choice.

4 On the right is Naresh, a security guard in India. He's guarding a building 4000 km away, in California! The CCTV pictures are sent by satellite. If he sees a problem he can quickly raise the alarm.
  You live in India. Write a letter to an Indian paper, in favour of, or against, the way the Californian company is employing Indian people.

5 And finally, you have a really important job. You are one of the G8 leaders. (Decide for yourself which one.)
  - a First, do you think it is possible to halt globalisation? Write a note to another G8 leader giving your views about this.
  - b You *are* worried about the power of the big TNCs. Write a set of guidelines you want TNCs to follow when they set up in LEDCs. (You will discuss these with the other G8 leaders.)
    Your guidelines should have at least 5 points.
    Think of big issues. Pay? Profits? The environment?

6 Plates, earthquakes and volcanoes

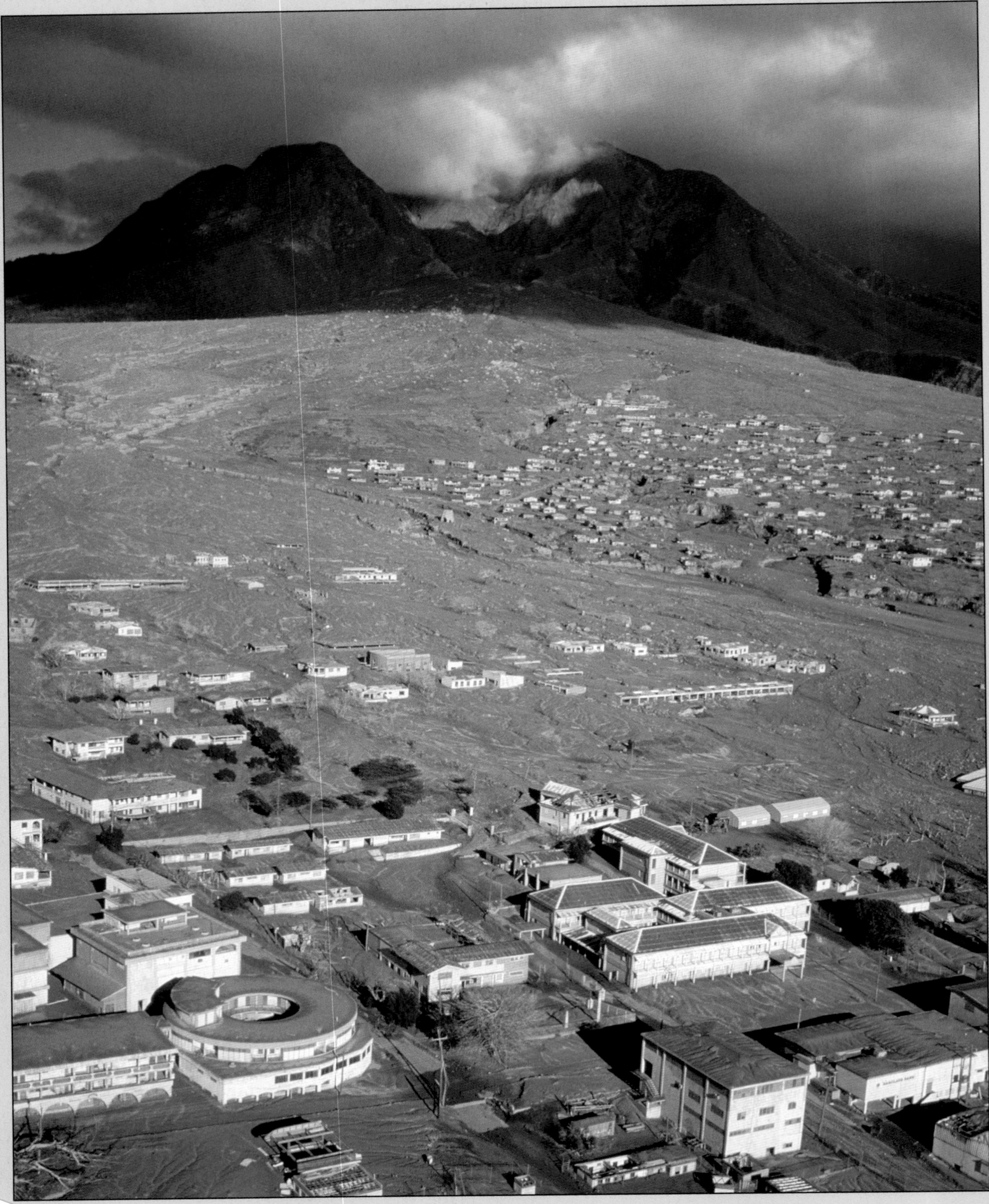

The big picture

This chapter is all about earthquakes and volcanoes, and the huge slabs or **plates** that the Earth's crust is broken into. These are the big ideas in the chapter:

- Earthquakes and volcanic eruptions have killed millions of people, and ruined millions of lives.
- They are caused by currents of hot soft rock inside the Earth, which drag the Earth's plates around.
- We can't stop them. All we can do is help the survivors, and find ways to protect people in the future.
- This can cost a lot of money. But poor countries don't have much, so their people may suffer more harm.

Your goals for this chapter

By the end of this chapter you should be able to answer these questions:

- What do these terms mean?

  crust *mantle* *core* *lithosphere* *convection current* *oceanic crust* *continental crust*

- What are the Earth's plates, and why do they move?
- What causes earthquakes, and what kind of damage do they do?
- What do these terms mean?

  fault *focus* *epicentre* *seismic wave* *aftershock* *tsunami*

- What causes tsunami? And what kind of damage do they do?
- What are volcanoes, and what kind of damage do eruptions do?
- What do these terms mean?

  magma *lava* *crater* *pyroclastic flow* *mudflow* *ash*

- What's the link between plates, earthquakes, and volcanoes?
- How do humans respond to earthquakes and volcanic eruptions?
- Why might these events be more disastrous in poor countries?

And then ...

When you finish the chapter, come back to this page and see if you have met your goals!

Did you know?
- You are living on a moving slab of rock.
- It's moving at about the speed your nails grow!

Did you know?
- China is the worst place in the world for earthquake deaths.
- In 1556, one earthquake in China killed 830 000 people.

Did you know?
- The UK has 200–300 earthquakes a year.
- Most are so small that people don't feel them.

Did you know?
- There is more volcanic activity under the oceans than on land!

Did you know?
- The country with most volcanoes is Indonesia.

Your chapter starter

Look at the photo on page 90. What do you think happened here?

Could anyone have stopped it?

How do you think the people felt about it?

Where do you think they've gone?

Do you think people will ever come back here to live?

6.1 A slice through the Earth

> **Did you know?**
> - The Earth is 4.6 billion years old.
> - We humans have been here for 200 000 years!

In this unit you'll learn about the three layers that make up the Earth – and then take a closer look at the layer you live on!

The three layers that make up the Earth

1 The crust
This is the layer you live on. It is a thin skin of rock around the Earth, like the skin on an apple (shown here by the thin blue line).

2 The mantle
It forms about half of the Earth. It is made of heavier rock.
The upper mantle is hard. But the rock below it is hot and soft, like soft toffee. It is runny in places.

3 The core
It is a mainly iron, mixed with a little nickel. The **outer core** is liquid. The **inner core** is solid.

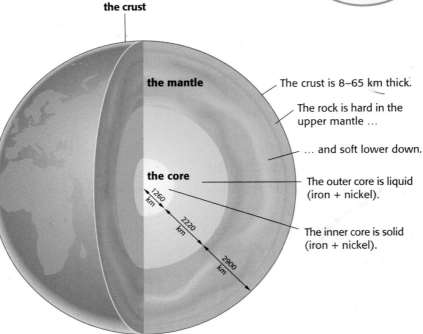

the crust
the mantle
the core
1260 km
2220 km
2900 km
The crust is 8–65 km thick.
The rock is hard in the upper mantle …
… and soft lower down.
The outer core is liquid (iron + nickel).
The inner core is solid (iron + nickel).

How did the layers form?

Some time after the Earth formed, it got so hot that everything inside it melted. The heavier substances in the liquid sank and the lighter ones rose, forming layers. As the Earth cooled, some of the layers hardened.

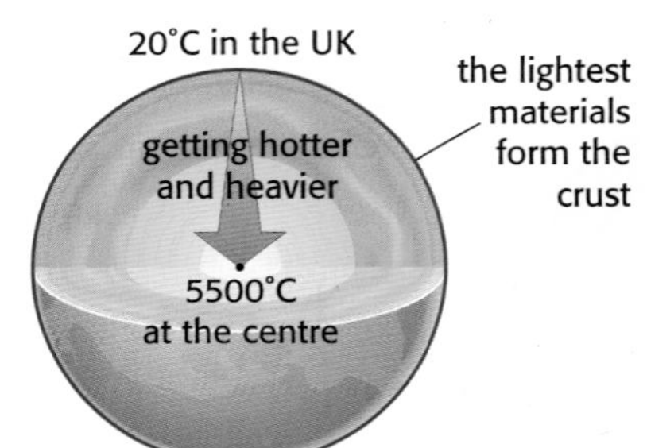

Hot hot hot

A great deal of heat is still trapped inside the Earth. That's why it gets hotter as you go down through it. 200 km down, the rocks are glowing white hot. At the centre of the Earth, the temperature is around 5500 °C.

▲ *A bubble of boiling rock reaching the Earth's surface in Hawaii.*

▲ *Several countries have dug holes to find out more about the Earth's crust. The deepest is in Russia – over 12 km!*

More about the Earth's crust

There are two types of crust. The crust under the oceans is called the **oceanic crust**. It's a thin layer of heavy rock. The **continental crust** is made of lighter rock, and forms the continents.

Did you know?

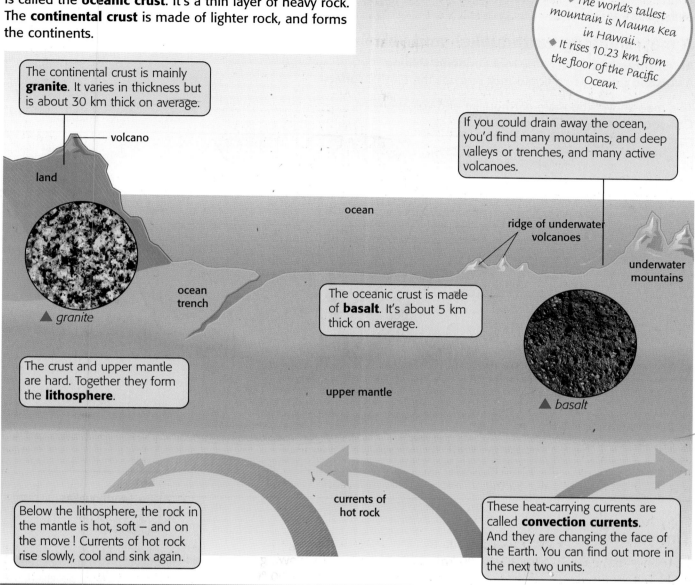

- *The world's tallest mountain is Mauna Kea in Hawaii.*
- *It rises 10.23 km from the floor of the Pacific Ocean.*

The continental crust is mainly **granite**. It varies in thickness but is about 30 km thick on average.

If you could drain away the ocean, you'd find many mountains, and deep valleys or trenches, and many active volcanoes.

volcano

land

ocean

ridge of underwater volcanoes

underwater mountains

ocean trench

▲ *granite*

The oceanic crust is made of **basalt**. It's about 5 km thick on average.

▲ *basalt*

The crust and upper mantle are hard. Together they form the **lithosphere**.

upper mantle

currents of hot rock

Below the lithosphere, the rock in the mantle is hot, soft – and on the move! Currents of hot rock rise slowly, cool and sink again.

These heat-carrying currents are called **convection currents**. And they are changing the face of the Earth. You can find out more in the next two units.

Your turn

1 Make a table like this, and fill it in for the Earth's layers.

Layer	Made of ...	Solid or liquid?	How thick?
crust			
mantle			
core – outer – inner			

2 a What is the Earth's radius, in km, at the thickest part of the crust?

b If you cycle at 20 km an hour, how long will it take you to cycle to the centre of the Earth?

3 Make a larger drawing like this, and complete the labels.

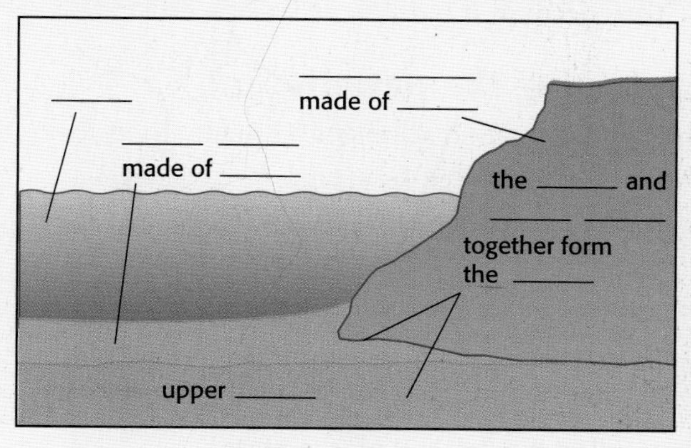

Earthquakes, volcanoes and plates

In this unit you'll learn what the Earth's plates are – and their link with earthquakes and volcanoes.

Did you know?
The ring of volcanoes around the Pacific Ocean is known as the Ring of Fire.

A map showing earthquakes and volcanoes

An **earthquake** is caused by rock suddenly shifting.
A **volcano** forms when liquid rock reaches the Earth's surface.

This map shows the main earthquake and volcano sites.
Can you see a pattern?

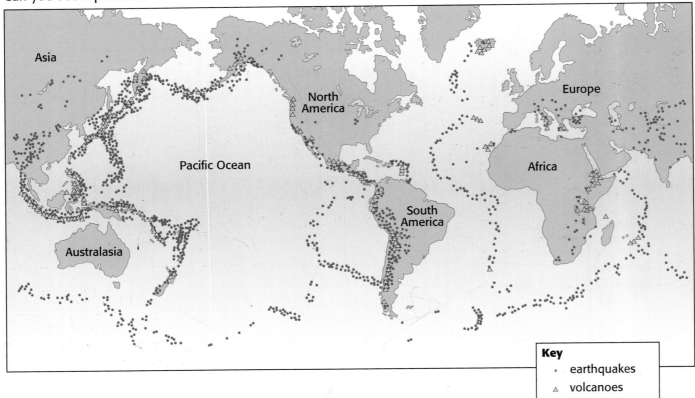

Asia
North America
Europe
Pacific Ocean
Africa
South America
Australasia

Key
- earthquakes
- volcanoes

The pattern

From the map you can see that:

- Earthquakes and volcanoes don't happen just anywhere. They tend to occur along lines.
- They often occur together.
- They occur in the ocean as well as on land.

Explaining the pattern

The pattern puzzled scientists for years. Then they found the explanation:

- The Earth's surface is cracked into pieces, like an eggshell.
- The pieces are continually moving.
- This movement causes earthquakes, and volcanic eruptions, along the cracks.

They called the cracked pieces **plates**.

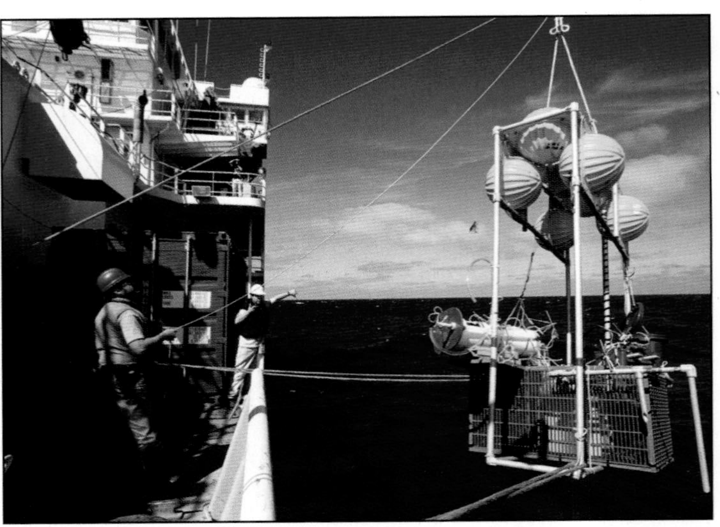

▲ *Research ships like this one helped scientists crack the plate puzzle. They are used to study the ocean floor.*

A map showing the Earth's plates

This map shows the main plates and their names. Some plates carry continents and ocean, others just ocean. They move slowly in different directions.

Key
- plate boundary (edge)
- uncertain plate boundary
- direction in which plate is moving
- earthquakes
- volcanoes

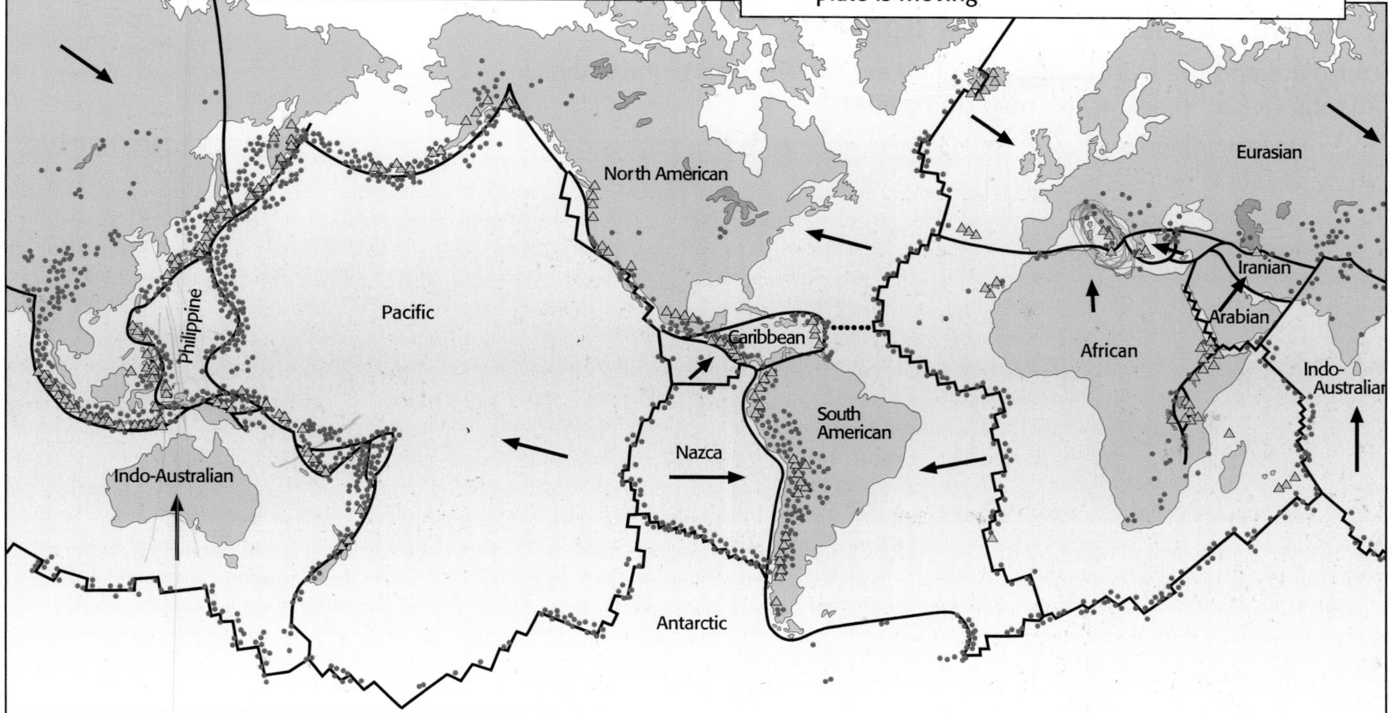

A closer look at plates

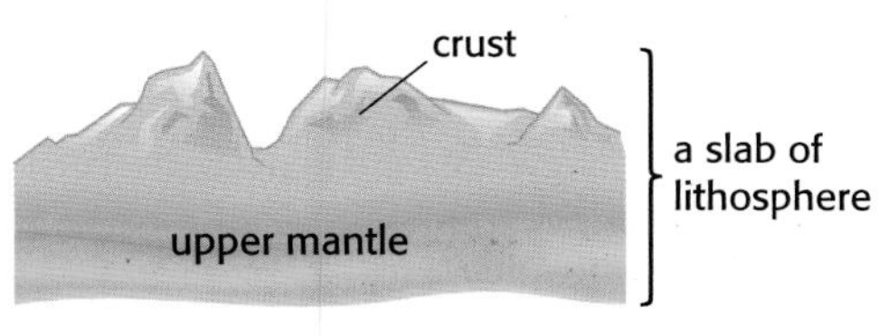

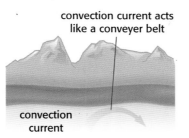

convection current acts like a conveyer belt

convection current

If I just lie still for 10 years I'll move half a metre.

Plates are slabs of the **lithosphere** – Earth's crust and upper mantle. They float on the soft hot rock below.

Plates move because they are dragged along by the powerful **convection currents** in the soft hot rock.

Plates move just a few cm a year – but it all adds up! For example India has moved 2000 km north in the last 70 million years.

Your turn

1 Earthquake and volcano sites tend to form a pattern. Explain why.

2 Name:
  a the plate you live on
  b a plate that is moving away from yours
  c a plate that is moving north
  d a plate that carries just ocean
  e the plate off the west coast of South America
  f the plate that's circled by the Ring of Fire.

3 Make a drawing of your own to show what plates are made of, and why they move. Give it a snappy title!

4 There are no active volcanoes in the UK. Suggest why.

5 Do you think a map of the Earth will look different 100 million years from now? Explain your answer.

6 A challenge! A move of 1° south equals 440 km. Suppose our plate starts moving south at 5 cm a year. About how long will it take Newcastle to reach the equator? (Newcastle is about 55° N.)

Plate movements

> **Did you know?**
> - The centre of London gets 2 cm further from the centre of New York every year ...
> - ... because the floor of the Atlantic Ocean is growing wider.

In this unit you'll learn how the Earth's plates are moving – and how their movements produce earthquakes, volcanoes, and even mountains!

1 Some plates are moving apart

Our plate and the North American plate are moving apart, under the Atlantic Ocean. (Look at the map on page 95.)

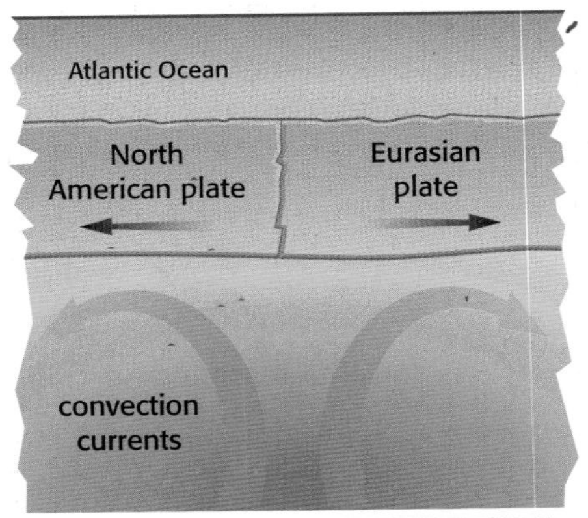

1 The plates are pulled apart by the convection currents in the soft rock below them.

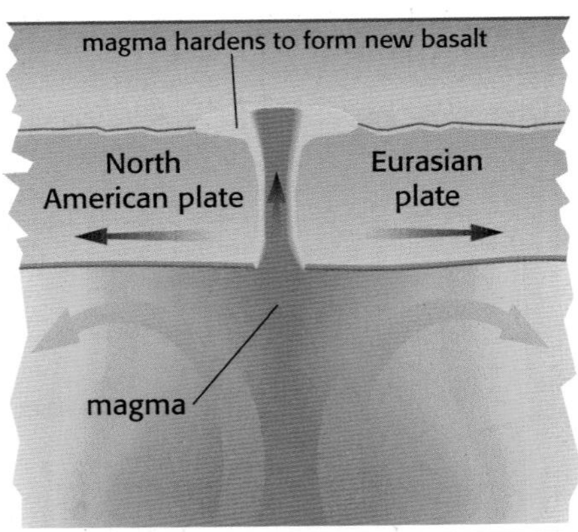

2 Liquid rock or **magma** rises between the plates. It hardens to basalt ...

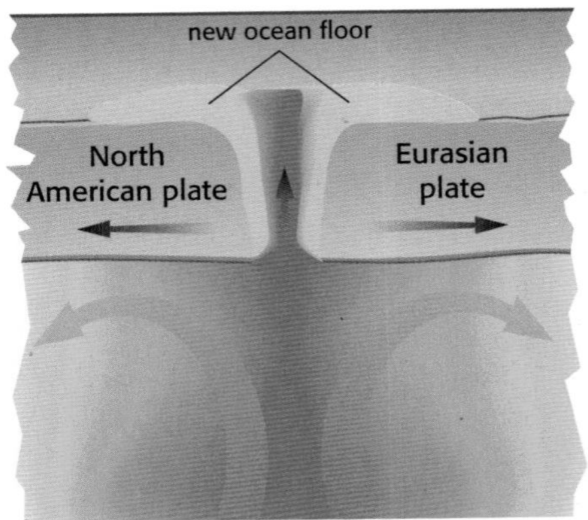

3 ... which forms new ocean floor. So the ocean floor is getting wider – by about 2 cm a year.

The rising magma is a form of volcanic eruption. And as the heavy plates move apart, you get earthquakes too! So, where plates move apart, you get earthquakes, and eruptions, and new ocean floor being formed.

2 Some plates are pushing into each other

The Nazca plate and the South American plate are pushing into each other, just off the west coast of South America. (Look at the map on page 95.)

The result is earthquakes and volcanoes.

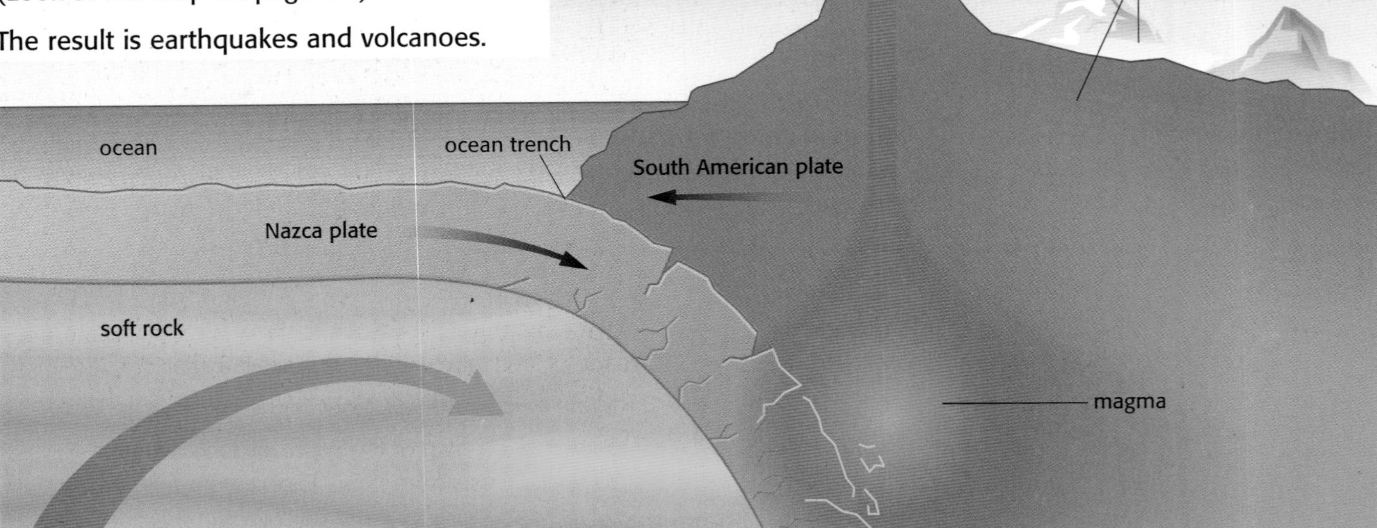

1 The Nazca plate is heavier. (Oceanic crust is heavier.) So it gets pushed under at an ocean trench.

2 The rock jolts and grinds its way down, causing earthquakes. At the same time ...

3 ... it heats up. Some rock melts, and forces its way up through the Andes to form a volcano.

When pushing makes mountains

Look at these two plates pushing into each other. Both are carrying land. One carries India, the other China.

As a result of the pushing, the rock has got crumpled and squeezed up to form mountains – the Himalayas.

The plates are still pushing. So the Himalayas are still growing – and China gets lots of earthquakes.

The Himalayas are called **fold mountains**. Can you see why?

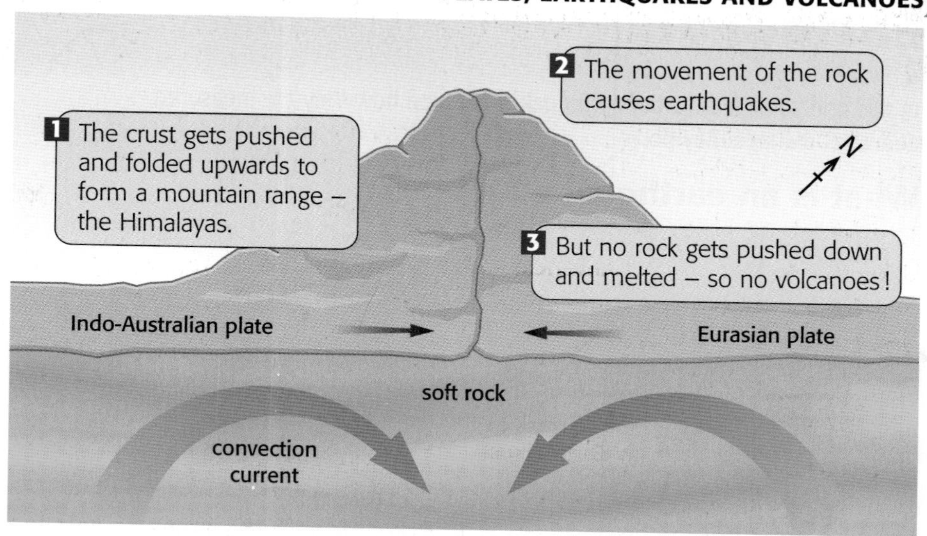

1 The crust gets pushed and folded upwards to form a mountain range – the Himalayas.
2 The movement of the rock causes earthquakes.
3 But no rock gets pushed down and melted – so no volcanoes!
N
Indo-Australian plate
Eurasian plate
soft rock
convection current

3 Some plates are sliding past each other

The Pacific plate is sliding past the North American plate. (Look at the map on page 95.)

Both move in the same direction, but the Pacific plate is moving faster.

The result is earthquakes now and then – but no volcanoes!

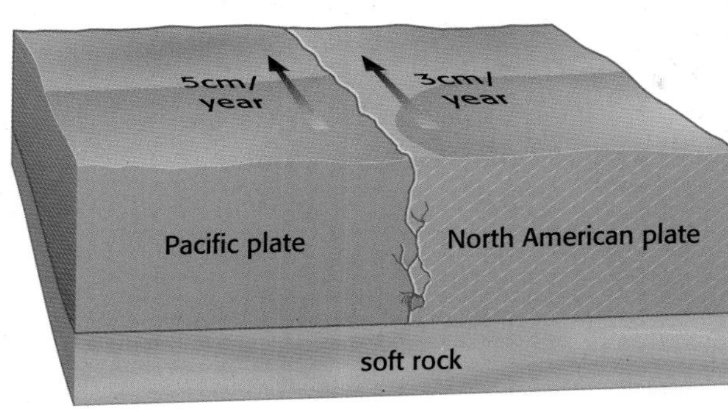

Your turn

1 The photo on the right shows the floor of the Atlantic Ocean. The grey ridge lies along plate edges.
  a Name the plates that lie on each side of the ridge.
  b What is the ridge made of?
  c Explain what is happening along the ridge.
  d Do you think earthquakes occur there? Explain.
  e Where else might you find a ridge like this?

2

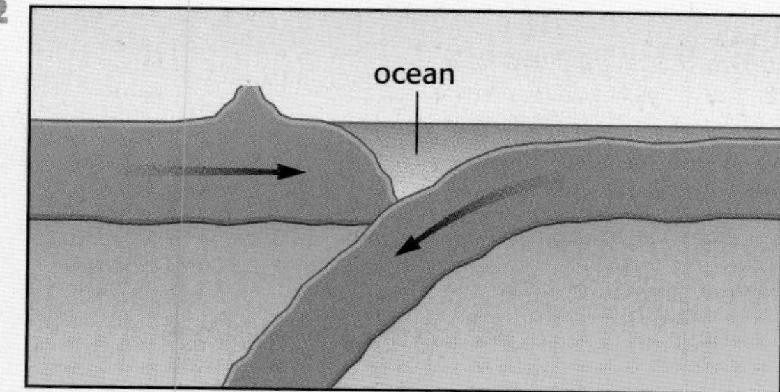

Make a drawing like this one. On your drawing:
  a label the ocean plate, the continental plate and a volcano.
  b mark in melted rock that feeds the volcano.
  c mark in and label an earthquake site.

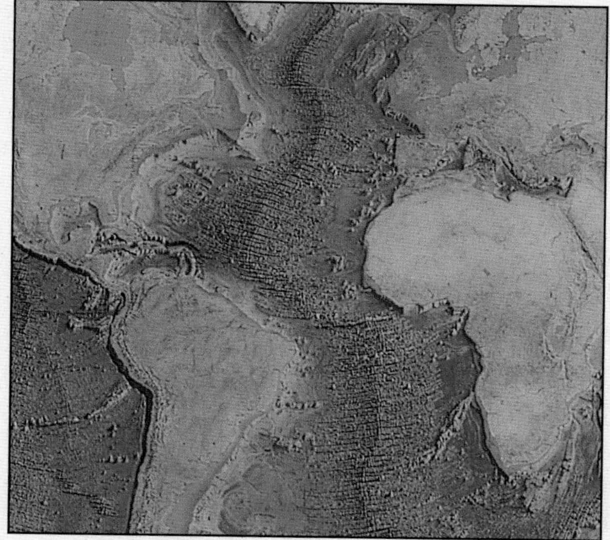

3 Now, using the maps on pages 95 and 128–129, explain why:
  a Peru has earthquakes and volcanoes
  b Iran has fold mountains
  c Italy has earthquakes and volcanoes
  d Japan has earthquakes and volcanoes.

Earthquakes

In this unit you'll learn what earthquakes are, and how they are measured, and what damage they do.

What is an earthquake?

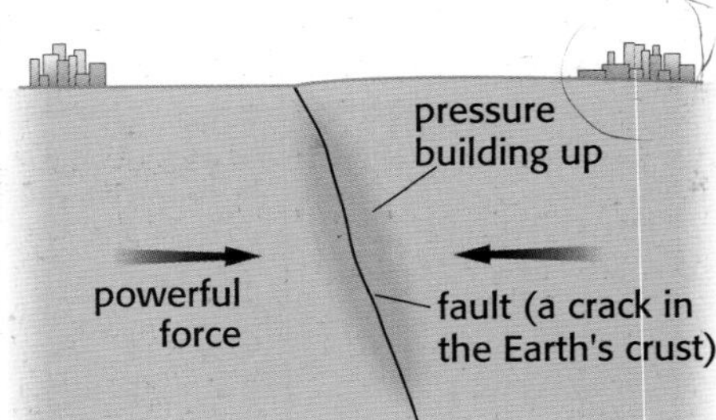

Imagine powerful forces pushing these huge masses of rock into each other. The rock stores up the pressure as **strain energy**.

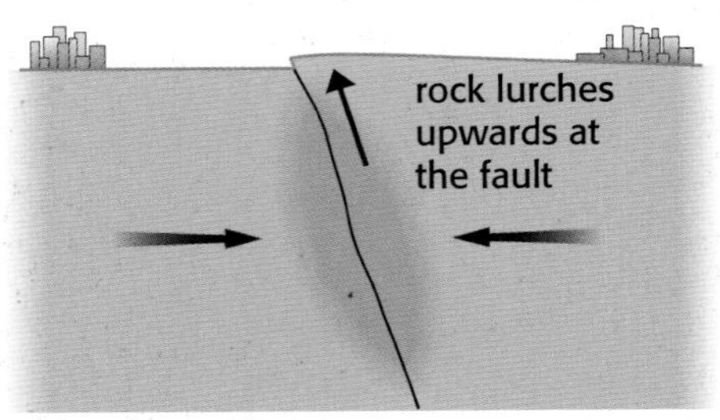

But suddenly, the pressure gets too much. One mass of rock gives way, lurching upwards. The stored energy is released in waves ...

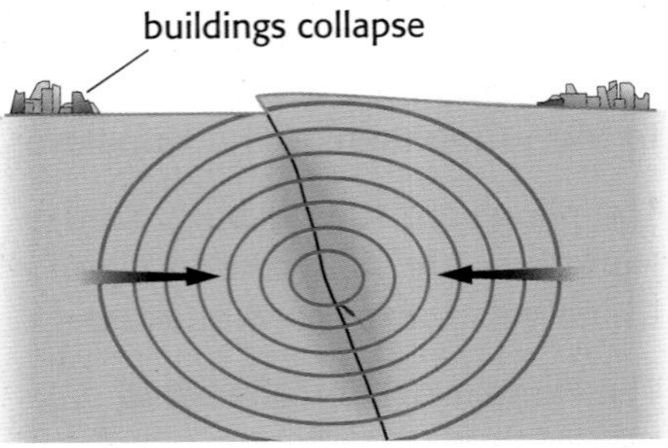

... called **seismic waves**. These travel through the Earth in all directions, shaking everything. The shaking is called an **earthquake**.

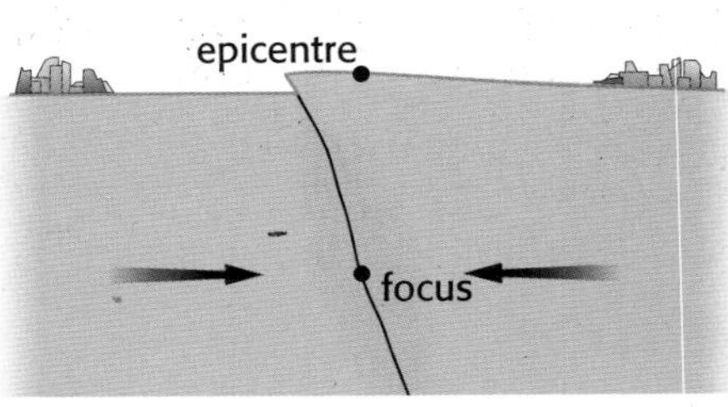

The **focus** of the earthquake is the point where the waves started. The **epicentre** is the point directly above it on the Earth's surface.

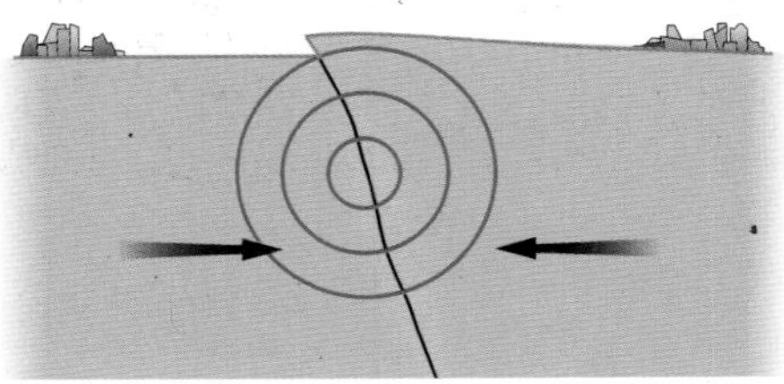

As the rock settles into its new position, there will be lots of smaller earthquakes called **aftershocks**.

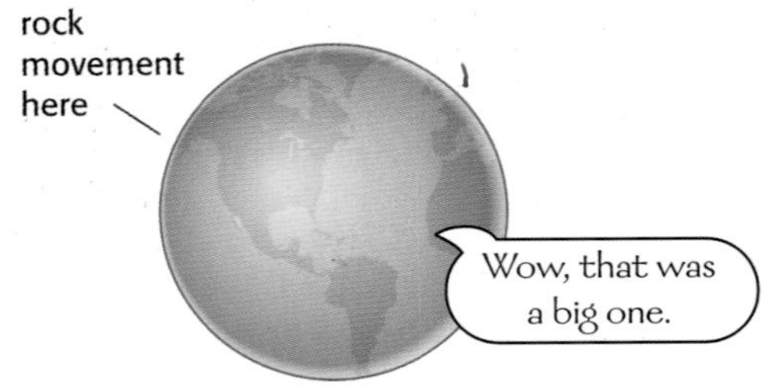

Seismic waves get weaker as they travel. Even so, a large earthquake can still be detected thousands of kilometres away !

Any sudden large rock movement will cause an earthquake. That's why there are so many earthquakes along plate edges. But even the collapse of an old mine shaft, or an underground explosion, can cause a small earthquake.

How big?

- Earthquakes are measured using machines called **seismometers**, which record the shaking as waves on a graph.
- From the graph, scientists can tell how much energy the earthquake gave out.
- The amount of energy an earthquake gives out is called its **magnitude**.
- We show it on the **Richter scale**. (On the right.)
- An increase of 1 on this scale means the shaking is 10 times greater, and about 30 times more *energy* is given out. (And that means a lot more damage !)

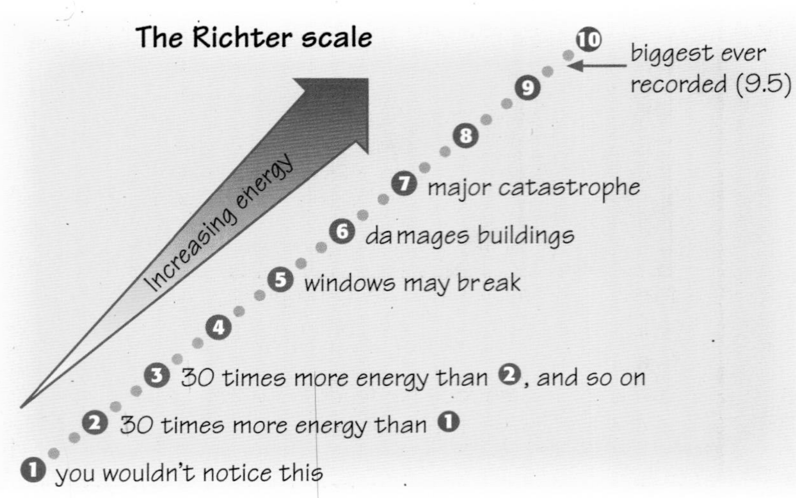

▲ *As a tsunami nears the coast, it sucks up water, exposing the ocean floor. This satellite image shows the water being dragged away, at the resort of Kalutara in Sri Lanka.*

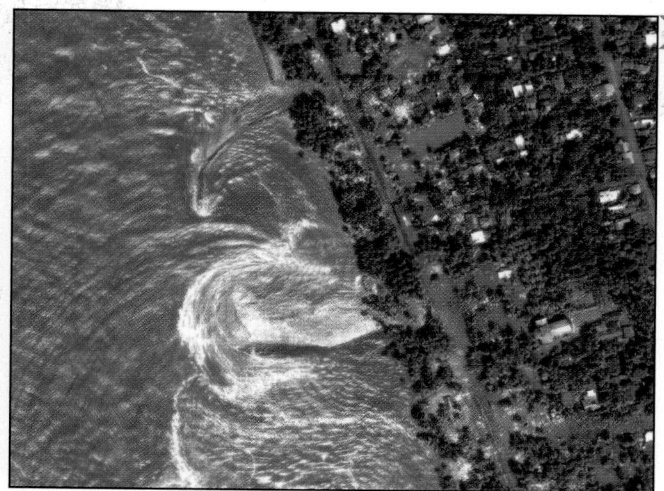

▲ *The same resort, after the tsunami has struck. The water churns and recedes, leaving destruction behind it. Both images were taken on 26 December 2004.*

The day they will never forget

Banda Aceh, Indonesia: I took an early ferry. I thought it was bouncing a bit, but that did not worry me. After an hour we got to Banda Aceh. I could not believe my eyes. The fishermen's homes along the water had gone. In the town, there were fishing boats on roof tops, and taxis stuck in trees. There were people sobbing, and corpses lying everywhere.

Telwatta, Sri Lanka: I was on the coast train, going see my family. Suddenly the train stopped. The sea started to pour in, very fast. The train turned over and over. I was trapped in there for nearly an hour, half drowned. But I'm lucky. They say there were 1500 passengers, and 800 of them died.

Khao Lak, Thailand: There was a hissing noise, and all the water along the beach got sucked out to sea. There were lots of fish left flapping on the ground. Children ran to look at them. Then there was a noise like thunder, and we saw a giant wave coming. The children had no chance.

Cuddalore, India: My two sons were playing cricket on the beach, with about 40 other children. I could hear them shouting and cheering. Then I looked down from the window and saw huge waves coming in, about 10 or 12 metres high. I froze. The water churned round and round. And then it sped out to sea, dragging them with it.

(Adapted from news reports, end December, 2004)

▲ *Three days after the tsunami, on the island of Phi Phi in Thailand.*

Did you know?

◆ In the Boxing Day tsunami, waves travelled nearly 5000 km from the epicentre to Africa.

Your turn

1 What causes a tsunami?

2 Try to explain these facts about the Boxing Day tsunami.
  - a Tsunami reached more than a dozen countries.
  - b The tsunami arrived at each at a different time.
  - c Indonesia suffered much greater loss than Somalia.
  - d People out at sea were not aware of the tsunami.
  - e The earthquake was detected in the Philippines, but no tsunami reached there.

3 People all over the world gave money to help the devastated places. Why was this essential? (Page 14?)

4 Before the Boxing Day tsunami, there was a tsunami warning system in the Pacific Ocean (see pages 128–129) but none in the Indian Ocean. Suggest a reason.

5 It's your job to invent a tsunami warning system for the Indian Ocean. It must warn countries in good time when tsunami are on the way. Tell us your ideas!

Volcanoes

In this unit you'll learn what volcanoes are, and what damage an eruption can do.

What's a volcano?

A **volcano** is where liquid rock or **magma** shoots out or **erupts** through the ground. Above ground, the liquid rock is called **lava**.

2 If the lava is thick and gassy, it can't run out of the volcano easily. The pressure builds up until it explodes out.

3 As it explodes it cools and hardens, giving a cloud of particles of all sizes – from dust and ash to big lumps – mixed with scorching gas, and rocks torn from the volcano's throat.

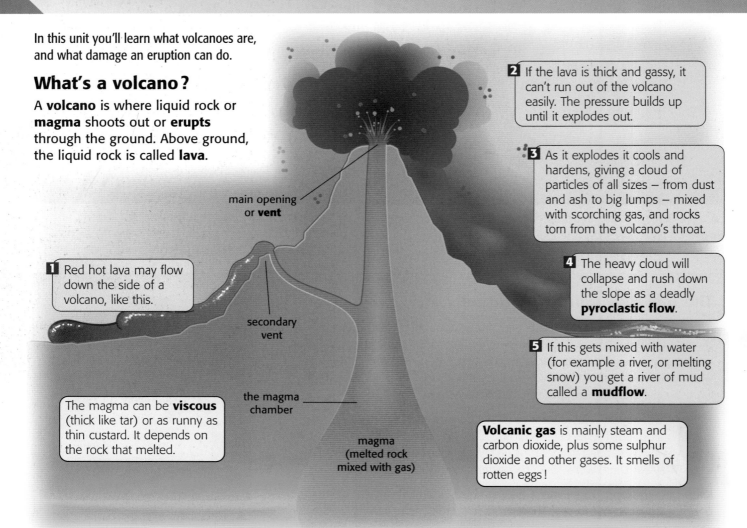

main opening or **vent**

1 Red hot lava may flow down the side of a volcano, like this.

4 The heavy cloud will collapse and rush down the slope as a deadly **pyroclastic flow**.

secondary vent

5 If this gets mixed with water (for example a river, or melting snow) you get a river of mud called a **mudflow**.

the magma chamber

The magma can be **viscous** (thick like tar) or as runny as thin custard. It depends on the rock that melted.

magma (melted rock mixed with gas)

Volcanic gas is mainly steam and carbon dioxide, plus some sulphur dioxide and other gases. It smells of rotten eggs!

Viscous gassy lava is the most dangerous kind. It builds up inside the volcano. Then the gas propels it out in an explosion.

▲ *An eruption of runny lava in Hawaii.*

▲ *A small eruption of steam, gas and ash from Mt St Helens (USA). The hollow around the vent is called a* ***crater****.*

What damage can eruptions do?

The dust from an explosive eruption may rise high in the atmosphere and block out the sun, causing temperatures around the world to fall.

A pyroclastic flow travels at up to 200 km an hour. You can't escape. It scorches and smothers everything.

Volcanic gas causes acid rain. This kills trees and plants over a wide area.

The dust can also cause planes to crash.

Mudflows can travel at 100 km an hour. They sweep everything along. You drown in mud.

A thick blanket of ash will ruin crops.

Lava flows destroy crops, and bury towns and villages. (They could kill you too – but you can just walk out of the way.)

A thick layer of ash is heavy enough to make roofs collapse.

The ash from an explosive eruption gets everywhere – in your eyes, your hair, your lungs. It can suffocate you.

This photo was taken on the island of Montserrat. **See next page for more!**

Your turn

1 What is: **a** magma? **b** lava?

2 Make a larger copy of this drawing. Then colour it in and add the missing labels.

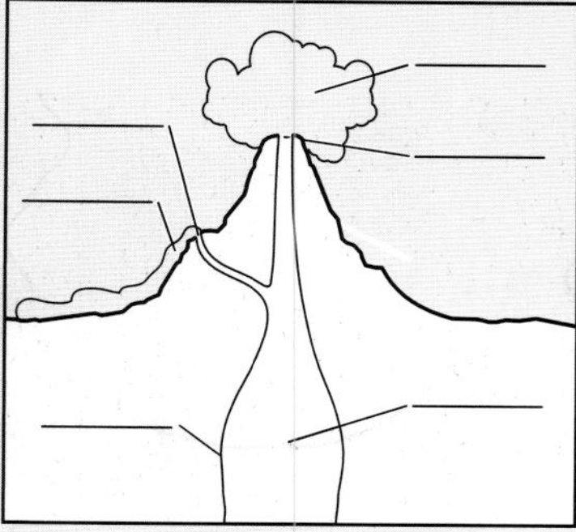

3 Look at the photo above. What do you think happened to:
a the roof of the church? **b** the trees near the church?

4 An active volcano can give out all of these:
showers of ash   a pyroclastic flow   a lava flow
plumes of dust   volcanic gases
a List them in order of danger, starting with what you think is the most dangerous one.
b Beside each item in your list, say what harm it does.

5 You were there when Mount Pinatubo in the Philippines erupted, in 1991. You took the photo below. E-mail your friend in New York telling him what you saw before you took it – and what happened next.

Montserrat: living with an active volcano

In this unit you will learn how an erupting volcano has changed a Caribbean island forever.

A paradise island

At the start of 1995, 11 000 people lived on the island of Montserrat in the Caribbean. Some farmed for a living. Some worked in the island's few factories. But most depended on the tourists who came to enjoy the peace on this paradise isle.

Then, on 18 July, life on the island began to change forever. The volcano, asleep for nearly 400 years, began to waken.

The volcano awakens

The first signs were rumbling noises, and showers of ash, and a strong smell of sulphur. The government acted quickly. It called in **vulcanologists** (volcano scientists) to check or **monitor** the volcano, and made plans to move people to safety.

That was way back in 1995. Twelve years later, in 2007, the volcano was still busy !

- Over the years, it has blasted out clouds of dust and ash that turned the sky black.
- It has grown domes full of lava that glowed at night before exploding.
- Many pyroclastic flows have raced down the slopes. Some have turned rivers into mudflows.

The vulcanologists watch it night and day. But they can't predict when it will go back to sleep again.

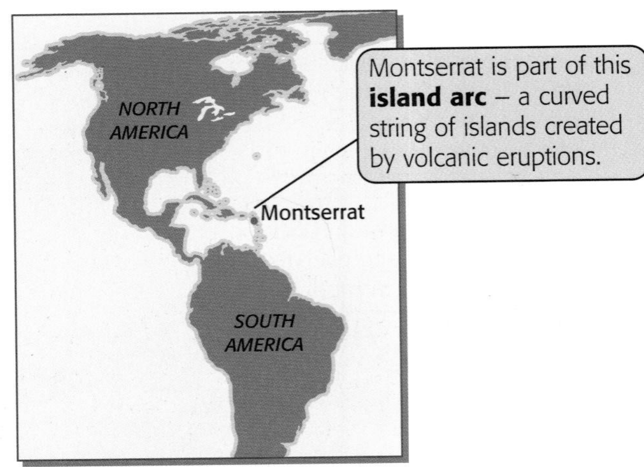
NORTH AMERICA
SOUTH AMERICA
Montserrat
Montserrat is part of this **island arc** – a curved string of islands created by volcanic eruptions.

▼ *Montserrat from the air. Spot the volcano !*

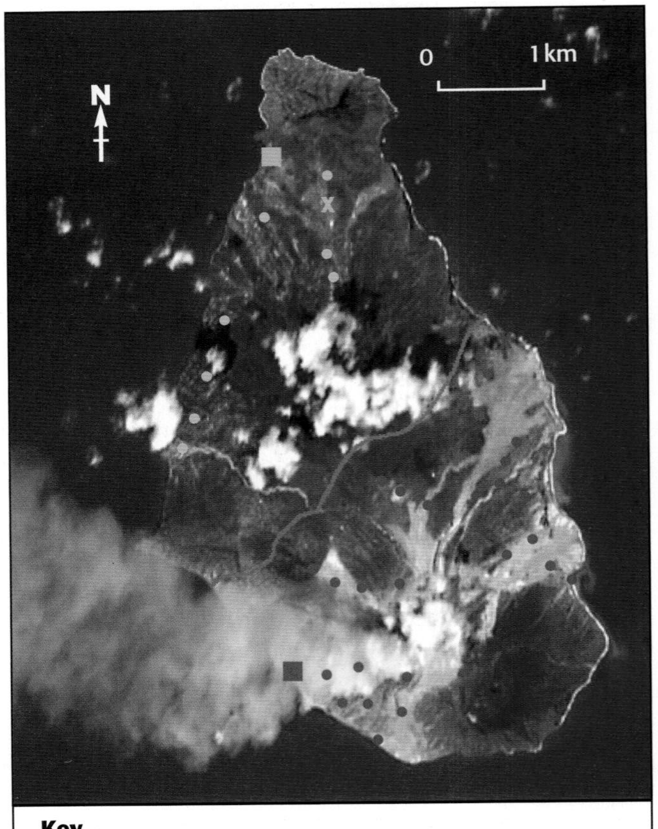
N
0
1 km

Key
- ■ capital (Plymouth) destroyed
- x airport (destroyed)
- • small settlements, abandoned or destroyed
- 〰 out-of-bounds below this line (January 2007)
- ■ proposed new capital (Little Bay)
- x new airport (2005)
- • undamaged small settlements

◀ *Just another pyroclastic flow on Montserrat.*

What's causing the eruptions?

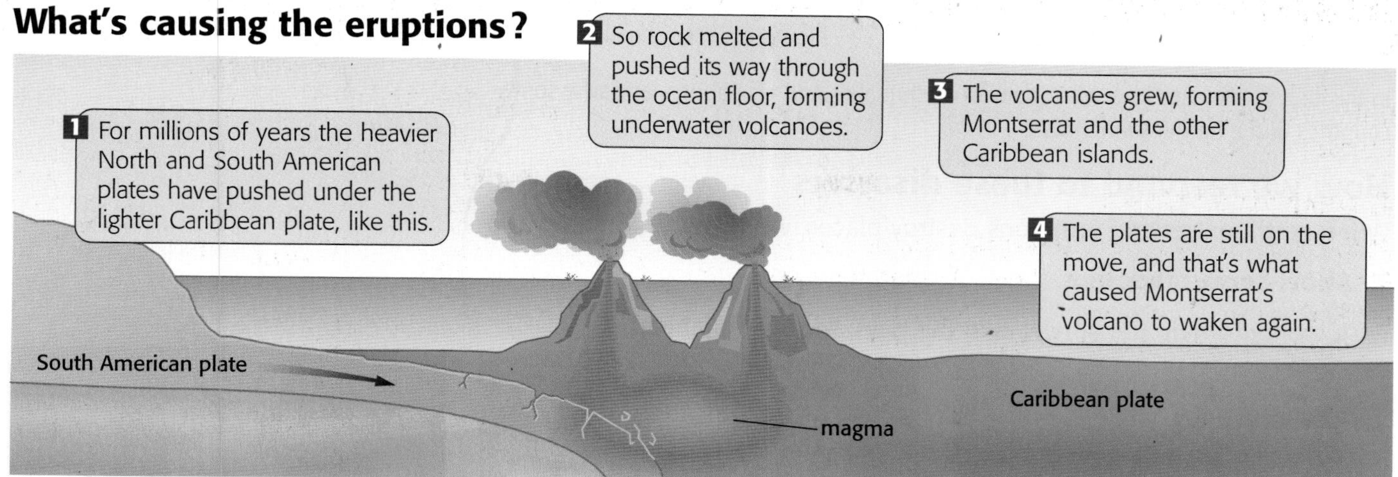

1 For millions of years the heavier North and South American plates have pushed under the lighter Caribbean plate, like this.
2 So rock melted and pushed its way through the ocean floor, forming underwater volcanoes.
3 The volcanoes grew, forming Montserrat and the other Caribbean islands.
4 The plates are still on the move, and that's what caused Montserrat's volcano to waken again.
South American plate
Caribbean plate
magma

People on the move

As the volcano grew more dangerous, people were moved from the south of the island. Some went to the 'safe' area in the north, to stay with friends or in shelters. Some went to other Caribbean islands, or to relatives abroad. By April 1996 the south of the island was empty.

But some refused to stay away. On 25 June 1997, pyroclastic flows killed 19 people who had crept back to work on their farms.

Life goes on

Today, only 4500 people are left on Montserrat, in the north of the island. The south is still out of bounds. (If you are caught there you will be fined and may even be sent to prison.)

There is not much farming now, since so much of the land is ruined. People depend on grants from the UK and the European Union. But they are trying hard to attract tourists again. A new airport was opened in 2005. A new capital is being built around the small port of Little Bay.

But people can't forget about the volcano. Every so often a dark plume in the sky, or a shower of ash, or a rattle of pebbles, reminds them.

▲ *Out of action… forever?*

Your turn

1 Explain in your own words why the volcano on Montserrat is erupting.

2 Look at the photo on page 90. It shows Plymouth, the capital of Montserrat, destroyed by the volcano. You used to live there. Write a letter to your cousin in Burnley describing what Plymouth looks like now.

3 How will the eruptions on Montserrat have affected:
a farmers? b hotel owners? c taxi drivers?

4 Montserrat hopes to attact tourists again – as a volcano island! You are in charge of tourism.
a Draw a sketch map of the island, showing the volcano, the new airport, and the safe zone.
b Mark in where you would put a new tourist hotel.
c What activities will you lay on for tourists?
d How will you make sure the tourists are safe?
e What kind of souvenirs will you sell them?
f Make up a slogan to attract tourists to the island.

5 Montserrat has received over £200 million in aid, since the volcano awoke. Much of this was from the UK, since it's a British Overseas Territory (or colony). Some people think the island should just be closed down.
a Give some arguments in favour of this.
b Give some arguments against it.
c If you had to make the final decision, what other information would you need?

Coping with earthquakes and eruptions

In this unit you'll learn how we cope with earthquakes and eruptions – and why some countries find it harder than others.

How we respond to these disasters

When earthquakes and eruptions destroy places, we respond in two ways.

1 Short-term response

First, we try to help the survivors in the days and weeks ahead.

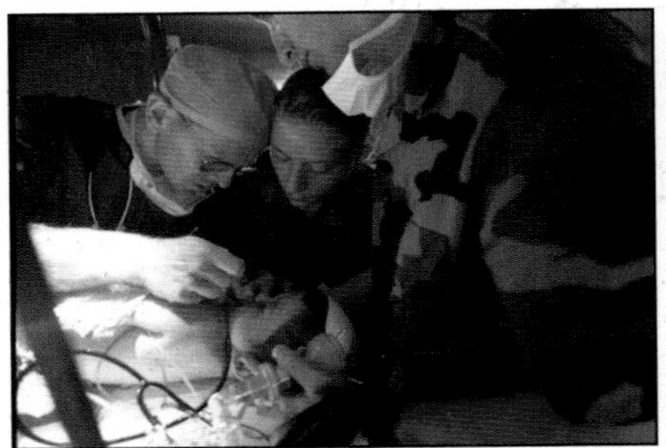

Doctors, nurses, firemen and the army rush there. Medical tents are set up. Aid agencies like Oxfam and the Red Cross arrive.

Tents, food, water and clothing are given to the people who have lost their homes. (These may be gifts from other countries.)

Ordinary people like you and me give money, to help the survivors of the disaster rebuild their lives and homes.

2 Long-term response

Then we try to prevent disasters like this happening in the future.

We can't stop earthquakes and eruptions. But at least we can identify the areas at risk.

Then we can make plans to protect the people living in these areas. Some of the plans ...

... can be put into action right away – for example plans to make buildings more quake-proof.

Other plans will be put into action the next time there's an emergency.

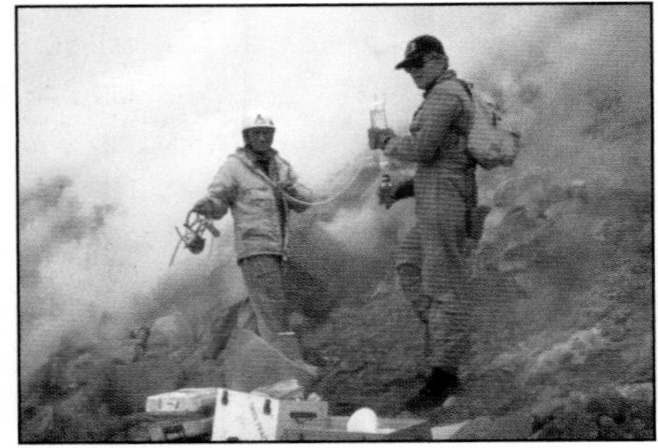

Meanwhile, scientists can monitor the areas at risk, and try to predict when earthquakes or eruptions ...

... will happen, so that they can warn people in time to move to a safe place.

Your turn

1 **A–G** below match words or terms used on page 108. For each, you have to pick out the matching word or term. Set out your answers like this:
B for the months and years ahead = long–t…

A for the next days and weeks
B for the months and years ahead
C a sudden dangerous situation
D to observe and check and take measurements
E to tell in advance when something will happen
F they study rocks (and earthquakes!)
G they collect money to help people in need
The glossary might help!

2 There is a big **earthquake** in a city in South America. 80 000 people are killed.
A–J below are responses to the disaster.

a Make a big table with headings like this:

Responses to the earthquake disaster	
Short-term	Long-term

b Now write out the sentences **A–J** in the correct columns. (With their label letters!)

A 30 firemen fly in from Italy to help.
B The government sets up a team of geologists to try to predict future earthquakes.
C A law is passed that all new buildings must be designed to cope with shaking.
D All bridges in the city are made stronger.
E South American countries set up a joint satellite system, to monitor plate movements.
F From now on, all schools in the country will teach pupils what to do in an earthquake.
G A city hospital sets up a tent for the injured.
H Reporters arrive from all over the world.
I Spain gives $500 million to help rebuild the city.
J In Stirling, S2 pupils collect £80 for the survivors.

3 Which of the responses above are:
a local (in the hit city)? **b** national?
c international?
To answer, underline each type of response in a different colour, in your table. Then add a colour key.

4 Now, imagine there's a huge **volcanic eruption** in Mexico that kills 9000 people. Make up six examples of responses to the disaster. You must include:
- at least two international responses
- at least one involving an aid agency
- at least one involving scientists.

5 This photo shows a sad father in Bam, Iran, after the earthquake in 2003. His children were buried by the earthquake. They were dug out after two days – but they died later in a tent hospital.
The things below might have helped to keep them safe. For each, try to explain why.
a a team of inspectors to enforce strict building rules
b money to buy strong building materials
c lots of money for research into predicting earthquakes, in Iran
d a good motorway network
e better emergency plans for earthquakes
f well equipped hospitals

6 Protecting people from disasters costs a lot of money. Look at the table below. It gives data for three countries at risk of earthquakes.
a Which of the three is wealthiest? (Glossary?)
b Which do you think is most likely to be able to:
i help people injured in disasters?
ii protect people from disasters in the long-term?
Give reasons for your answers.

Comparing some countries

Country	Iran	Mexico	USA
GDP per capita (US dollars PPP)	$7500	$9800	$39 700
% of houses with TV	77	92	97
Number of doctors per 10 000 people	11	20	26
Number of hospital beds per 10 000 people	14	10	30
Length of motorway per 1000 sq km of the country	0.54 km	3.34 km	8.17 km

7 Crime

The big picture

Geography is brilliant. It even covers crime! This chapter is all about crime. These are the big ideas behind the chapter:

- Crime affects all of us, not just the victims.
- It's easier to commit crimes in some places than others – so criminals have to think about geography!
- Maps are good for showing where crimes occur, and working out why.
- Today, when we build new streets and housing, we try to make them more 'crime proof'.
- Some crimes involve many people, in different countries. Drug trafficking is an example.

Your goals for this chapter

By the end of this chapter you should be able to answer these questions:

- What do these terms mean?

  crime *victim* *offender* *sentence* *secure accommodation*
- Crime affects all of us – not just the victims. In what ways?
- What do these terms mean?

  fraud *burglary* *vandalism* *domestic violence*
  assault *environmental crime* *terrorism* *crime hotspot*
- Why is some crime *not* reported to the police?
- In what ways can a location help to make crime easier?
- What kind of things can we do to cut down burglary, and street crime?
- Where does most of the world's heroin come from, and why? And how is heroin linked to crime?

And then …

When you finish this chapter you can come back to this page and see if you have met your goals!

Did you know?

- *There are about 89 000 people in prison in the UK right now.*
- *That's about 1 in every 670 of the population.*

Did you know?

- *The UK has over 4 million CCTV cameras, in buildings and on streets.*
- *That's more than any other country, per person.*

Did you know?

- *There are about 300 000 known thefts from shops in England and Wales each year.*

Your chapter starter

Page 110 shows policemen on patrol. They're looking out for crime.

What's a crime?

What kind of crimes could happen in that area?

Who decides what counts as a crime?

Has it got anything to do with you?

7.1 A crime story

In this unit you will explore how crime affects more than just the victim.

The offender's story

It happened a year ago when I was 13.

I was walking through the park with my friend and we were talking about things we like. You know, clothes and all. There was a woman in front of us, quite old. My friend said 'I'm going to get her bag'. He ran and grabbed the bag. She held on and screamed. He gave a tug. So did I. She fell back on to the iron railings.

Now she's paralysed. I am sorry about her. I got an 18-month sentence. It wasn't even my idea but they said I was guilty too.

I wish it had never happened. But it did and I can't change it. Now I have a criminal record and the police will always be watching me.

At school they teach you things like cooking, and crossing the road safely, and what to do in a fire. But they never teach you not to steal – not really.

▲ *The offender.*

The victim's story

It has ruined my life. 46 years old, and in a wheelchair.

I had a good job at the hotel. My children were doing well. We were an ordinary family. And then in just a few minutes everything changed. What did I do to deserve this?

The worst part is the effect on my family. It's like a big dark cloud over all of us. We can never have a normal life again.

My husband had to leave his job and take a part-time job to look after me. My children worry all the time. My son has got really depressed. He used to do well at school but now he's getting bad reports, and he'll probably fail his exams.

I never go out now – I sit out the back in the garden. When my husband wheeled me down the street once, I got panicky. I felt everyone was staring at me.

Those two boys just got a few years between them. I got a life sentence.

▲ *The victim.*

So – who pays the penalty?

In this sad story, the offenders were punished for their crime. The victim was punished too. But they were not the only ones who suffered, as you'll see next.

Key

The victim and her family

- The victim and her family live here.
- This is the park where the crime took place.
- The victim had to have several serious and expensive operations in this hospital.

The offenders and their families

- The secure accommodation where the two boys are being held. They are not allowed out.
- The families of the two boys live in these houses. Their neighbours won't talk to them now.

Other people

- Five people in these houses need operations. But the hospital had to delay them in order to treat the victim. (It ran short of money.)
- Eleven people in these houses used to walk in the park. Not any more. They are too afraid.
- The owner of this house was about to sell it – but the crime put the buyers off.
- The police and prisons cost a lot to run. The money comes from taxes …
- … so everyone who pays taxes pays more because of crime.

Your turn

1 Why do you think the boy wanted the bag?

2 Who suffered because of this crime? Make a list.

3 The boy who snatched the bag was 11. He got an 18-month sentence too. Do you think it was fair that:
   a both boys got the same sentence?
   b they got 18 months?

4 Write down the meaning of each term. (Glossary?)
   victim offender sentence
   secure accommodation

5 We all pay for crimes other people commit. You pay every time you go shopping! Look at this:

Theft from UK shops costs £billions every year!

To see how you pay for shop theft, write these sentences in the correct order.
   A The shop has to find money to pay for the stolen goods, and the security staff.
   B So the shop hires security staff to stop theft.
   C Shoplifters steal things from a shop.
   D So you pay more when you go shopping.
   E So it charges more for the things it sells.

6 Mugging and shoplifting are crimes. So is dumping poisonous chemicals in rivers. Which do you think is the best definition of a crime?
   a An action that harms a person.
   b An action that breaks the law.
   c An action that offends people.

7.2 Different kinds of crime

In this unit you'll explore and compare different kinds of crime.

A bad bad day in the city …

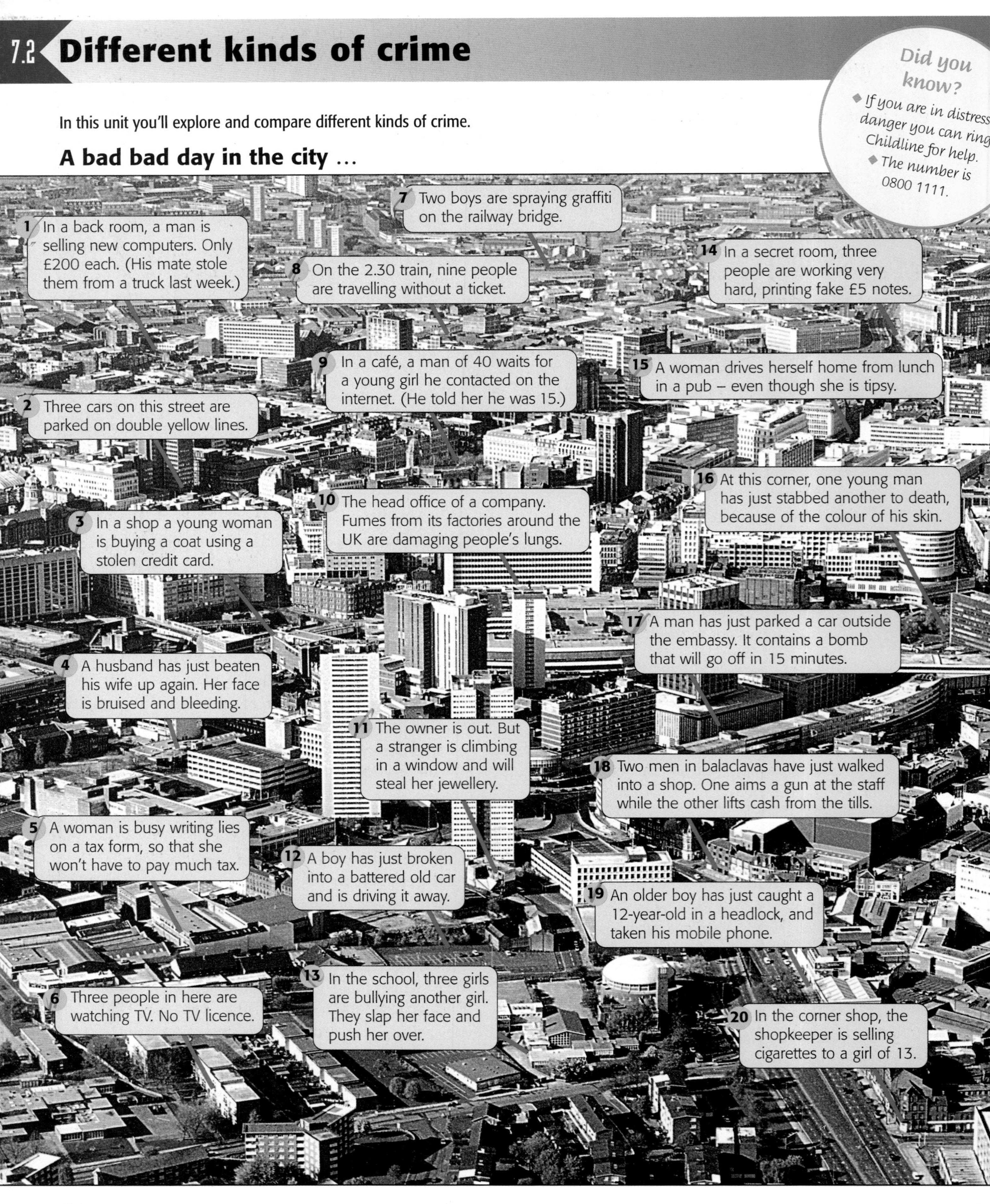

Did you know?
If you are in distress danger you can ring Childline for help.
The number is 0800 1111.
1 In a back room, a man is selling new computers. Only £200 each. (His mate stole them from a truck last week.)
2 Three cars on this street are parked on double yellow lines.
3 In a shop a young woman is buying a coat using a stolen credit card.
4 A husband has just beaten his wife up again. Her face is bruised and bleeding.
5 A woman is busy writing lies on a tax form, so that she won't have to pay much tax.
6 Three people in here are watching TV. No TV licence.
7 Two boys are spraying graffiti on the railway bridge.
8 On the 2.30 train, nine people are travelling without a ticket.
9 In a café, a man of 40 waits for a young girl he contacted on the internet. (He told her he was 15.)
10 The head office of a company. Fumes from its factories around the UK are damaging people's lungs.
11 The owner is out. But a stranger is climbing in a window and will steal her jewellery.
12 A boy has just broken into a battered old car and is driving it away.
13 In the school, three girls are bullying another girl. They slap her face and push her over.
14 In a secret room, three people are working very hard, printing fake £5 notes.
15 A woman drives herself home from lunch in a pub – even though she is tipsy.
16 At this corner, one young man has just stabbed another to death, because of the colour of his skin.
17 A man has just parked a car outside the embassy. It contains a bomb that will go off in 15 minutes.
18 Two men in balaclavas have just walked into a shop. One aims a gun at the staff while the other lifts cash from the tills.
19 An older boy has just caught a 12-year-old in a headlock, and taken his mobile phone.
20 In the corner shop, the shopkeeper is selling cigarettes to a girl of 13.

How much crime is there in the UK?

The UK has quite a lot of crime. (Most is not very serious.) But not all of it gets reported to the police, or recorded by them.

So every year the government carries out its own survey. Households in England and Wales are asked about crimes they suffered over the past twelve months.

The survey shows many more crimes than the police records do – in fact over three times as many!

This table shows the results for one year. The numbers are all in thousands. So there were 6660 thousand (or over six million) thefts in England and Wales that year.

But the survey does not ask about crimes like fraud or drug dealing. So you need to look at police records too, to get a better picture.

British Crime Survey: one year's results

Type of crime		Number of times committed (thousands)
1 Vandalism		2465
2 Thefts	burglary	943
	of or from cars	2121
	of bicycles	370
	other household thefts	1283
	thefts from people	622
	other thefts of personal property	1321
	Total	6660
3 Violent crimes	mugging (to rob)	283
	wounding (in fights)	655
	common assault (hitting)	1654
	Total	2592
Total of all crimes		**11 717**

Your turn

Did you know?

- Murder is quite rare compared with other crimes.
- There are about 13 000 times more thefts than murders!

1 First, pick a number from the photo to match each term below. (A different number for each.)

a murder b forgery
c vandalism d armed robbery
e burglary f domestic violence
g fraud h handling stolen goods
i a traffic offence j environmental crime
k terrorism l common assault
m car theft n mugging

If you get stuck the glossary may help.

2 Both young people and adults commit crime. Look at the list of crimes a – n above. Pick out:
  a one that's more likely to be carried out by younger people (under 16) than older people
  b five that are more likely to be carried out by adults
  c two you think just as likely for either group.

3 Young people are often victims of crime. From the photo, pick out five crimes where young people are, or could be, victims.

4 All the crimes on the photo took place in a city. But some of them could take place in a rural area. Give the numbers for four crimes that:
  a could easily take place in a tiny rural hamlet
  b are unlikely to take place in a rural area.

5 Many crimes are not reported to the police. Suggest a reason why these crimes from the photo were not reported.

a 12 b 4 c 20 d 13

6 Look at the table above.
  a How many crimes did the survey find altogether? (Check the heading of the last column!)
  b Of the three main types of crime, which one was the most common?
  c There were about two and a half million acts of vandalism. Give four examples of vandalism.
  d Which type of theft was the most common? Suggest reasons.
  e Which type of theft was the least common? Suggest reasons.

7 All crime is wrong. But some crimes are more serious than others.
  a Draw a scale like the one below. Make it the width of your page, and divide it into three equal parts. Label the divisions.

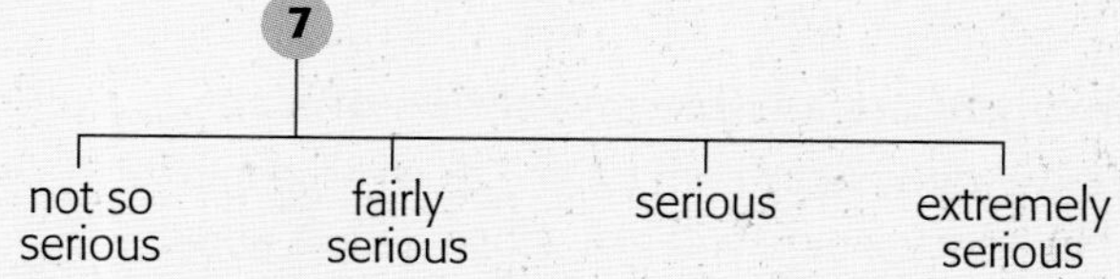

  b Now mark in these six crimes (from the photo) on your scale, where you think they should go:

1 2 8 9 10  17

One number has been put in as an example.

  c In b, how did you decide on the *most* serious and *least* serious crimes? Explain your thinking.

Criminal geography !

In this unit you'll explore the links between location and crime. And find out who's most likely to get burgled !

The criminal's mental map

We all have **mental maps** (maps in our mind) of areas we know well. Look at this mental map for a criminal.

The criminal will head for areas:
- that he knows well
- that offer opportunities for crime
- where he can get away without being seen.

This criminal has three areas to target – near home, near work, and near where he goes for shopping and entertainment.

And now it's time to go exploring !

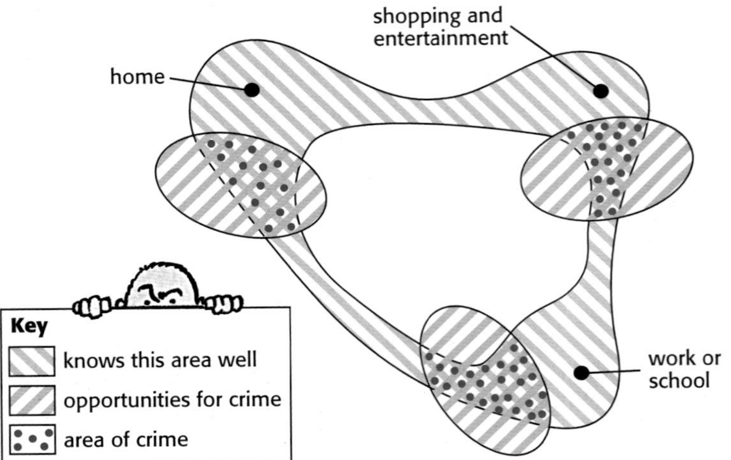

Your turn

First, put yourself in a criminal's shoes.

1 You are a house burglar. You know all the places in the photos on the opposite page.
 a Which two places would you target ?
 b For each, give reasons for your choice.

2 What kinds of crimes might occur in the places shown in these photos ? Give reasons for your answers.

Now, back to being yourself.

3 In which place in the photos would you feel safest, walking around by yourself:
 a during the day ? b at night ?
 Give the numbers of the photos, and your reasons.

4 In which place would you feel least safe, walking around by yourself:
 a during the day ? b at night ?
 Again give the photo numbers, and your reasons.

Next, you are a crime prevention officer.

5 Choose one photo from page 117 with people in. What advice would you give those people about protecting themselves from crime, in that situation ?

6 If a place shows **physical disorder** it means it looks run-down and messy.
 a Which photo do you think shows highest physical disorder ?
 b Do you think there's a link between physical disorder and risk of crime ? How could you check ?

And finally, think about being burgled.

7 The table below shows the risk of burglary. 3.4 % of households in rural areas are likely to be burgled, and 5.6 % of all households.

The risk of household burglary	%
Head of household aged 16–24	15.2
Living in an area of high physical disorder	12.0
Living in rented property	9.7
Living in the inner city	8.5
Living in a council estate	8.1
Living in a flat	7.2
On a main road	6.6
Average risk of being burgled	5.6
Earning more than £30 000 a year	5.0
Living in property they own	4.2
Living in a detached house	4.1
Head of household 65 or older	3.8
Living in rural areas	3.4

Draw a bar graph to show the data in the table. It will be a wide graph so you can turn your page sideways. Start like this:

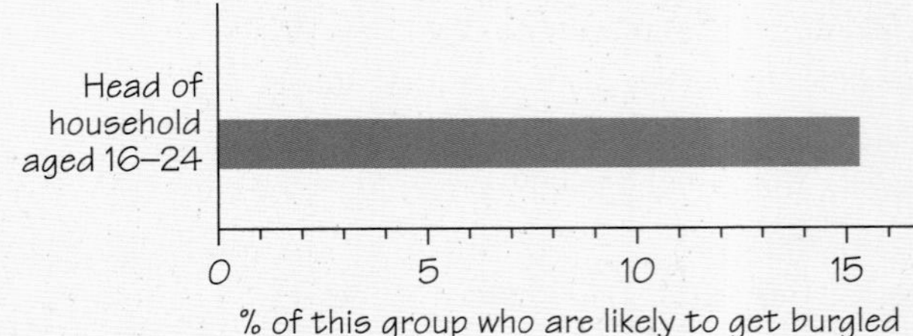

8 Now it's time to analyse the data in your bar graph. The text on the opposite page will help. This clue box might help too !

Suggest reasons why the risk of being burgled is:

a lowest in rural areas
b low for people over 65
c lower if you own your home than if you rent it
d above average if you live on a main road
e below average if you earn more than £30 000
f higher for flats than for detached houses
g highest where the head of the household is only 16–24.

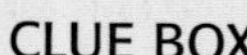

CLUE BOX

Not everyone can afford burglar alarms and good locks.

Lots of us don't know our neighbours.

In busy places nobody pays much attention to strangers.

Burglars prefer places with no-one at home.

If you own lots of things you might fit a burglar alarm and good door and window locks.

We take more care of our own things.

1

2

3

4
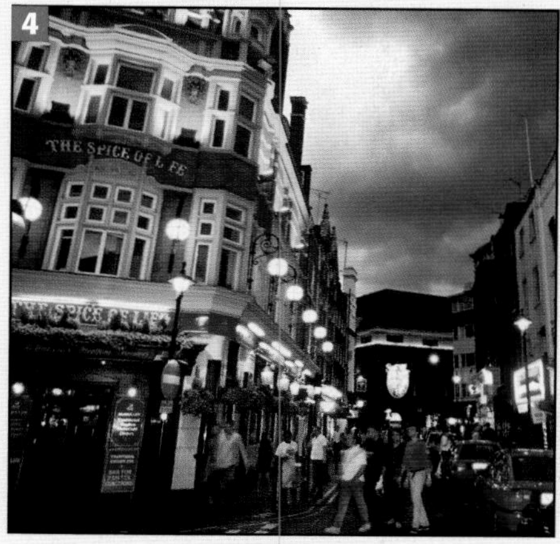

5

6

7

8

9

7.4 Mapping crime

In this unit you'll explore crime spots, using a map and an aerial photo.

Put your police hat on !

You are in charge of crime control for the area on the map below.
The matching photo on page 119 will help you answer these questions.

Your turn

1 There were several fights along one part of the High Street, in the last six months.
  a Suggest a reason for this. (Check building use !)
  b What could you do to prevent trouble here? Come up with some suggestions. Then put them in order, with the best one first.

2 Now look at square 1436.
  a What was the main crime here?
  b Suggest a reason for this. (Check the photo.)
  c What will you do to prevent this crime? Put your suggestions in order, best one first.

Key

railway and railway bridges

embankment

Businesses

shops (all types)

financial centres (banks, building societies, post office)

places of entertainment (pubs, clubs, wine bars, cafes, restaurants)

Abbreviations

PW place of worship
PO post office
Mkt market
Sta station

Crime over last 6 months

household burglary
repeat household burglary
break-ins to businesses
assault (fighting)
theft of or from cars
illegal dumping of rubbish
vandalism
mugging

0 600 m

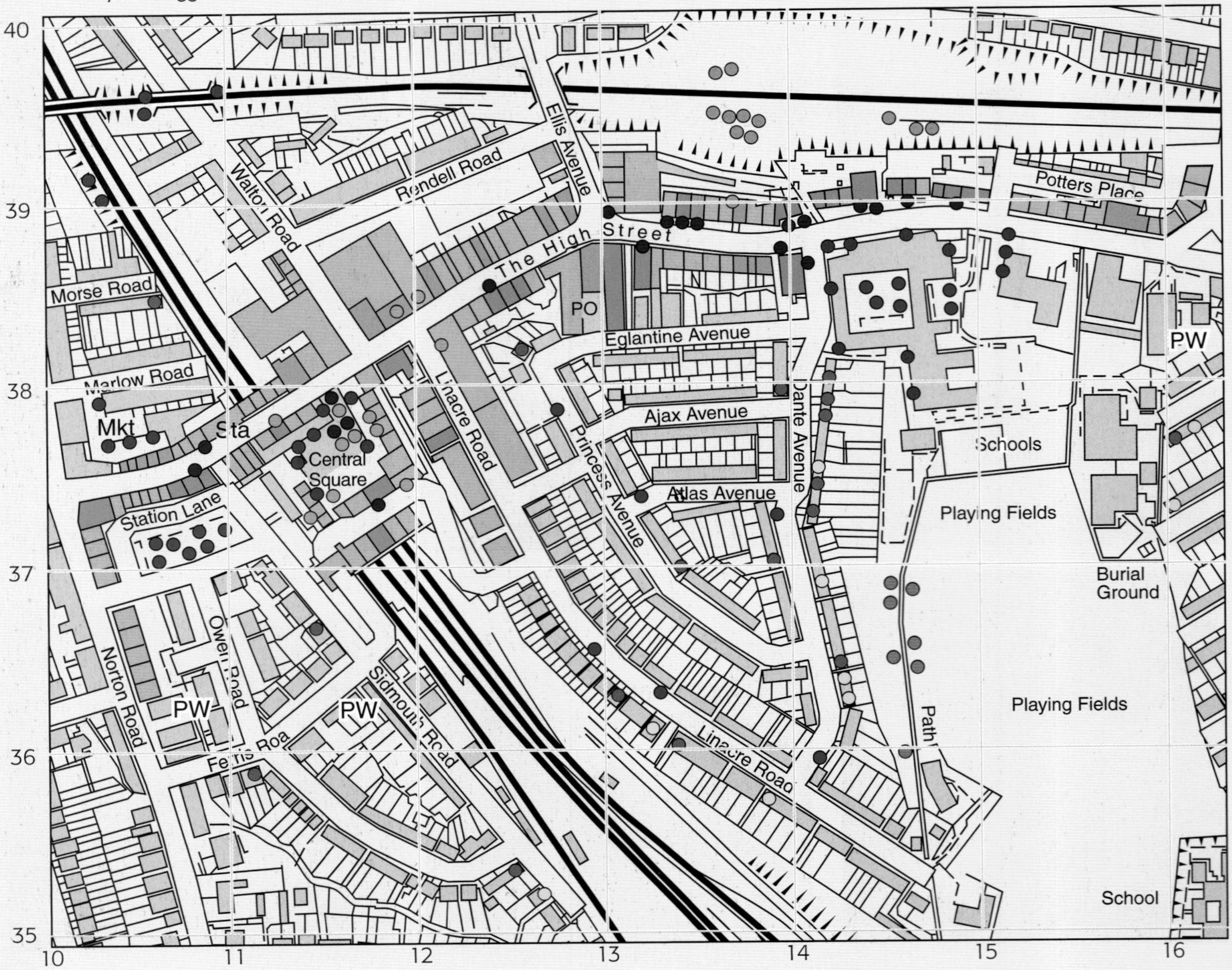

Rendell Road
Ellis Avenue
Walton Road
Potters Place
The High Street
Morse Road
PO
Eglantine Avenue
PW
Marlow Road
Mkt
Sta
Central Square
Linacre Road
Ajax Avenue
Dante Avenue
Princess Avenue
Schools
Station Lane
Atlas Avenue
Playing Fields
Burial Ground
Norton Road
Owen Road
PW
PW
Sidmouth Road
Ferris Road
Linacre Road
Path
Playing Fields
School

40 39 38 37 36 35

10 11 12 13 14 15 16

3 Yesterday two of your police team visited each house on the right of Dante Avenue (going north). They offered to write the postcode on valuable things like computers, with a special invisible ink.
 a What is a *postcode*?
 b Why did they want to write it on things?
 c Why did they choose this road?

4 Houses on the left of Dante Avenue are burgled far less often than those on the right. Suggest a reason.

5 Say which two grid squares were worst for this crime, and give reasons:
 a theft of or from cars
 b illegal dumping of rubbish

6 Vandalism is a problem too. Windows get broken, phone boxes smashed and walls sprayed with graffiti. It is a special problem in squares 1438 and 1137. Suggest reasons for this.

7 A **crime hotspot** has more crime than the other places around it. Where is the main crime hotspot in the map area? Try to give reasons for this.

8 Mr Williams rang yesterday to say he has now been burgled 6 times in 6 months. He lives at 126353. The photo below shows his house from the road.
 a Suggest reasons why his house is burgled so often. Look at the map *and* the photo.
 b Now write to Mr Williams with some advice about how he could stop his house being burgled.

7.5 In the fight against crime

In this unit you'll learn about things we can do to deter criminals.

Protecting property

Criminals like an easy target – and not to get caught. So we can make their lives more difficult. Here are two ways to protect property …

1 Make the target harder to get at. This is called **target hardening**. You could put in high fences, window bars, and strong locks.

2 Make it easier to spot that a crime is being committed. You could fit burglar alarms and bright lights, and hire security guards.

Did you know?

Burglars like you to …
- leave windows open
- have high hedges
- leave ladders and garden tools lying around outside.

Did you know?

- Geese are often used as guards in Europe and Asia …
- … because they have very sharp eyesight and honk loudly at intruders.

Designing out crime

The **built environment** means all the built things around us – houses, streets, shopping centres and so on. As you have seen, it can give lots of opportunities for crime.

Now people are starting to think about crime before they build something new. They try to design it so as to prevent crime.

That is called **designing out crime**. Look at this new housing estate.

Target hardening is built in.
- All windows have locks, and glass that's very hard to break.
- The outer doors are strong, with strong locks.
- Every house has a burglar alarm.

The layout makes crime easier to spot.
- People can easily keep an eye on each other's homes and cars.
- There's only one way in and out of the estate. So burglars can't escape easily.
- All paths are out in the open, easy to see from the houses.

A space to watch over

In the estate above, there is a **defensible space** around the houses. That means a space people can watch over and protect.
There are no hidden alleys or corners. People can see if strangers are trying to break into houses, or steal cars.

Space like this, that people can watch over, is a good way to fight crime.

Today, the police are happy to check the plans for new developments, to make sure they are anti-crime. They will even suggest which kinds of doors, windows and locks to use.

Did you know?

- You can 'rent' patrol dogs and their handlers.
- Some dogs are trained to find drugs and explosives.

Your turn

1 What does *target hardening* mean?

2 a First, make a larger copy of this Venn diagram.

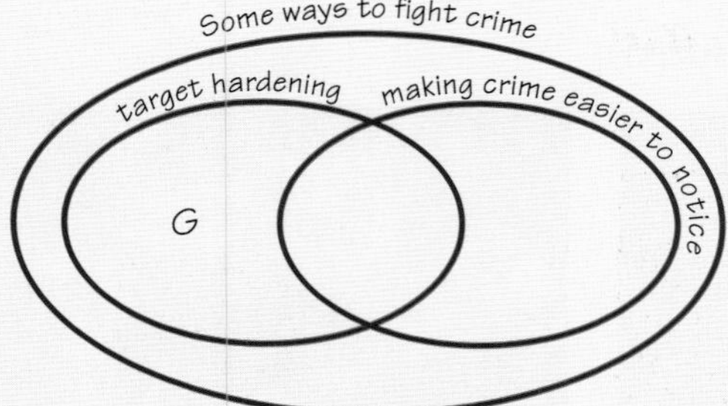

b Now look at the list below.
In which loop of your Venn diagram should each item go? Mark its letter in. (One is done already.)
If you think an item belongs to both loops, put the letter where they overlap.

A a lock for your bicycle
B a bullet-proof vest
C a 'krooklok' for a car steering wheel
D a CCTV camera (like the one shown on the right)
E security tags on clothes in a shop
F a guard dog
G a high wall with metal spikes on top
H a shatterproof glass screen in the post office
I a Neighbourhood Watch scheme (Glossary!)
J a bodyguard

3 CCTV (or closed circuit TV) is used in shops and on streets. Some years ago, CCTV cameras were installed in the town centre in Airdrie in Scotland.
Look at this table.

	In the 12 months … before CCTV	after CCTV
Car break-ins	480	20
Theft of cars	185	13
Serious assaults	39	22
Vandalism	207	36
Break-ins to business premises	263	15

a Overall, did CCTV reduce the number of crimes?
b Which type of crime did it reduce most?
c Which did it reduce least? Try to give a reason.

4 You are (still) in charge of crime for the area on page 118. You have money for just two CCTV cameras. Below is a list of grid references.
From this list, pick out the two best places for your CCTV cameras, and give your reasons.

a 145365 b 138375 c 113374
d 139389 e 145385 f 115382

5 What do these terms mean?
a designing out crime b defensible space
Answer in your own words, using the photo at the bottom of page 120 to help you.

6 The methods in this unit help to reduce crime. But they don't stop it altogether! Look at these opinions:

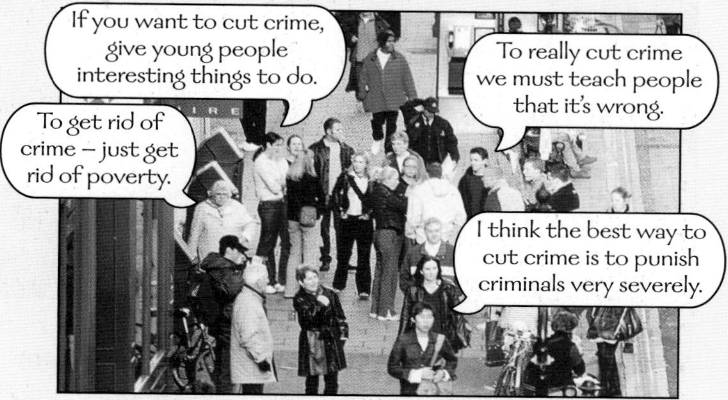

If you want to cut crime, give young people interesting things to do.
To really cut crime we must teach people that it's wrong.
To get rid of crime – just get rid of poverty.
I think the best way to cut crime is to punish criminals very severely.

a Choose any *two* of the four opinions.
b For each, decide whether you agree or not.
Then write down what you will say to that person in reply.

a CCTV camera – it can turn, tilt and zoom

The heroin trail

Here you'll explore an example of crime that involves many people, in different countries.

> **Did you know?**
> ◆ A farmer in Afghanistan can earn over 100 times more by growing opium rather than wheat.

The heroin story starts here

For most heroin, the story starts in Afghanistan – the world's top producer.

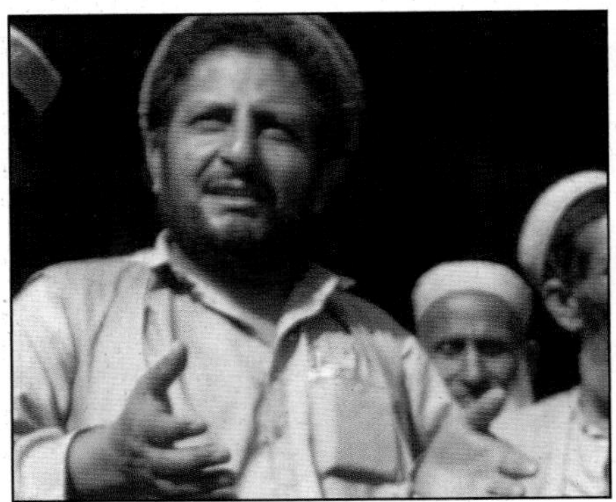

This is Hamid, a poor farmer. He needs money for his family. He can earn most by growing opium poppies …

… so he goes to the local drug trader, who gives him the seeds, and enough money to last him for several months.

He plants the poppy seeds in October on land where he used to grow wheat. By the following May the poppy is ready to harvest.

He takes a white liquid from the seed heads. This is **opium gum**. He sells it to the trader for about £30 a kilo. The gum …

… is then turned into **heroin**. (1 kg of gum gives 100 g of heroin.) It is smuggled across the border to Iran, past the border patrols.

Three weeks later, in London, it is being sold for £25 000 a kilo. Emma is just about to buy a little. In time it will ruin her life.

From Afghanistan to the UK

This map shows one route used to get heroin from Afghanistan to the UK.

- The heroin enters Iran by camel, bike, truck.
- A big drug trader may send 10 or 12 trucks at a time, loaded with several tonnes of heroin – and with armed guards to protect it.
- From Iran, most of it goes through Turkey. From there it gets smuggled into the UK in trucks, ships, boats and planes.

A lot of heroin gets sold along the way. So Iran now has the world's highest % of heroin addicts.

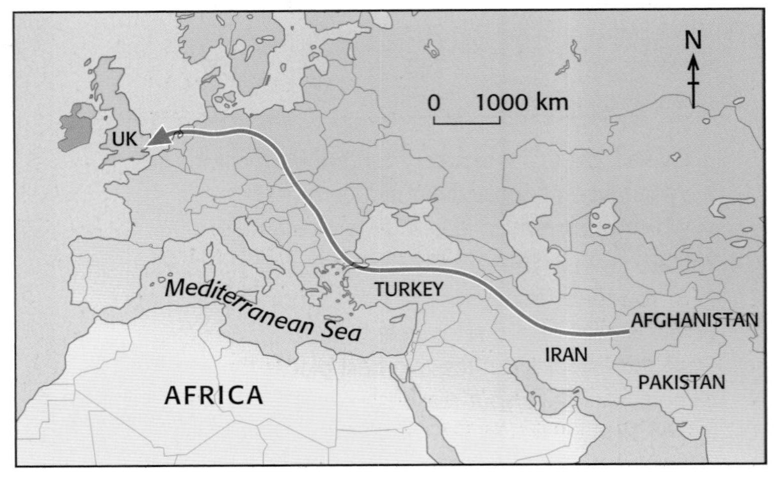

It's big business!

- The heroin trade is big business – worth billions of pounds a year. (The opium farmers get only a fraction of this.)
- It relies on people getting addicted.
- Some addicts then rob and steal to pay for the drug.
- Experts think that some of the money from the heroin trade gets used to fund terrorists.

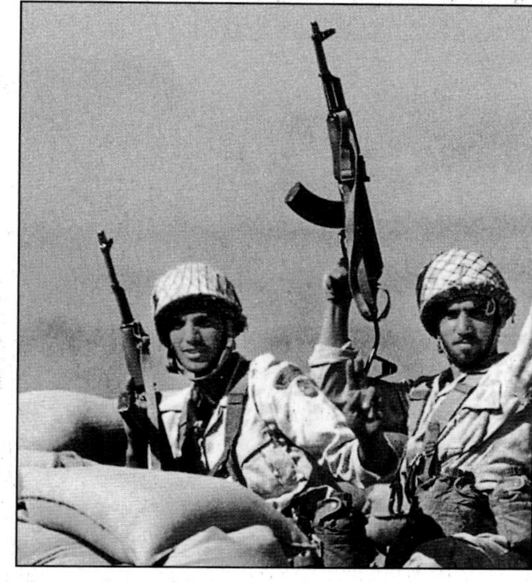

▲ *Iranian soldiers scan the border.*

Iran fights back

- Iran tries hard to stop heroin getting across the border from Afghanistan.
- It has spent millions putting up border fences and barriers.
- 42 000 soldiers and policemen patrol the border.
- On average, 3 per day get killed in clashes with heroin smugglers, and many more get injured.

Even if Iran wins its battle, that won't solve the heroin problem. Smugglers will just find other routes out of Afghanistan.

Your turn

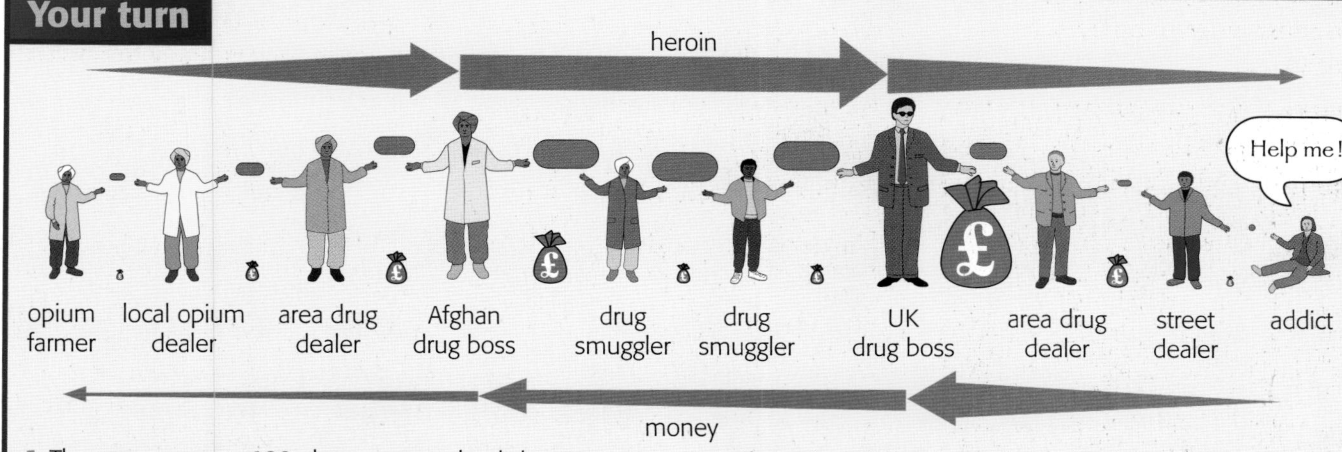

1 The map on page 122 shows an overland drug route. List the countries the heroin passes through on this route, to get to the UK. (Pages 128–129 will help.)

2 a About how long is the border between Iran and Afghanistan? (Use the map scale.)
   150 km   950 km   1800 km
  b It is hard to patrol. Why? (Clues in photos!)

3 Other countries help Iran to fight drug trafficking. For example the UK has helped with training, night-time binoculars, and bullet-proof vests for the patrols.
  a What is *drug trafficking*? (Glossary.)
  b Why do other countries want to help Iran?

4 Many drug traffickers now avoid the Afghanistan / Iran border. They get to Iran through other countries. Which country do you think a trafficker would choose, to get to Iran from:
  a southern Afghanistan? b northern Afghanistan?

5 Drug trafficking is an example of *organized crime*. Explain the term in italics. (Glossary?)

6 Above is a chain of people involved in the heroin business.
  a Most got involved for one reason. What was it?
  b Is each person in the chain a criminal? Explain your answer.
  c Why did the user start taking heroin? Suggest some possible reasons.

7 You're a world leader. You want to persuade Hamid and other farmers never to grow opium poppies again. What will you do? Write an action plan.

8 Look at this opinion.
  a Do you agree that drug dealing has no victims?
  b Write a response to this person. Answer as fully as you can, giving reasons for what you think.

Drug dealing is a crime with no victims – people buy drugs because they want to!

Power stations in the British Isles

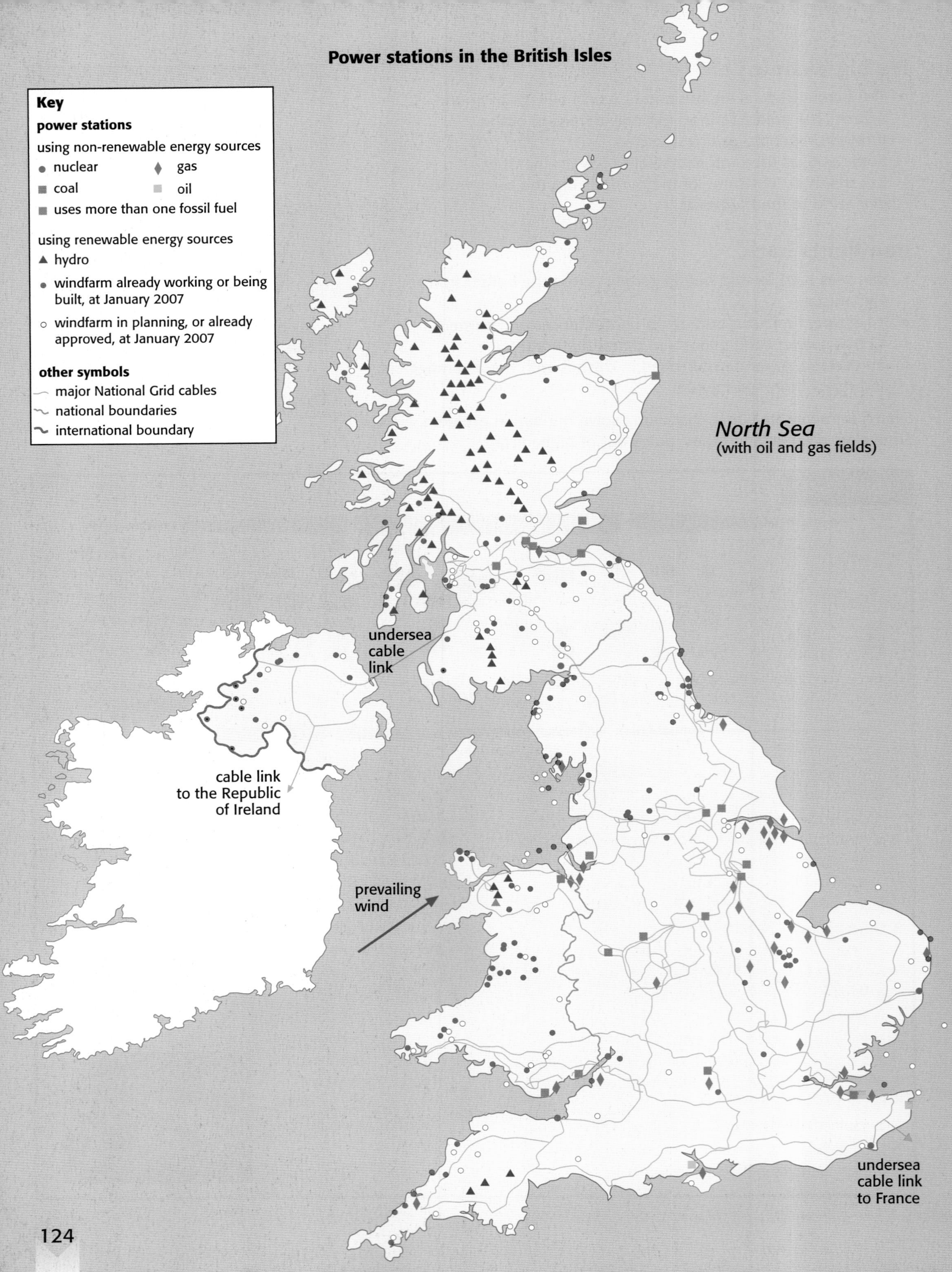

Key

power stations

using non-renewable energy sources

- nuclear
- gas
- coal
- oil
- uses more than one fossil fuel

using renewable energy sources

- hydro
- windfarm already working or being built, at January 2007
- windfarm in planning, or already approved, at January 2007

other symbols

- major National Grid cables
- national boundaries
- international boundary

North Sea
(with oil and gas fields)

undersea
cable
link

cable link
to the Republic
of Ireland

prevailing
wind

undersea
cable link
to France

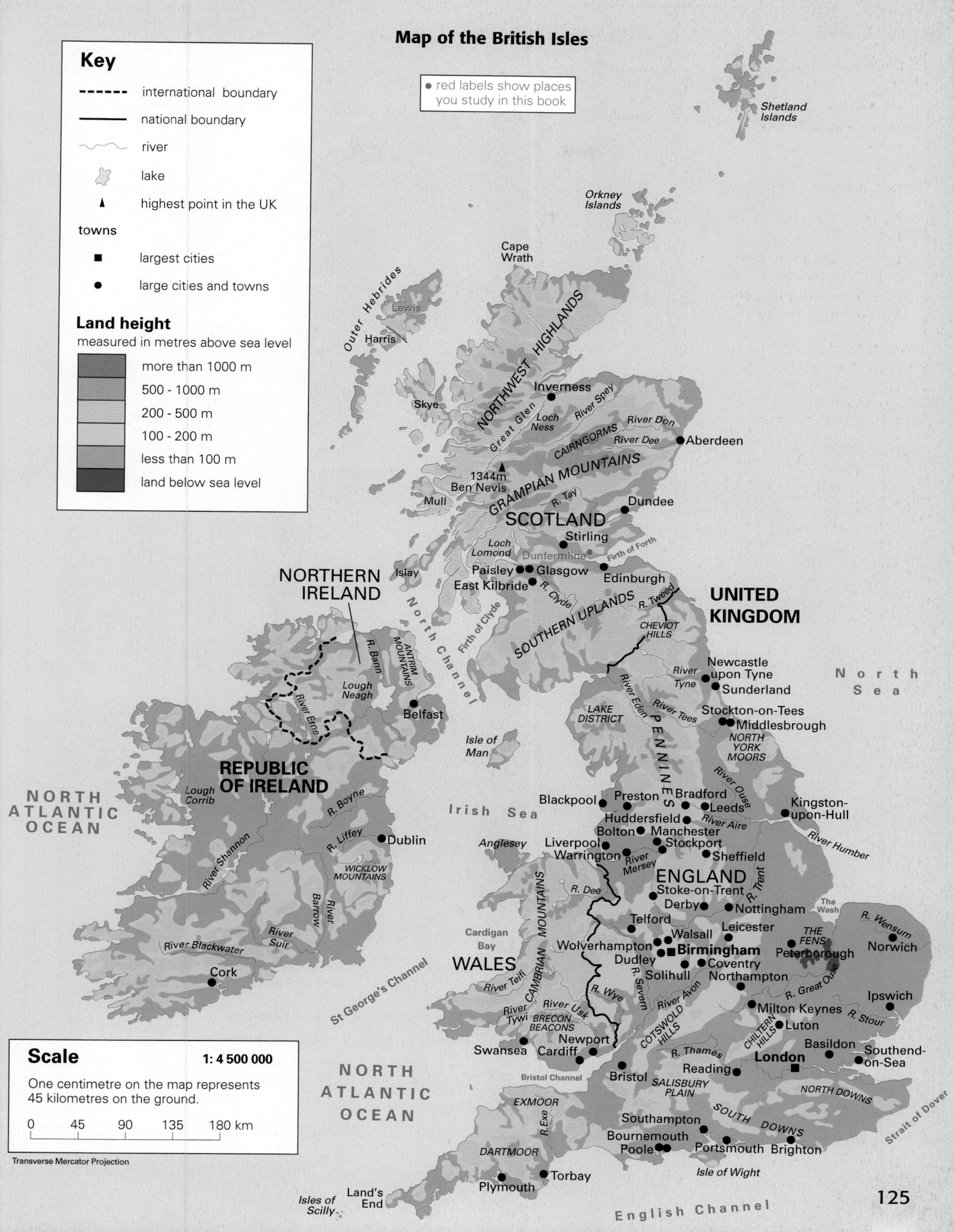
Map of the British Isles
Key
international boundary
national boundary
river
lake
highest point in the UK
towns
largest cities
large cities and towns
Land height
measured in metres above sea level
more than 1000 m
500 - 1000 m
200 - 500 m
100 - 200 m
less than 100 m
land below sea level
red labels show places you study in this book
Scale
1: 4 500 000
One centimetre on the map represents 45 kilometres on the ground.
0
45
90
135
180 km
Transverse Mercator Projection
Shetland Islands
Orkney Islands
Cape Wrath
Outer Hebrides
Lewis
Harris
Skye
Mull
Islay
NORTHWEST HIGHLANDS
Inverness
Great Glen
Loch Ness
River Spey
River Don
River Dee
Aberdeen
CAIRNGORMS
GRAMPIAN MOUNTAINS
1344m
Ben Nevis
R. Tay
Dundee
SCOTLAND
Stirling
Loch Lomond
Dunfermline
Firth of Forth
Paisley
Glasgow
Edinburgh
East Kilbride
R. Clyde
Firth of Clyde
SOUTHERN UPLANDS
R. Tweed
CHEVIOT HILLS
UNITED KINGDOM
NORTHERN IRELAND
North Channel
R. Bann
ANTRIM MOUNTAINS
Lough Neagh
River Erne
Belfast
REPUBLIC OF IRELAND
Lough Corrib
R. Boyne
R. Liffey
Dublin
River Shannon
WICKLOW MOUNTAINS
River Barrow
River Suir
River Blackwater
Cork
NORTH ATLANTIC OCEAN
Isle of Man
Irish Sea
Newcastle upon Tyne
River Tyne
Sunderland
River Eden
River Tees
LAKE DISTRICT
PENNINES
Stockton-on-Tees
Middlesbrough
NORTH YORK MOORS
River Ouse
North Sea
Blackpool
Preston
Bradford
Leeds
Kingston-upon-Hull
Huddersfield
River Aire
Bolton
Manchester
River Humber
Anglesey
Liverpool
Stockport
Warrington
River Mersey
Sheffield
ENGLAND
R. Trent
R. Dee
Stoke-on-Trent
Derby
Nottingham
The Wash
CAMBRIAN MOUNTAINS
Telford
Leicester
R. Wensum
THE FENS
Walsall
Cardigan Bay
Wolverhampton
Birmingham
Peterborough
Norwich
WALES
Dudley
Coventry
Solihull
Northampton
R. Severn
River Teifi
R. Wye
River Avon
R. Great Ouse
Ipswich
St George's Channel
River Usk
River Tywi
BRECON BEACONS
COTSWOLD HILLS
Milton Keynes
R. Stour
CHILTERN HILLS
Luton
Newport
Basildon
Swansea
Cardiff
R. Thames
London
Southend-on-Sea
Reading
Bristol Channel
Bristol
SALISBURY PLAIN
NORTH DOWNS
EXMOOR
SOUTH DOWNS
Strait of Dover
R. Exe
Southampton
Bournemouth
Poole
Portsmouth
Brighton
DARTMOOR
Isle of Wight
Plymouth
Torbay
Land's End
Isles of Scilly
English Channel

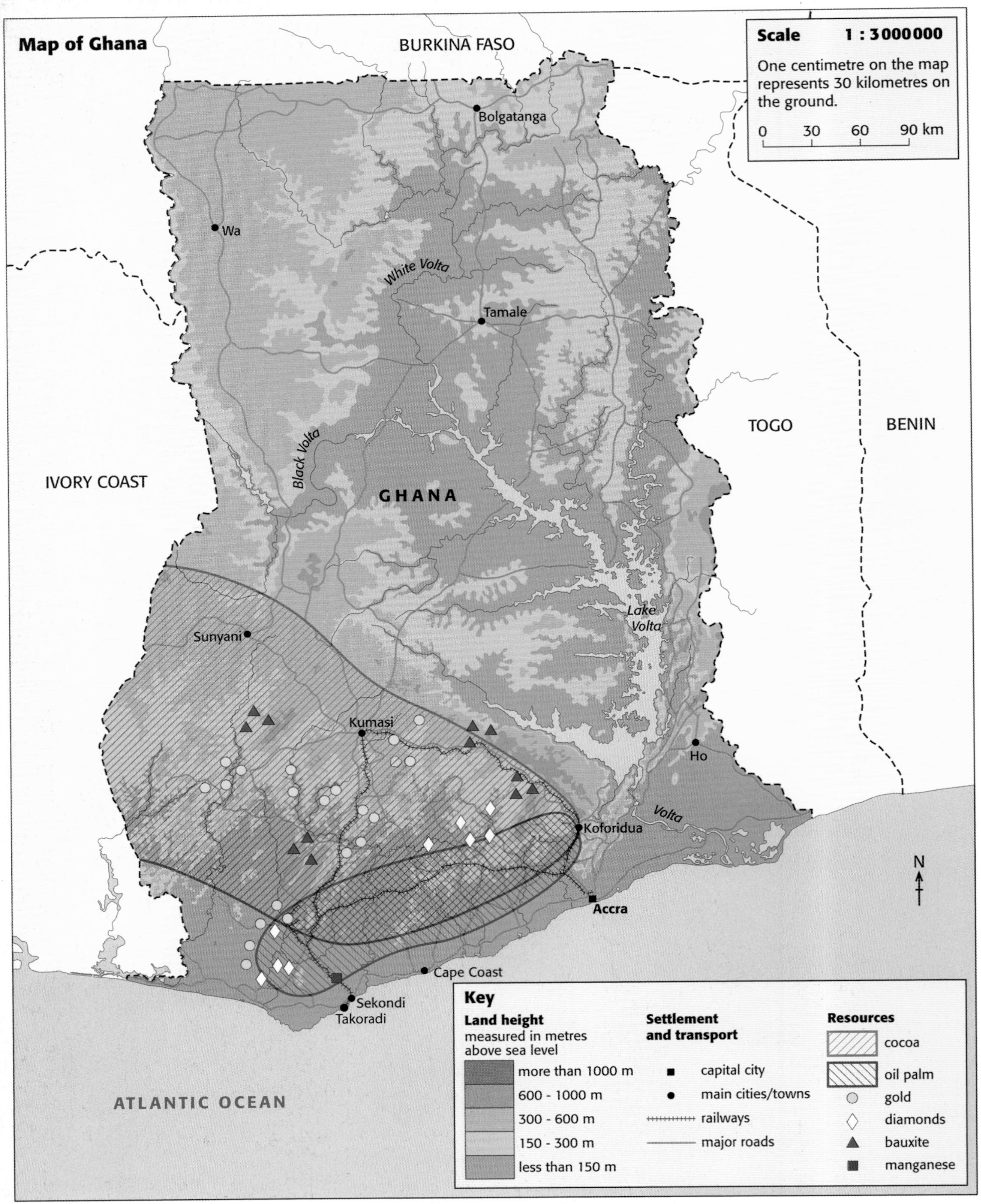
Map of Ghana
BURKINA FASO
Scale 1 : 3000000
One centimetre on the map represents 30 kilometres on the ground.
0
30
60
90 km
Bolgatanga
Wa
White Volta
Tamale
Black Volta
GHANA
IVORY COAST
TOGO
BENIN
Lake Volta
Sunyani
Kumasi
Ho
Koforidua
Volta
Accra
N
Cape Coast
Sekondi
Takoradi
ATLANTIC OCEAN
Key
Land height
measured in metres above sea level
more than 1000 m
600 - 1000 m
300 - 600 m
150 - 300 m
less than 150 m
Settlement and transport
capital city
main cities/towns
railways
major roads
Resources
cocoa
oil palm
gold
diamonds
bauxite
manganese

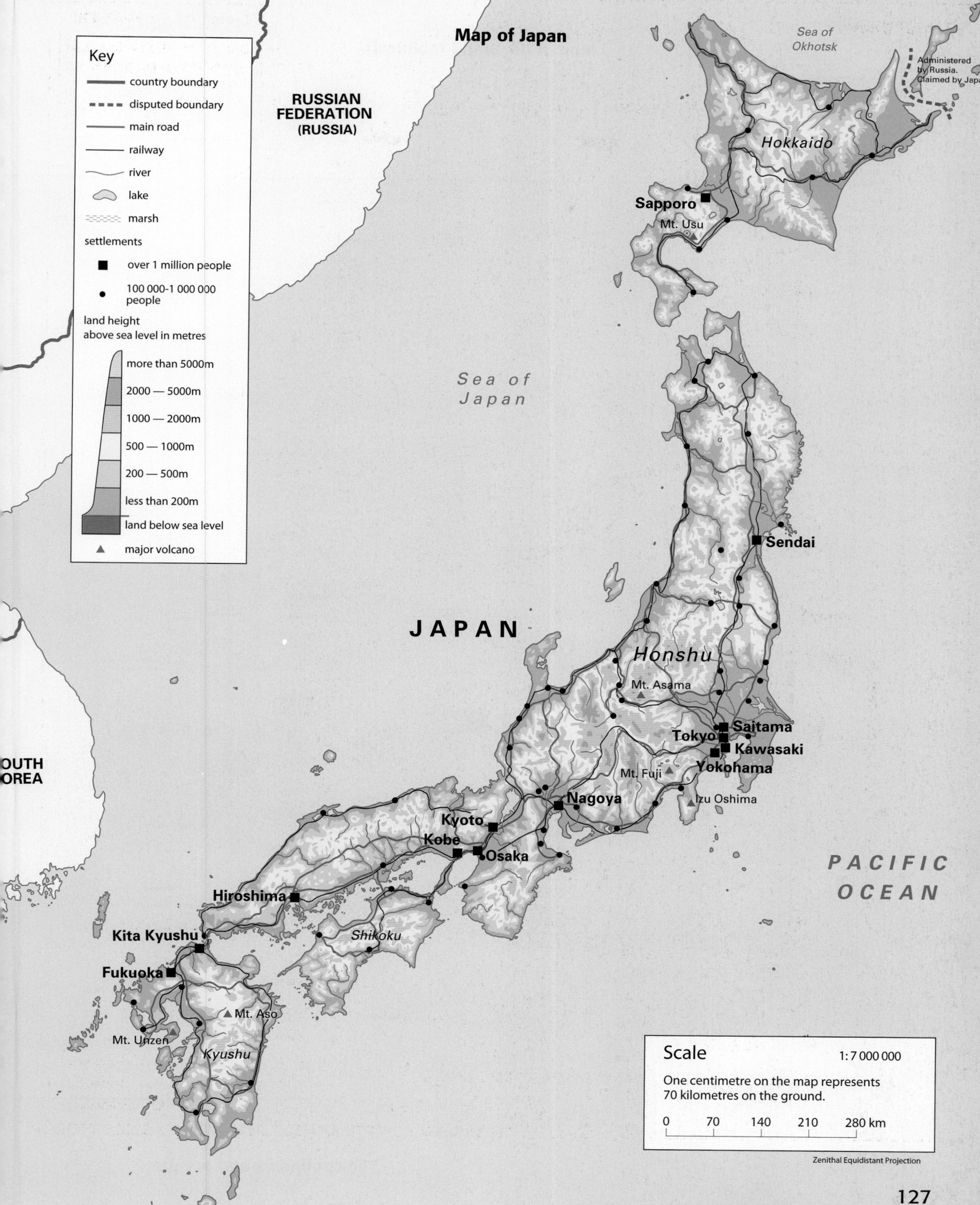
Map of Japan
Key
country boundary
disputed boundary
main road
railway
river
lake
marsh
settlements
over 1 million people
100 000-1 000 000 people
land height above sea level in metres
more than 5000m
2000 — 5000m
1000 — 2000m
500 — 1000m
200 — 500m
less than 200m
land below sea level
major volcano
RUSSIAN FEDERATION (RUSSIA)
Sea of Okhotsk
Administered by Russia. Claimed by Japan.
Hokkaido
Sapporo
Mt. Usu
Sea of Japan
Sendai
JAPAN
Honshu
Mt. Asama
Saitama
Tokyo
Kawasaki
Yokohama
Mt. Fuji
Izu Oshima
Nagoya
Kyoto
Kobe
Osaka
Hiroshima
Shikoku
Kita Kyushu
Fukuoka
Mt. Aso
Mt. Unzen
Kyushu
OUTH OREA
PACIFIC OCEAN
Scale
1:7 000 000
One centimetre on the map represents 70 kilometres on the ground.
0 70 140 210 280 km
Zenithal Equidistant Projection

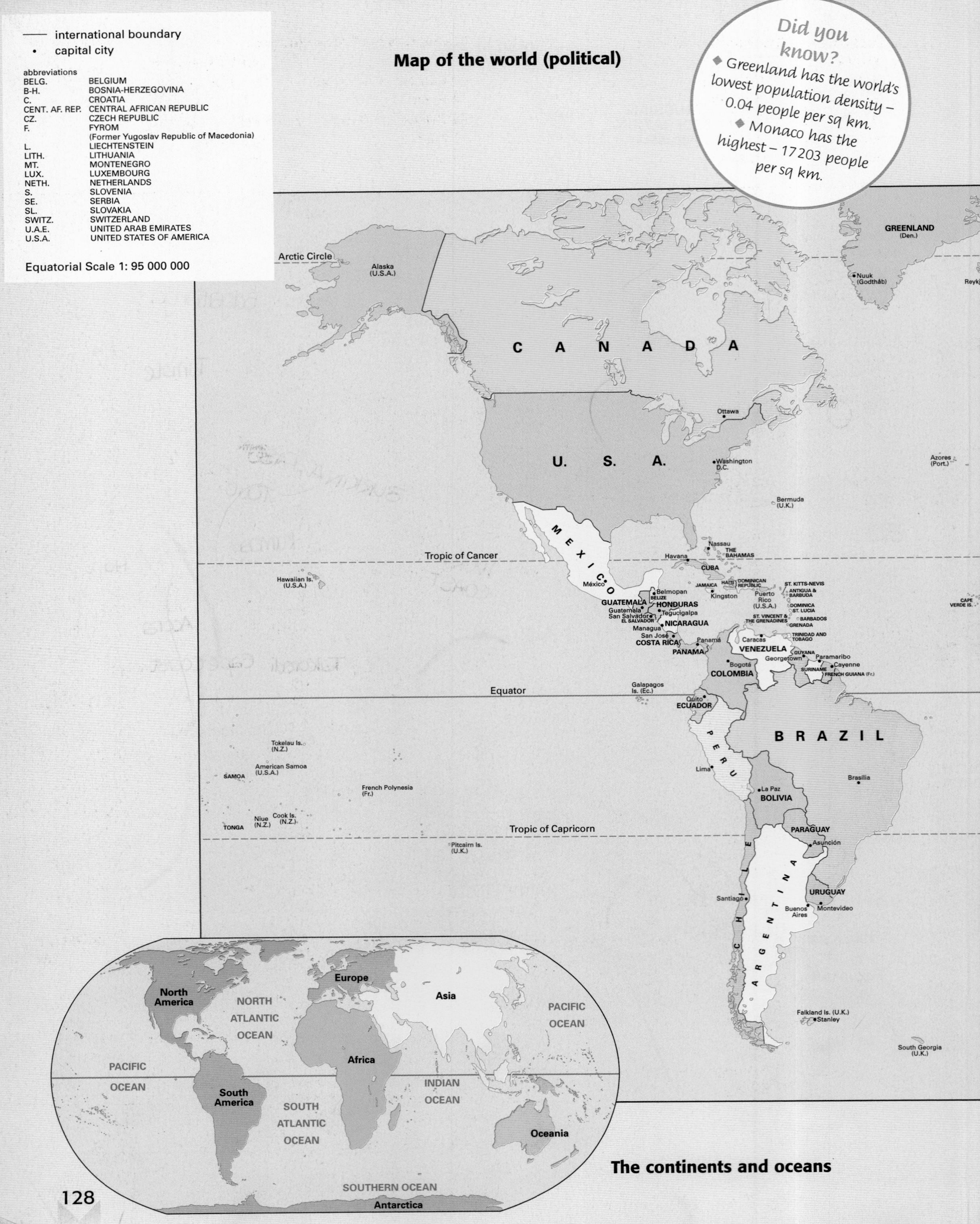
international boundary
capital city
abbreviations
BELG. BELGIUM
B-H. BOSNIA-HERZEGOVINA
C. CROATIA
CENT. AF. REP. CENTRAL AFRICAN REPUBLIC
CZ. CZECH REPUBLIC
F. FYROM
(Former Yugoslav Republic of Macedonia)
L. LIECHTENSTEIN
LITH. LITHUANIA
MT. MONTENEGRO
LUX. LUXEMBOURG
NETH. NETHERLANDS
S. SLOVENIA
SE. SERBIA
SL. SLOVAKIA
SWITZ. SWITZERLAND
U.A.E. UNITED ARAB EMIRATES
U.S.A. UNITED STATES OF AMERICA
Equatorial Scale 1: 95 000 000
Map of the world (political)
Did you know?
Greenland has the world's lowest population density – 0.04 people per sq km.
Monaco has the highest – 17203 people per sq km.
Arctic Circle
Alaska (U.S.A.)
CANADA
GREENLAND (Den.)
Nuuk (Godthåb)
Ottawa
U.S.A.
Washington D.C.
Azores (Port.)
Bermuda (U.K.)
MEXICO
México
Tropic of Cancer
Hawaiian Is. (U.S.A.)
Nassau
THE BAHAMAS
Havana
CUBA
JAMAICA
Kingston
HAITI
DOMINICAN REPUBLIC
Puerto Rico (U.S.A.)
ST. KITTS-NEVIS
ANTIGUA & BARBUDA
DOMINICA
ST. LUCIA
BARBADOS
ST. VINCENT & THE GRENADINES
GRENADA
TRINIDAD AND TOBAGO
CAPE VERDE IS.
Belmopan
BELIZE
GUATEMALA
Guatemala
HONDURAS
Tegucigalpa
San Salvador
EL SALVADOR
NICARAGUA
Managua
San José
COSTA RICA
Panamá
PANAMA
Caracas
VENEZUELA
GUYANA
Georgetown
Paramaribo
SURINAME
Cayenne
FRENCH GUIANA (Fr.)
Bogotá
COLOMBIA
Equator
Galapagos Is. (Ec.)
Quito
ECUADOR
BRAZIL
PERU
Lima
Brasília
La Paz
BOLIVIA
Tokelau Is. (N.Z.)
American Samoa (U.S.A.)
SAMOA
French Polynesia (Fr.)
Niue (N.Z.)
Cook Is. (N.Z.)
TONGA
Tropic of Capricorn
Pitcairn Is. (U.K.)
PARAGUAY
Asunción
CHILE
ARGENTINA
Santiago
URUGUAY
Buenos Aires
Montevideo
Falkland Is. (U.K.)
Stanley
South Georgia (U.K.)
North America
Europe
Asia
NORTH ATLANTIC OCEAN
PACIFIC OCEAN
Africa
PACIFIC OCEAN
South America
SOUTH ATLANTIC OCEAN
INDIAN OCEAN
Oceania
SOUTHERN OCEAN
Antarctica
The continents and oceans

Population of the world's continents

- Asia 3.92 billion
- Africa 0.90 billion
- Europe 0.72 billion
- N America 0.48 billion
- S America 0.35 billion
- Oceania 0.03 billion

The world's top five languages

	(native speakers)
◆ Chinese (Mandarin)	over 1 billion
◆ Hindi	498 million
◆ Spanish	391 million
◆ English	512 milion
◆ Arabic	245 milion

Glossary

A

adult literacy rate – the % of people aged 15 and over who can read and write a simple sentence

agricultural economy – term used for a country that depends mainly on farming

aid – help given by richer countries to poorer countries

B

birth rate – the number of births in a country in a year, per thousand people

brand name – a name that shoppers recognize (like McDonald's)

built environment – everything around us that is built, such as homes and streets

C

call centre – where people are employed to work all day long on the phone

cash crop – you grow it to sell, not eat

CCTV – closed circuit television, used in shops and on streets to fight crime

climate – the 'average' weather in a place

colonised – taken over by another country

colony – a country taken over and ruled by another country

common assault – hitting or threatening to hit someone

congestion – overcrowding; traffic jams

convection current – a current of warmer material; when air or water or soft rock is heated from below, the warmer material rises in convection currents

core – the inner layer of the Earth, made mainly of iron plus a little nickel

crime – an action that breaks the law

crime hotspot – an area or location with a high level of crime

criminal – a person who commits a serious crime, or lives a life of crime

crust – the Earth's thin outer layer of rock

D

debt – money you owe someone

defensible space – a space that people can watch over and protect from criminals

deforestation – when forests are cut down

delta – flat land around a river mouth, built from sediment deposited by the river

densely populated – lots of people live there

depopulated – has lost population (for example the young people have all left)

desertification – when soil in a savanna region gets dried out, and useless

developed country – enjoys good public services and a high standard of living

development – a process of change to improve people's lives

development indicators – data used to compare how developed countries are

domestic violence – violence in the home; for example a man punching his wife

drug trafficking – smuggling and selling illegal drugs such as heroin

E

earthquake – the shaking of the Earth's crust caused by rock movement

economic – to do with the economy, money and earning a living

electronic goods – goods such as mobile phones, that contain a computer chip

employment structure – tells you what % of the workforce is in each employment sector (primary, secondary, tertiary)

environmental – to do with the environment (eg the air, water, wildlife)

environmental crime – an action such as dumping harmful waste in rivers, that breaks the law

exploit – to make use of someone, in an unfair way, for profit

F

fair trade – where the producer of the goods gets a fair share of the profits

forgery – faking a document or signature

fossil fuels – coal, oil and natural gas; they are the remains of plants and animals that lived millions of years ago

fraud – making false claims, usually in order to make money

free trade – when countries trade freely with each other, with no restrictions

G

GDP – (gross domestic product) – the total value of all the goods and services produced in a country in a year

GDP per capita – the GDP divided by the population: it gives you an idea of how wealthy the people are, on average

GDP per capita (PPP) – GDP per capita, taking into account that a dollar buys more in some countries than others

globalisation – the way companies, ideas and lifestyles are spreading round the world with increasing ease

global warming – temperatures around the world are rising; this is linked to carbon dioxide from burning fossil fuels

GNI (gross national income) – the total amount earned in a country in a year (including money from other countries), minus any money paid out to other countries

greenhouse gases – gases such as carbon dioxide that trap heat around the Earth

groundwater – water held in rocks below the ground (where rain soaked down)

H

hazard – a source of danger; earthquakes and typhoons are natural hazards

HDI (human development index) – a 'score' between 0 and 1 to indicate how developed a country is; higher = better

heavily indebted countries – poor countries with large loans they can't repay

hemisphere – half the globe; the northern hemisphere is north of the equator

hydroelectricity – electricity generated when running water spins a turbine

I

IMF (International Monetary Fund) – a fund set up by governments to make loans to countries, especially for trade

in decline – coming to an end, dying away

indented – jagged, not smooth

Industrial Revolution – the period of British history (around the 18th century) when many new machines were invented and many factories built

infant mortality – the number of babies out of every 1000 born alive, who die before their first birthday

interdependent – depending on each other

interest (on a loan) – the charge for taking out a loan; it is a % of the loan

irrigation – bringing water to water crops

isolated area – cut off from other areas

L

lava – melted rock erupting from a volcano

LEDC – less economically developed country (one of the poorer countries)

life expectancy – how many years a new baby can expect to live, on average

lithosphere – the hard outer part of the Earth; it is broken into large slabs called plates which are moving slowly around

M

machete – a large broad knife used for harvesting crops, and other tasks

magma – melted rock below the Earth's surface; at the surface it is called lava

magnitude – how much energy an earthquake gives out

mantle – the middle layer of the Earth, between the crust and the core

manufacturing – making things in factories

MEDC – more economically developed country (one of the richer countries)

megapolis – a huge built-up area formed when a string of towns and cities spread out and run into each other

mental map – a map that you carry in your mind; it might not be very accurate !

metropolis – a city plus the surrounding area that is very closely linked to it, socially and economically

migrate – to move from one area or country to another (perhaps for work)

Millennium Development Goals – goals, agreed by world leaders, to reduce poverty in the world by the year 2015

millet – a type of cereal crop

mudflow – a river of mud; it can form when the material from an eruption mixes with rain or melting ice

mugging – an attack on a person in the street, in order to steal something

N

National Grid – the network of power stations and cables that supply our electricity

natural resources – resources that occur naturally, eg coal seams and fertile soil

Neighbourhood Watch – a scheme where neighbours keep an eye on each others' homes to help prevent crime

newly industrialised country (NIC) – has only recently developed lots of industries

non-renewable resource – a resource such as oil or gas that will run out one day

nuclear power – electricity made using the energy given out by nuclear fuel

O

offender – a person who commits a crime (often used for people under 18)

organized crime – crime that's planned and carried out by a group of people; usually on a large scale and over a long period

P

peatland – has wet spongy ground, made of partly decayed vegetation

plain – large area of flat land

plates – the large slabs that the Earth's surface is broken into

political – about how we are governed

pollution – anything that spoils the environment, such as exhaust fumes

poor south – a term sometimes used for poorer countries (since many are in the southern hemisphere)

population – how many people live there

population density – the average number of people per square kilometre

population distribution – how the population is spread around the country

population pyramid – a bar chart showing the population divided into males and females, and different age groups

primary sector (of the economy) – where people are employed in collecting things from the earth (farming, fishing, mining)

processing – converting a material from one form to another (for example cotton to denim, or milk to cheese)

profit – left when you subtract the cost of something from what you sold it for

PV cell – or photovoltaic cell, gives electricity when sunlight strikes it

pyroclastic flow – a flood of gas, dust, ash and other particles rushing down the side of a volcano, after an eruption

R

raw material – has not yet been processed; eg cotton before it is woven into cloth

relief – the shape of the land (how high or low it is)

renewable resource – a resource that we can grow or make more of; for example wood

resources – things we need to live, or use to earn a living; for example food, fuel

revenue – money you take in from selling goods and services

rich north – a term sometimes used for the richer countries (since most are in the northern hemisphere)

Richter scale – a scale for measuring the energy given out in an earthquake

Ring of Fire – the ring of volcanoes around the Pacific Ocean

rugged – rocky and steep

rural – to do with the countryside

rural depopulation – when a rural area is left with fewer and fewer people

S

secondary sector (of the economy) – where people work in manufacturing and building

secure accomodation – a type of prison for young offenders

seismic wave – wave of energy given out in an earthquake; it shakes everything

seismometer – an instrument for recording the vibrations during an earthquake

sentence – the punishment for a crime

service sector – see *tertiary sector*

slave trade – the buying and selling of people to work as slaves (without pay)

social – to do with the way people live

solar power – electricity obtained from sunlight, using a PV cell; see *PV cell*

sparsely populated – few people live there

street vendor – a person who sells things, such as soft drinks, out on the streets

subsidies – grants (eg for growing a crop)

summit meeting – a formal meeting between leaders of different countries, to discuss things

sustainable – can be continued into the future without harm

sustainable development – development that contributes to social, economic and environmental well-being

sweatshop – a place where people are forced to work long hours for low pay

T

target hardening – installing things to make it harder for criminals to get at their targets (for example steel shutters)

tariff – a tax that a country places on goods being imported or exported

terrorism – violent acts (such as bombings) carried out for political reasons

tertiary sector (of the economy) – where people are employed in providing services (like medical care and transport)

Third World – a name sometimes used for the world's poorer countries

TNC (transnational corporation) – company with branches in many countries

traffic offences – offences to do with driving and parking vehicles

treaty – an agreement between countries

typhoon – another name for a hurricane

U

under-five mortality rate – the % of babies born alive who die before they reach five

undernourished – when you don't get enough food to live a normal healthy life

urban area – a built-up area, eg town or city

V

vandalism – wilful damage to property; for example smashing up phone boxes

vent – an opening on a volcano through which lava erupts

victim – a person against whom a crime is committed

volcano – a place where lava erupts at the Earth's surface

vulcanologist – studies volcanoes

W

water table – the upper surface of the groundwater held in rocks

windfarm – a group of wind turbines set up to generate electricity from the wind

wind turbine – a tower with blades that spin in the wind, giving electricity

World Bank – a joint bank owned by governments of over 180 countries, set up to provide loans for development

WTO (World Trade Organisation) – a body set up to help trade between countries; over 140 countries belong to it

Index